AFTER KATRINA

AFTER KATRINA

RACE, NEOLIBERALISM, AND THE END OF THE AMERICAN CENTURY

Anna Hartnell

SUNY
PRESS

Any royalties earned by the author as a result of the sale of this book will be donated to Jane Place Neighborhood Sustainability Initiative, a non-profit that promotes affordable housing in New Orleans.

Published by State University of New York Press, Albany

© 2017 State University of New York

All rights reserved

Printed in the United States of America

No part of this book may be used or reproduced in any manner whatsoever without written permission. No part of this book may be stored in a retrieval system or transmitted in any form or by any means including electronic, electrostatic, magnetic tape, mechanical, photocopying, recording, or otherwise without the prior permission in writing of the publisher.

For information, contact State University of New York Press, Albany, NY www.sunypress.edu

Production, Diane Ganeles
Marketing, Michael Campochiaro

Library of Congress Cataloging-in-Publication Data

Names: Hartnell, Anna, author.
Title: After Katrina : race, neoliberalism, and the end of the American century / by Anna Hartnell.
Description: Albany, NY : State University of New York Press, [2017] | Includes bibliographical references and index.
Identifiers: LCCN 2016031489 (print) | LCCN 2016054551 (ebook) | ISBN 9781438464176 (hardcover : alkaline paper) | ISBN 9781438464183 (pbk. : alkaline paper) | ISBN 9781438464190 (e-book)
Subjects: LCSH: New Orleans (La.)—Social conditions. | Hurricane Katrina, 2005—Social aspects—Louisiana—New Orleans. | African Americans—Louisiana—New Orleans (La.)—Social conditions. | New Orleans (La.)—Environmental conditions. | Social change—United States. | United States—Race relations—Political aspects. | Neoliberalism—United States. | Capitalism—Social aspects—United States. | United States—Social policy—1993– | Environmental policy—United States.
Classification: LCC HN80.N45 H37 2017 (print) | LCC HN80.N45 (ebook) | DDC 306.09763/35—dc23
LC record available at https://lccn.loc.gov/2016031489

10 9 8 7 6 5 4 3 2 1

For Bart, Maddy, and Luke

Contents

Acknowledgments

Many people have helped me write this book, which has been on my mind since the late summer of 2005. While the perspectives on New Orleans offered here are undoubtedly those of an outsider, many "insiders" have kindly helped me shape them. So, first and foremost, I must thank the many wonderful friends, acquaintances, and colleagues who I have met on my numerous trips to New Orleans between April 2008 and October 2014. Linetta Gilbert, formerly of the Ford Foundation, cofounder of the Declaration Initiative, and long-time New Orleans resident, has been a friend to this project from the beginning. Benjamin Morris has lent this project his time, knowledge, and enthusiasm. Catherine Michna has been a tirelessly supportive friend and colleague who has generously introduced me to a wide variety of people and ideas, in ways that have enormously enriched my understanding and appreciation of New Orleans.

Huge thanks to all the people who have given up their time to talk to me about their invaluable work in the city, and whose interviews inform this book: Carol Bebelle of the Ashé Cultural Arts Center; parent advocate and education activist Ashana Bigard; the ecologist Michael Blum of Tulane University; Reverend Donald Boutte of St. John Baptist Church, New Orleans; New Orleans geographer Richard Campanella of Tulane University; the filmmaker Luisa Dantas of JoLu Productions; Mai Deng of the Mary Queen of Vietnam Community Development Corporation; Abram Himelstein of the Neighborhood Story Project; Hannah Krieger-Benson of the Music and Culture Coalition of New Orleans (MaCCNO); Darryl Malek-Wiley of the Sierra Club; jazz musician and scholar Brice Miller; Bill Quigley, the social justice lawyer based at Loyola Law School; Ashley Shelton of the Louisiana Disaster Recovery Foundation; Nick Slie of Mondo Bizarro; Audrey Stewart of Loyola Law School's Katrina Clinic; visionary architect David Waggonner of Waggonner & Ball; the award-winning writer Jesmyn Ward; and Mary Williams of the Deep South Center for Environmental Justice.

I owe a huge debt to the English Department at Tulane, which has been welcoming to and supportive of my work for a number of years. Special thanks to Molly Rothenberg for making me a Visiting Scholar there in 2010. Huge thanks also to Mike Kuczynski, for renewing that status for a three-month visit in the autumn of 2013, and for extending the hospitality to my husband, Bart Moore-Gilbert, who was able to take advantage of Tulane's amazing resources in order to conduct his own research on Palestine and postcolonialism. Thanks also to Joel Dinerstein of the New Orleans Center for the Gulf South at Tulane, which kindly hosted the conference I organized in November 2013, "After Katrina: Transnational Perspectives on the Futures of the Gulf South." Thank you to the many inspiring participants of this conference, in particular the two keynote speakers, writer and activist Kalamu ya Salaam and Richard Campanella. I am indebted to Rich's scholarship and guidance during the course of writing this book, which I imagine he would probably disagree with in many respects, but which I hope nonetheless pays quiet tribute to his meticulous and illuminating contributions. Finally, the Gulf South Center then supported my work again in 2014 by offering me a Global South Fellowship which enabled me to return to the city and complete the research for this book.

Thank you to a network of supportive friends and colleagues in the UK and beyond who have in various ways engaged with and helped me with this work, especially Rick Crownshaw, Zara Dinnen, Danielle Fuller, Barnor Hesse, Cedric Johnson, and Steve Hewitt. Thanks also to my fantastic colleagues in the Department of English and Humanities at Birkbeck, especially Alison Finlay, Roger Luckhurst and Sue Wiseman. During the course of this project I was lucky enough to be the holder of an Arts and Humanities Research Council Early Career Fellowship. I am very grateful to the AHRC, both for the time this allowed me to work on this book, and for the support for the two conferences that book-ended the fellowship, the one in New Orleans and the one held in London at Birkbeck in November 2014, "Rupture, Crisis, Transformation: New Directions in US Studies at the End of the American Century." Thanks to everybody who participated in that conference, especially the two keynote speakers, Wai Chee Dimock and Caryl Phillips. Huge thanks also to two of my PhD students, Pippa Eldridge and Alex Williamson, for their enthusiasm and hard work on this conference. They are among some of the wonderful students I've had the privilege of working with at Birkbeck, and who make teaching there so stimulating and special.

Thanks to Michael Rinella at SUNY Press for his interest in and commitment to this book, and to Rafael Chaiken for his kind assistance.

Their patience is much appreciated! I am also grateful to the two anonymous reviewers for providing such detailed and helpful feedback.

Special thanks to Caroline Hartnell, who I am unbelievably lucky to call my mother. I first visited New Orleans with her in 2003, and on many subsequent return trips she has not only supported my work—providing company, childcare, connections—but shared my love of the city. Thanks also to my wonderful father, John Strawson, for always being there.

Above all, I must thank my own little family unit, primarily my husband, Bart, and our daughter, Maddy. They have supported and tolerated this project, respectively, and have accompanied me on numerous trips to New Orleans. In autumn 2013 we lived there for three months, during which New Orleans became another home to all of us. Thanks to Maddy for her enthusiasm not only for the adventure of relocation but for the city itself. It was in New Orleans that she first started stringing sentences together at just two years old. I'm sure it's no coincidence that it was in this city that she learned her love of telling stories. Thanks to Bart for his insatiable interest in everything, which extended to an openness to a city that he also learned to love, despite the fact that it sits within a national context that he found so politically unpalatable. It's thanks to conversations with Bart that this book found its shape through the conceptualization of various types of temporality. Bart helped me appreciate the particularly sharp distinction between the dystopian qualities that pervade the Crescent City in the name of a racialized neoliberalism—imagined here as "Katrina time"—and the more utopian currents that I have called in this book "New Orleans time."

Bart was diagnosed with kidney cancer in April 2015, and he died eight, painfully short months later. This book is dedicated to Bart, my best friend and love of my life, not to mention my most exacting academic critic—among so many other things. It is also dedicated to the other members of the family we share, our darling Maddy, and our son Luke, the gift that arrived just nine days before Bart died. Bart lives on in so many ways, not least in his own considerable body of writing. But most of all he lives on in our beautiful children.

Introduction

"Is This America?"

In the aftermath of Hurricane Katrina, which struck the U.S. Gulf Coast in the late summer of 2005, and which led to the flooding of 80 percent of New Orleans, people imprisoned in the city for offenses as minor as traffic violations found themselves lost in the system, doing what came to be known as "Katrina time."[1] Prior to this period of unbounded time, many Orleans Parish prisoners were abandoned in their flooded cells and it seems likely that at least a handful drowned.[2] Those who were eventually evacuated found themselves, along with many other New Orleans residents, quite literally imprisoned on overpasses, for days exposed to the burning sun and the abuse—often physical—of police guards. It is in many ways fitting that New Orleans' overpasses, which have defined the contours and guaranteed the boundaries of the ghettoization of the city's black neighborhoods, were in Katrina's wake transformed into actual prisons for this segment of New Orleans' overwhelmingly African-American incarcerated population.[3] The meaning of "Katrina time" might be expanded here to encompass the temporalization of the unravelling of a state self-defined by the rule of law and the protection of its citizenry, one that has unapologetically turned its attention to endless wars, hitched the fate of its citizens to the brutalizing trajectory of market logic, and turned a blind eye to the devastation of the environment that inevitably follows. This is the time of a neoliberal state that warehouses people indefinitely because it has no vision of the future—its focus is on short-term gains at the expense of long-term investments—even if its political rhetoric still pays lip-service to a narrative of progress. The hollowed-out security state so visibly on display after Katrina can thus be read as the repudiation of the ideals that animated the mirage of the "American Century."

First coined by *Time* editor Henry Luce in *Life Magazine* in 1941, the "American Century" anticipated various forms of U.S. leadership and supremacy and drew on exceptionalist understandings of U.S. history that were consolidated in the Cold War period.[4] The idea of the American Century conjured the image of a triumphant national narrative motored by a Protestant work ethic that might vindicate a vision of special destiny via the achievement of a U.S.-led global capitalism. This mirage is the product of a particular and optimistic postwar moment that embraced the idea that capitalist enterprise and technological advancement would make peoples' lives better—both in the U.S. and in the wider world that the U.S. would lead. Time-keeping was central to understandings of efficiency and indeed fairness that animated the Fordist economy of this particular capitalist moment. Time-keeping also supported a narrative of progress that in the larger national mythology of the United States has always been uniquely oriented toward the future.[5] The nebulous, lawless, and unbounded nature of "Katrina time," which gestures to other extra-legal zones of U.S. authority like Guantánamo Bay, is a flagrant negation of this optimism. The expanded variant of "Katrina time" that I formulate in this book suggests that the time of the fleeting American Century—which itself was only ever an aspiration, a dream—is over. The postwar "golden" era of controlled capitalism, a Keynsian system that enabled the growth of a social safety net that might mitigate capitalism's worst effects, has given way to rampant deregulation and thus an age of asset-stripping that redistributes wealth upwards—impoverishing the majority and severely weakening the middle classes. "Katrina time" offers a disturbing glimpse of the unsustainability of a system that prioritizes profit over people, privatizes the public commons, and privileges an ideology of individualism at the expense of our collective futures.

This book proposes that post-Hurricane Katrina New Orleans offers a unique vantage point from which to understand the narrative of U.S. decline that is emerging as a pivotal feature of the twenty-first century. While "Katrina time" is read here as symptomatic of a much larger neoliberal project that had destroyed aspects of New Orleans and a host of other American cities long before Katrina, arguably New Orleans itself has historically offered an alternative vision and experience of the United States. In so doing it has brought into focus aspects of America's racial, transnational, and environmental coordinates routinely suppressed in official national narratives. The interaction between this disruptive temporality that I argue New Orleans has come to represent vis-à-vis the nation, and the dystopian and brutal register of "Katrina time," is key to the ways in which the post-storm city might be viewed as a microcosm for reading contemporary America. Both registers, I argue, exceed the temporal horizons of the so-called American Century and thus offer new ways of conceptualizing its end.

A gateway to the Caribbean, Africa, and the imperial past, New Orleans' spatial and temporal coordinates contradict the central tenets of U.S. exceptionalism: geographical isolation, the idea that the nation is an inherently anti-imperialist endeavor—a unique experiment in freedom—and the myth that America is always already bound for the future. While New Orleans' ambivalent status in the last few decades as a predominantly service economy aimed at tourists has meant that its branding as a culturally back-ward-looking "museum," as well as an excessive "party town," is a superficial aspect of the city's marginality within the larger nation, these characteristics combine with a genuinely transgressive cultural legacy derived in large part from the traditions of ex-slaves. New Orleans' annual calendar of festivities, at the center of which is Mardi Gras, might be read as part of the city's critique of the ideology of work and production so prevalent within a main-stream Puritan U.S. culture. The city's blues tradition—encompassing not just its black musical legacy but its history of insurrectionary activity and its long tradition of societies dedicated to both social aid and pleasure[6]—argu-ably speaks powerfully to an increasingly privatized, post-industrial America that is yielding decreasing returns to a shrinking middle class.[7]

Post-Katrina New Orleans showcased the convergence of the city's exceptional and representative features, and it is within this context that this book explores a widespread response to the images of the city's destruction in Katrina's immediate aftermath: "Is this America?"[8] There are so many ways in which this disorientation of the national perspective was expressed in the storm's wake. The scenes in New Orleans, numerous commentators have suggested, were reminiscent of "Third world disaster zones."[9] The largely African-American population stranded in New Orleans and then ruthlessly evacuated were routinely described by the press and politicians as "refu-gees."[10] The controversy and understandable sense of insult that circulated around this term—which to some seemed to approximate a racist denial of U.S. citizenship—belied a deeper truth: these internally displaced persons had been brutally abandoned by their own government, their plight not dissimilar to the growing number of the world's population that are on the move, fleeing conflict zones, government persecution and, increasingly, environmental destruction. In other words these were citizens on whose behalf the government did not seem to be *working*. The sense that scenes in post-Katrina New Orleans were somehow "un-American" was the result of denial and misrecognition. Denial that New Orleans itself, often viewed as "foreign" to the larger national imaginary, was really part of America at all. And misrecognition of the myriad ways in which the dystopian aspects of post-Katrina New Orleans reflect on a larger national condition.

The deeply ambivalent reaction to post-Katrina New Orleans—which involved both populist compassion and outright disgust at the conditions on the ground[11]—is worlds away from the mainstream national reaction to 9/11 just four years before. The horrifying intrusion of an external enemy that indiscriminately murdered innocents and toppled the symbols of U.S. prestige and domination consolidated a sense of national unity and led to a powerful resurgence of U.S. exceptionalist discourse in the latter part of 2001. Katrina, in stark contrast, challenged some of the most deeply held ideas about what it means to be American: to be a member of the most industrialized, most militarily, economically, and politically capable nation on the planet; to be protected by the laws of the most advanced democracy in the world; and, for some, to be the proud carrier of the legacy of America's liberal tradition, the crowning achievement of which is arguably the triumph of the Civil Rights movement. The so-called war on terror which followed in 9/11's wake had already exposed the limits of U.S. power—both soft and hard varieties. The growing influence of the power of corporations and lobbies in U.S. politics has long offered a warning sign about the priorities of the political elite and the curtailment of democratic rights.[12] And the racialized poverty and decaying environments of many American inner cities, including those of New York and New Orleans, testify to the fundamentally incomplete project of the Civil Rights movement, which failed to deliver substantive economic power or social capital to the vast majority of African Americans. Despite the veritable inevitability of Katrina in all its revelatory powers, the spectacle of post-Katrina New Orleans was experienced by politicians and media commentators as a profound shock.

September 11 was mobilized rhetorically and ideologically as representative of a break, a cultural and political faultline, one which clearly divided "them" from "us," American from non-American. All academic scholarship responding to this designation, even that which seeks to question the idea that 9/11 represented a cultural cleavage, has to wrestle with the seductive power of this deeply problematic and culturally narcissistic narrative. This book proposes that we might temper such post-9/11 perspectives on U.S. culture by centralizing an event that has not been properly assimilated into the national imaginary precisely because it questioned all of the divisions that 9/11 so comfortably consolidated: between past and present, American and non-American, the innocent and the enemy. As Diane Negra suggests, it is worth noting that

> most 9/11 victims were killed while at work or going to it while
> Katrina victims died in the homes they were perceived to have

fully "chosen" to stay in. In this way 9/11 victims were emphatically linked to the idealized daily rhythms of American capitalism and seats of financial and governmental power while Katrina victims were presented in compliance with a set of pre-existing stereotypes about the idle urban poor in a city where "black gangsterism" was understood to thrive. In many respects, then, Katrina can be seen as an event that punctured 9/11 mythologies and unraveled many of its associated certitudes.[13]

Unlike the 9/11 story, which presented the western world with a deceptively simplistic face, Katrina immediately confronted us with its complexity, its challenge.

By focusing on Katrina as a flashpoint for reading the contemporary moment, we are confronted with a crisis that fits the myriad dictionary definitions of that word: indicative not just of instability and danger, but also of a possible turning point that demands a decision.[14] I suggest that part of this decision might involve the embrace of a narrative that demythologizes and de-centers the United States—as opposed to the relentless re-centering that took place after 9/11—in ways that might simultaneously interrupt the national decline narrative by offering an alternative projection of the future. This book seeks to invoke the disparity between "Katrina time," understood here as the time of neoliberalism, and the potentially interruptive temporality of New Orleans itself, which has resisted aspects of state and market oppression. Of interest is the fact that both temporal registers offer alternatives to the narrative of the United States as progress in the twentieth century. By exploring these strikingly different possibilities that emerge from the shadow of the American Century, this book suggests that a city that has long been associated with ideas of decline and obsolescence might, in its post-storm manifestation, offer alternative ways of imagining a national culture increasingly stalked by images of its own destruction.

New Orleans and the Death Drive

New Orleans' status as a premier tourist destination throughout the twentieth century, alongside the fact that it has been the object of myriad literary constructions since at least the late nineteenth century, means that the external gaze has had a perhaps unusually decisive role in determining popular perceptions of the city.[15] The post-storm spectacle magnified the sense of the city as a giant goldfish bowl to be consumed after a fashion:

variously the object of compassion, scorn, and fascination. Indeed, Lynnell Thomas argues that not only were images of the storm filtered through the city's tourist narrative, but that this narrative "had paved the road to the damage inflicted by Hurricane Katrina."[16]

In a radio program broadcast in the UK in 2012 called "Re-imagining the City: New Orleans," British rock journalist Nik Cohn begins by saying, "New Orleans functions for me and for many others as a drug, it was compulsive, you could never have enough, and it really wasn't good for you." In trying to explain New Orleans' paradoxical appeal, Cohn refers to the fact that much of the city lies below sea level: "when you step out of the airport into the air," Cohn explains, "you get a smell, swampy, over-ripe, slightly rotten smell . . . and you think of course, I'm underwater."[17] The idea that New Orleans is a heady yet unhealthy place of intoxication is absolutely central to the way that the city has been commonly conceptualized in tourist and imaginative literature, as is the idea that the city is slightly rotten, a place associated with decay and decline.

Tennessee Williams's *A Streetcar Named Desire* is the most famous literary example of this narrative. Its appearance in 1947 makes its representation of an assertive, brutal, and relentlessly future-oriented America being wrested from the trappings of the past particularly timely. Williams's vision of New Orleans contrasts starkly with the post-second world war U.S. ascendancy in economic, political, and cultural terms. Instead, *Streetcar* depicts the New Orleans geography as the death-rattle of an old, neurotic, southern order, pointing to the fact that the city itself, as the veritable playground of the South, was unable to make the transition into a productive and profitable "New South." As Barbara Eckstein explains in her book on literary constructions of New Orleans, Williams's depiction of Blanche Du Bois as neurotic, sensual, exotic and, crucially, obsolete, reflects not simply an image of New Orleans, but an image that the city has come to rely on in order to sell itself to the visitors who keep it financially afloat.[18]

Whether evoked romantically and nostalgically or ghoulishly and crudely, New Orleans in the popular imagination is intimately associated with death. On arrival in the city tourists will immediately be greeted with the idea that New Orleans is "America's most haunted city"; New Orleans is a center for the literary gothic as well as the horror film. From the myriad ghost tours on offer in the city's above-ground cemeteries, to the zombies associated—problematically, stereotypically, and sometimes offensively—with the city's ongoing and West-African-derived traditions of voodoo, it is impossible to ignore the idea that the tourist industry in the city is deeply invested in the sale of death.

Revealingly, just after he has talked about the city's racial makeup and the widespread poverty and crime, Nik Cohn goes on to explain the personal psychodrama that New Orleans has represented for him:

> When I first came here I was in my mid-twenties and I really had no idea what I was about . . . . What it was about New Orleans that got me was I now realize a sort of extended love affair with low-life and a dance with death, which probably had always been inside me, which needed to be played out so that I was able to come out the other side . . . for me it was a huge cleansing process, of cleansing through getting even dirtier, layered in dirt, until that washed off finally.

These deeply problematic associations articulated by this white British tourist demonstrate that the various ways in which New Orleans acts imaginatively, fantasmatically, as a kind of limit figure, a force for negation, is not unrelated to its black population. In this way New Orleans has long functioned as a rite of passage for its visitors. "Long before I visited New Orleans I would visit it in my imagination," writes Tom Piazza, a much more subtle commentator than Nik Cohn, though not immune to caricature and cliché.[19] "The air smelled different; it felt different, heavier, on your arms, more like a liquid than like air." Where New York might be associated with the mind, Piazza suggests, New Orleans is more an experience of the body: "New Orleans was like finding yourself in some electrically charged soup."[20]

Borrowing Jacqueline Rose's suggestion that we should recognize the role that fantasy plays in public life, it might be helpful to think of New Orleans as an imaginative site that has been appropriated to inform a larger "state fantasy." In *States of Fantasy*, Rose writes: "fantasy surely ceases to be a private matter if it fuels, or at least plays its part in, the forging of the collective will. More simply, you don't have to buy into Freud's account of hidden guilt to recognize the force in the real world of the unconscious dreams of nations."[21] Donald Pease picks up Rose's insights to suggest that American exceptionalism should be understood along these lines, as the key U.S. "state fantasy." The fantasy of the blank slate that has become a staple of exceptionalist discourse—functioning as possibly the key ideological motor of the project of settling America and which has continued to drive the marginalization of history in U.S. national ideology—might be said to function in this way, just beneath the surface of national consciousness.[22]

Arguably, the idea of the blank slate finds its exception in a city that has been constructed by outsiders as a haunted place of death, decay, decline.

Where in his 1986 study another foreign tourist to the United States, Jean Baudrillard, presented a remarkable and clichéd vision of "America" as identified with the blankness of the desert and the surface play of the signifier,[23] New Orleans has been consistently associated with the imagination of depth. As Nik Cohn claims of the city: "if you stay here it's almost impossible to skim along the surface." It is a city, Cohn suggests, that constantly confronts you with things normally buried, with realities elsewhere repressed.

I suggest that in this sense the "City that Care Forgot"—as New Orleans has often been known and indeed treated—has posed as a kind of playground for the American imagination, an unruly id that has notably transgressed the rules laid down by the national superego. Catholic where the national mainstream is Protestant, openly transnational where the national mainstream claims to be exceptional, black where the national mainstream imagines itself white, a place of pleasure and play against a national Protestant work ethic. In this sense sustaining the paradox so prevalent in discourse on New Orleans, that it is both foreign to the national imaginary and quintessentially American, is inadequate: it might be better seen as the nation's excessive supplement, one that has been variously appropriated as a national other to consolidate national unity, but which ultimately refuses to be assimilated into the official story of America.

It is this latter point that begins to push beyond the clichéd formulations that have made New Orleans the object of an external gaze, and which instead points to the ways in which the city's organic culture and traditions do perhaps genuinely resist the national mainstream. Piazza's description of the New Orleans tradition of the jazz funeral is helpful in this regard:

> Most funeral traditions in our society are there to remind us that we are dust, and to dust we shall return. In New Orleans the funerals remind us that Life is bigger than any individual life, and it will roll on, and for the short time that your individual life joins the big stream of Life, cut some decent steps, for God's sake . . . This isn't escapism, or denial of grief; it is acceptance of the facts of life, the map of a profound relationship to the grief that is a part of life.[24]

This acceptance of death in life is part of a larger appreciation of what Piazza calls "thereness" or, in other words, a present that is accentuated by an acute awareness of finitude. Piazza characterizes New Orleans culture as "part of a ritual in which the finiteness, the specificity and fragility and durability and richness and earthiness and sadness and laughter of life, are all mixed together, honored, and given tangible form in sound, movement, and communal cuisine."[25] The various ways in which the city's evident appetite for pleasure often exists in close proximity to pain are indicative of the blues tradition so central to African-American culture. The jazz funeral is a remarkable example of this proximity, and the kind of ecstatic grief that these events often display might be seen as forms of *jouissance*, that joy that exists "beyond the pleasure principle" and which Jacques Lacan associated with the death drive. While for Freud the death drive was primarily aggressive, for poststructuralist thinkers its destructive powers have been identified in a host of tendencies that challenge the symbolic order of the social. New Orleans' deeply rooted traditions of the carnivalesque, with Mardi Gras being only the most prominent example, regularly enact symbolic reversals that not only mock the social order but which threaten to dissolve the order of the symbolic entirely. In this sense, certainly some aspects of the city's culture have, on a much deeper level than its tourist industry implies, embraced an understanding of finitude in ways that conflict with American exceptionalist discourse and its veritable colonization of the future.

In *No Future* (2004) Lee Edelman appropriates the death drive as part of his polemical critique of the fantasy of the future as projected via what he describes as "reproductive futurism." For Edelman it is the figure of the child who "has come to embody for us the telos of the social order and come to be seen as the one for whom that order is held in perpetual trust."[26] In this way the social structure authenticates itself by presenting us with an unquestioned and unquestionable figure—the innocent child of the future—while diverting attention from the curtailment of rights in the present. In opposition to the future-oriented nature of all politics, Edelman poses the figure of the queer, a figure that he argues embraces negativity—the death drive—in order to unsettle the fiction of identity and the myth of political progress. While he argues that lesbians and gay men are likely to be just as invested in reproductive futurism as their straight counterparts, he suggests that they *should* embrace their queerness within the social order, which is constituted by their association with its end. By analogy we might argue that aspects of New Orleans are queer in Edelman's sense—or that the city should embrace its own stereotypic representations as the negation of the larger national culture. Its associations with ritual, death and indeed—in popular imagination at least—with sterility, arguably circumvent the linear model of time that has delimited the teleological imagination of life in the modern West. And yet this appropriation of the symbolic possibilities of New Orleans might also be read as another grotesque distortion of this city and its rich material culture.

In the aftermath of Katrina New Orleans' associations with death became literal rather than figural. Images of the bloated bodies of the drowned—compared by some to lynching photographs[27]—were accompanied by rhetoric in some quarters that a city residing largely below sea level ought to be left to die a "natural" death. Others suggested that Katrina was an act of God sent to "cleanse" what they viewed as a center of abortion, homosexuality, and the racialized spectres of "welfare dependency" and voodoo. As Michael Bibler suggests, Katrina confirmed for many "the perception of New Orleans as a tragic city that has already sealed its own doom."[28] For Bibler, the city's apparent links with "blackness and femaleness" are key to this sense of tragedy, and to these racialized and gendered associations we might also want to add a sexual orientation similarly associated with negation.

Threatened with destruction on all sides, the future and the myriad agendas that might shape it have loomed large in post-storm New Orleans. The Katrina crisis demands decisions on all kinds of levels that have inexorably drawn the city into the orbit of repair, recovery and reconstruction—survival activities that have no alliance with the death drive. For Cohn Katrina seems to have exorcised New Orleans of that "death-haunted quality": Katrina "was so serious, they got all the death they could handle . . . Something happened with Katrina, that washed away that miasmic feeling. It's less addictive now, and it's a lot better for your health." Though not a cause for personal celebration, Katrina has, according to Cohn, "cleansed" the city. Cohn's simultaneous and indulgent nostalgia for the fantasy of a hedonistic city in love with death brings into relief the myriad ways in which a critical embrace of the death drive can paradoxically coexist with the rhetoric of redemption and opportunity which has characterized the neoliberal response to post-Katrina New Orleans.

Edelman's work is a case in point. Quite apart from the problematic gender politics of his attack on reproductive futurism, Edelman's commitment to a queerness that disrupts any articulation of a politics, that can only commit to the "undoing of civil society"—that is in fact so disturbing to the symbolic order that the task of articulating it (in language), Edelman admits, is futile—in effect fails to offer any resistance to the status quo. This is symptomatic of a larger problem in academic scholarship that reifies the self-deconstructing qualities of so much that is problematic in social and cultural life, as if this discourse in itself enacted real change, while rejecting the compromising and muddying work of politics. The effects can be not so dissimilar to the rightist positions that nurture the neoliberal status quo and which so many of these academic arguments claim to contest.

A similar slipperiness can be identified in the New Urbanist philosophy that has played such a central role in reconstructing post-Katrina New Orleans. New Urbanism supports the creation of mixed-income housing that nurtures community by constructing built environments that are walkable and on a human scale. It is hard to disagree with these principles. And yet, as will be discussed in detail in chapter 4, they have been appropriated to justify the demolition of much of the city's public-housing stocks which had been under threat before the storm, and which, contrary to some claims, weathered Katrina remarkably well. The claim that these housing projects, which, so the argument goes, concentrated poverty and incubated environments ripe for crime and drug abuse, were unfit for human habitation, rang hollow when residents and campaigners launched an impassioned campaign against the demolition plans and for the right of former residents to return to their homes.[29] This was further reinforced when the United Nations called on the city and the U.S. government to halt the demolitions, for fear that the human rights of particularly the city's African-American population were under threat.

In this way New Urbanist philosophy collaborates with agendas that disenfranchise the city's poor and disproportionately black population, even if its outlook and aspirations are ultimately well-intentioned. New Urbanist principles also function to erode the city's distinctive features even as it pays lip-service to them: Andres Duany, a leading light of the New Urbanist movement, champions the idea that New Orleans should be thought of as a "Caribbean city" (an idea explored in chapter 1)—one that has developed differently from the rest of the United States. He claims: "if New Orleans were to be governed as efficiently as, say Minneapolis, it would be a different place—and not one that I could care for. Let me work with the government the way that it is." In this vein, as Cedric Johnson explains, "Duany argues in favour of laissez-faire building practice as a means of preserving the city's famous *laissez le bon temps roulez* culture."[30] This is one among many examples of the appropriation of New Orleans' exceptional status within the United States in the name of an ideological and profit-driven agenda that is itself very much an expression of the mainstream; it is the same paradox to be noted within a tourist industry eager to sell the city's unique cultural legacy and in doing so constantly threatening its "Disneyfication."

It is also a good example of the way in which the city's historic repudiation of the national exceptionalist conceit of the "blank slate" has been appropriated and subverted after Katrina. The physical destruction of much of New Orleans during the storm has seemingly offered the city up to planners and developers to be both literally and metaphorically levelled and reimagined: in this sense the hurricane has transformed the city into the mythological blank slate of the national imaginary. For some, this spells opportunity, for others tragedy; the debates are thorny and complicated.

In the aftermath of Katrina, when the rhetoric of redemption and opportunity threatened first the destruction and then the neoliberal remaking of the city, it was crucial that this vision of the future be met with alternative possibilities. Particularly given the fact that pre-Katrina New Orleans was no paradise for the vast majority of its residents, even if it nonetheless constituted "home" in the deepest possible sense. And yet this fantasy of the future that has been so central to the idea of the "American dream," and which Edelman and others have been so critical of, is not without real dilemmas in this context. This threat of the neoliberal destruction of post-Katrina New Orleans—some of which has been realized, although not without significant resistance—is fundamentally linked to "Katrina time," to that unbounded time that has no end, that is in fact the negation of the future. This does not prevent the neoliberal authorities abusing the rhetoric of the future, ruthlessly appropriating the figure of the future child, and this is precisely Edelman's point. Simultaneously and paradoxically, in order for the city to survive as a transgressive and resistant site within U.S. culture, it needs to conjure its own vision of the future child. This vision has become a battleground upon which different constituencies—including many looking in, often greedily, to the goldfish bowl—have sought to stamp their formula for the future.

What seems to be at stake here is the extent to which the vision of the future that wins out maintains the traces of its genesis in a city that has played an important cultural role as whistleblower in relation to the larger national imaginary—a place that has arguably enacted a queer time in relation to America in part because many of its traditions have mocked the kind of taken-for-granted future that has been such a central part of U.S. political ideology. These constitute key questions for this book: is it possible for the city to resist "Katrina time" without sacrificing the unique temporality by which it appears to resist key aspects of United States ideology? Is it possible to embrace the idea that aspects of New Orleans offer a unique and resistant cultural experience without adopting the stereotypes that have routinely maligned the city and its inhabitants?

On Ruins, Redemption, and a Post-American World

As soon as the storm hit real estate developers and politicians began announcing quite publicly that from the ruins of post-Katrina New Orleans would come redemption. Most notoriously, Republican Senator Richard Baker told lobbyists "we finally cleaned up public housing in New Orleans. We couldn't do it but God did." The financial and social opportunities that the storm presented to some were spelled out by real estate magnate Finis Shellnut: "The storm destroyed a great deal and there's plenty of space to build houses and sell them for a lot of money . . . Most importantly, the hurricane drove poor people and criminals out of the city and we hope they don't come back."[31] As Naomi Klein argues in *The Shock Doctrine* (2007), post-Katrina New Orleans became a laboratory of neoliberal opportunity, an opening—a moment of shock—that was exploited by an agenda already fully envisioned before the storm but one which might only be swallowed by residents caught unawares.[32]

As many journalists and scholars have now charted, residents in their numbers in post-storm New Orleans have been engaged in an ongoing struggle with the authorities for the right to return to and shape the future of their home. They may have been caught unawares but the response has nonetheless been phenomenal. Rebecca Solnit is one of the many commentators who has been deeply moved by the emergent grassroots movements in the city, and post-Katrina New Orleans forms a key chapter of her book, *A Paradise Built in Hell: The Extraordinary Communities that Arise in Disaster* (2009). For Solnit it is the sense of solidarity witnessed in the aftermath of disaster, the improvised, usually transitory and often quasi-utopian communities that are formed, that offer an opening, a glimpse of redemption. The redemptive trajectory that Solnit favors in her text is belied by much of the evidence she cites: Solnit wants to argue that disaster highlights something that is ultimately good in "human nature," despite the fact that her thorough research frequently uncovers instances of social injustice either created or exacerbated by disaster and which paint a patchy picture of "human nature"—at least at the top of the socioeconomic ladder.[33] The unevenness that Solnit reveals tells against her frequent invocation of the commonly held view that disasters are socially levelling. As Naomi Klein writes, with post-storm New Orleans in mind:

> Not so long ago, disasters were periods of social leveling, rare moments when atomized communities put divisions aside and pulled together. Increasingly, however, disasters are the opposite: they provide windows into a cruel and ruthlessly divided future in which money and race buy survival.[34]

While in many ways inadvertently affirming this less redemptive view, Solnit's assessments of post-Katrina New Orleans often—and again, almost certainly inadvertently—reinforce the logic of privatization that creates these bifurcated futures. Solnit's enthusiasm for post-Katrina volunteerism leads her to espouse "the viability of a dispersed, decentralized system of decision making";[35] while her text is rhetorically opposed to the divestment of public services in New Orleans and is passionate in its critique of shameful government neglect in the storm's immediate aftermath, she ultimately implies that this "shadow government" of engaged citizens offer a better alternative.[36] Solnit suggests that "one reason that disasters are threatening to elites is that power devolves to the people on the ground in many ways," but in so doing she misses the fact that the "do-it-yourself" society is precisely what the neoliberal roll-back of public services is all about.[37]

That Solnit's text might inadvertently support the logic behind Baker and Shellnut's statements on the economic opportunities available in post-Katrina New Orleans demonstrates the dilemmas posed by any discourse of redemption—that seeks to turn a negative into a positive and make something *work*. Interestingly, the figure that Solnit chooses to end her text with is the ruin. The epilogue is entitled "The Doorway in the Ruins." *A Paradise Built in Hell* does not centralize this figure—although Solnit has written about ruins elsewhere[38]—but it is indicative of the ways in which this figure as conceptualized in journalistic and academic discourse can blunt critical functions. This is particularly significant here given that not only has New Orleans been historically associated with ruins, but that post-Katrina New Orleans has been linked to the ruins that might define the United States' post-imperial decline at the end of the American Century.

William Faulkner's evocation of New Orleans in his 1927 novel, *Mosquitoes*, exemplifies the city's status as a metaphoric and literal ruin in the literary imagination. Faulkner's French Quarter is simultaneously a place of vivid sensory experience—it smells "overripe"—and the terminus for the senses, a place that threatens stasis: in an early scene one of the novel's cast of characters strikes a match and leads his companions "up the dark tortuous stairs while their three shadows aped them, rising and falling monstrously upon the ancient wall."[39] This architectural ruin houses the jagged figure of an artist with a "hawk's face" who, like the other artists we are presented with later in *Mosquitoes*, turns out to be in the process of staving off his own inevitable decline, financially parasitic on those who cannot ultimately avert his eventual ruin.[40]

The ludicrous figure of the artists' patron in the novel is historically contemporary with the emergence of an increasingly formalized preservation movement dedicated to retaining the Quarter's unique historic features, long shaped by the process of memorialization. These developments culminated with a 1936 amendment to the Louisiana Constitution which named the Vieux Carré a historic district with special privileges.[41] Like Faulkner's patron, supporters of the preservation movement in New Orleans fight a quaint and ultimately losing battle against the juggernaut of "progress" by actively embracing ruins. Though socially conservative in one sense, these forces for preservation arguably gesture toward a more radical understanding of ruins and their social function.

As part of a larger tradition of "ruin-gazing," the preservation movement in New Orleans romantically and nostalgically invests in a locale that guarantees origins by stamping the past on our image of the present. Yet as Andreas Huyssen writes, the nostalgia for the past that is part of our investment in the ruin is one shadowed by the fact that the past can only be grasped in its decay. The ruin, writes Huyssen, represents "the hardly nostalgic consciousness of the transitoriness of all greatness and power, the warning of imperial hubris, and the remembrance of nature in all culture."[42] This latter remembrance can be witnessed all over the city as erupting tree roots, forced up by the ground swell of water-logged soil, result in cracked and potholed roads and sidewalks; a vivid and treacherous reminder that the urban colonization of "nature" is only temporary. Huyssen's insight becomes even more complex when transplanted to perceptions of the French Quarter, the architecture of which gestures back to the Spanish and French colonial periods. Not only do these "ruins" represent pasts "other" to the United States, they also gesture to an unacknowledged aspect of U.S. history wherein it picked up the imperial mantle from its French predecessor by purchasing the largest chunk of its continental empire. The United States was not a conquering power in the region but the Louisiana Purchase is a reminder that its status as a U.S. possession was not a foregone conclusion, and neither was its transition to statehood, which happened in 1812. The ghost of an old order that haunts the Quarter is fascinating not because it excludes the United States but for the ways in which it includes it, thus enacting a memory of the nation's transnational and indeed imperial origins.

In their collection *Ruins of Modernity*, Julia Hell and Andreas Schönle suggest that the familiar cyclic story of imperial legacies and their ruination "seemed to be a story of European ruins. But after 9/11 and the invasion of Iraq, it has become an American story, too."

> America used to set little store by ruins, venerating its prehistoric natural heritage at the expense of historical artifacts . . . Yet in a post-Fordist, post 9/11 reality, the imaginary of imperial ruin and ruination has become pervasive.[43]

For Hell and Schönle, the "ruins" of post-Katrina New Orleans are central to their narrative in which the United States discovers its own tradition of ruins in a post-industrial reality of imperial decline. Crucial to this embrace of U.S. ruins would be a simultaneous acknowledgment of the imperial nature of the American national project. But arguably Hell and Schönle's analysis falls victim to the tendencies it warns against: "soon our gaze at the rubble piling up before our eyes is clouded by the iconic wreckage of ages."[44] If the ruins that resulted from Katrina are a "wake-up call" of some kind, as they suggest, this call needs to be considered in its specificity rather than in the nebulous and all-encompassing lexicon of "ruin discourse."

This is perhaps best illustrated by the collection's impulse to talk about the ruins of post-industrial Detroit and post-Katrina New Orleans in the same breath. Long before the city of Detroit declared itself bankrupt in July 2013 it had been viewed as the symbol of U.S. post-industrial decline. Detroit was the motor city that was in the postwar period hailed as the symbol of the American Century. Shiny Art Deco buildings and towering skyscrapers were architectural signs of the city's faith in the larger national dream of progress; as George Steinmetz puts it, "Detroit occupied a central place in the imaginary of twentieth-century industrial modernity."[45] But arguably by the 1960s, even before the race riots which many name as the beginning of the city's descent, Detroit started showcasing the symptoms of post-industrial decline and by the 1980s its golden era was long over and the city was widely viewed as a key instance of urban blight and the social desperation that accompanies it. The combination of the postwar "white flight" and the loss of its manufacturing base mean that contemporary Detroit features the decaying inner city that has become the norm for many U.S. urban environments. New Orleans' trajectory is in many ways not so dissimilar. It too has suffered from the disinvestment in public services that attends "white flight" and the consequent loss of the tax base, bears the marks of the nationwide commitment to the construction of freeways at the expense of public transportation, and suffered job losses as a result of the decline of the industrial sector—which gave way to a low-wage tourist economy. Like Detroit, New Orleans in the 1990s became infamous for its drug trade and the attendant high crime rates, turf wars, and urban suffering. Unlike Detroit though, New Orleans was never viewed as a symbol of U.S. aspirations—it has never been considered the embodiment of a national future.

In this sense the "ruins" that we see post-Katrina are fundamentally different from those that were imagined in New Orleans pre-Katrina. Where the appreciation of the pre-Katrina "ruins" might be seen as part of a European narrative of ruins indicative of the ways in which the city departs from national norms, including America's general lack of appreciation for historical ruins, the ruins of post-storm New Orleans arguably bring the city back into the national fold by not only inserting it into an emergent discourse of *U.S.* imperial ruins, but also by centralizing it as a site for America's future redemption. Where pre-Katrina ruins only pointed backward, post-Katrina ruins point remorselessly forward. At least from the perspective of those who want to ignore the lessons of history floating in the storm debris and "move on."

"The ruin is a ruin precisely because it seems to have lost its function or meaning in the present, while retaining a suggestive, unstable semantic potential."[46] The transtemporal language of "ruins" is potentially radical because it unsettles stable notions of place and time, but this process of unsettling, of "destruction," which clears a "space" and creates an "opportunity," simultaneously draws our attention—strikingly in the New Orleans context—to the disturbing tendencies unleashed by the elision of crucial historical and geographical distinctions.

Donald Pease's contemplation of the rubble not of New Orleans but of New York calls our attention to another mode of temporal dislocation that arguably does not threaten the disappearance of history, the revelation of a "blank slate": trauma. For Pease, the image of the collapsing twin towers returns to U.S. spectators the knowledge of the nation's violent origins—the disavowal of which forms the comforting foundation of American exceptionalism. According to Pease, 9/11 provided a "conclusive ending" to the Cold War as well as reinstating the imagined presence of a national enemy that might inaugurate "the dynamic structure of American exceptionalism as a collectively shared state fantasy."[47] In this way 9/11 conveniently furnishes the U.S. government with a means of masking U.S. economic and political aggression abroad as national defense. And yet Pease also suggests that 9/11 performs a deconstructive role in relation to national mythology. His argument draws on the mythology of the "Virgin Lands" that was mobilized by the early settlers to perpetuate the lie that the so-called New World was an empty one, while they went about their genocidal campaign to eliminate the native population. Pease points out that George W. Bush mobilized this myth to talk about the way in which 9/11 violated U.S. territory, but suggests that in doing so Bush hints at this narrative's own undoing. Pease writes:

> At Ground Zero, U.S. Virgin Land had not merely been violat-
> ed by foreign invaders; this violation assumed the form of the

forcible dislocation of a settled population. The buildings that had been erected to symbolize the U.S. rise to world dominance were turned into horrific spectacles of the violent removal of occupants from their site of residence.[48]

Pease's arguments are persuasive and chime with a number of accounts that read 9/11 as an uncanny return of various U.S. national crimes. Yet his sense that the spectacle of 9/11 gestured back to the violence of national founding and thus the impossibility of American innocence does not account for the very robust articulations of American innocence and exceptionalist discourse that were mobilized in 9/11's wake. Pease's treatment of post-Hurricane Katrina New Orleans registers the strain of this particular narrative of U.S. ruins. Pease suggests that the post-storm city produced "unforgettable representations of the vulnerable and homeless persons that the Homeland had abandoned," and so for him, "these images meant that the state fantasy of the Homeland Security State had been drowned in the same waters as the city of New Orleans."[49] While this seems to be undeniably the case, Pease's implication that the predominant emotion inspired by post-Katrina New Orleans among the American public was identification and compassion seems to overlook the role played by politicians and journalists, many of whom shaped an atmosphere in which the victims of Katrina were blamed for their own need and subject to countless racist and classist misrepresentations.

Where 9/11 shored up notions of American unity by providing an external enemy as focus, Katrina similarly led to exclusive constructions of Americanness, but variants that, by involving various "enemies within," were less robust because shot through with profound ambivalence. Again, while the links between 9/11 and Hurricane Katrina are substantive and important, it is not possible to appropriate both events seamlessly into a narrative about the "ruin" or deconstruction of American exceptionalism, even if this particular account moves in opposition to the mythology of the "blank slate" and the evacuation of history that this mythology supports. Both events relate to a larger story of U.S. decline, but in fundamentally different ways.

Pease's account of the post-9/11 unravelling of American exceptionalism suggests that this process has come about as a result of contact with a "traumatic real"—with this narrative's "obscene underside." Part of the problem with this account seems to be that it relies on the logic of exception that grounds our understandings of trauma. Both 9/11 and Hurricane Katrina are construed as moments of rupture that return a "traumatic real" (the knowledge of the genocidal origins of U.S. settlement and a deeply ingrained legacy of racism that supported slavery and its afterlife) that fracture investments of U.S. citizens in exceptionalist narratives. In fact the understanding of particularly 9/11 as an instance of "trauma" seems to have been a barrier to the ethical moment of recognition that Pease identifies. Not only did 9/11 reinforce in myriad ways an understanding of the U.S. subject as innocent (victim of trauma), as numerous commentators have argued.[50] Its visual imagery and media portrayal was also constructed as a traumatic rupture, a cultural faultline. "We will never be the same again." While some portrayed 9/11 as returning the United States to the scene of historical struggle after a period of postmodern stupor,[51] this was nonetheless understood as a singular event that belied context. The "day of fire"[52] identified by George W. Bush came for many commentators "out of the blue."

Katrina too was sensationalized by the media as a singular event, a story that momentarily highlighted social realities that were soon forgotten. Unlike 9/11 it was not as clear in coverage of Katrina who the victims of trauma were—those who actually suffered at the hands of the storm and subsequent government neglect or those who witnessed the scenes with a mixture of compassion and scorn. Nonetheless, the hurricane was construed as exceptional, "the big one" that had destroyed a city that was somehow itself exceptional in the levels of social malaise it harbored. Liberal accounts that portrayed Katrina as a "national tragedy" that expressed a specifically "American dilemma" of racial disenfranchisement failed to open the discussion to one that properly included class, and neither did they keep the conversation about race on the table long enough to have a meaningful debate.

In contrast it is the task of scholarship in Katrina's aftermath to return to the "ruin" of pre-Katrina New Orleans, the one that hosted levels of social despair comparable to Detroit but which also pointed back to transnational and imperial histories that always already deny the mythology of the blank slate and the related enigma of the level playing field. This return allows us to view post-Katrina New Orleans not as a traumatic rupture but rather as part of the "slow violence"[53] that has afflicted impoverished communities in this city and this region for decades. But it also enables us to understand the ways in which aspects of New Orleans culture have bypassed the "cruel optimism" that has long been the product of investments in the American dream. Lauren Berlant writes that "a relation of cruel optimism exists when something you desire is actually an obstacle to your flourishing."[54] She argues that neoliberal capitalism has ushered in an increasingly unstable reality in which fantasies of the good life are increasingly unrealizable. For Berlant any attachment or investment, even if negative, is by definition optimistic;

and by her reckoning life-building investments in the twenty-first century yield increasingly cruel results. As a city whose postwar mythology was steeped in the promise of the American dream, contemporary Detroit might be cited as a casualty of cruel optimism. New Orleans on the other hand might exemplify the failure of the American dream, but it was never viewed as its realization, and neither was it culturally so in love with the idea. I understand this lack of love—which should not be interpreted as wholly positive or negative—as an untimeliness that in the twentieth century was in marked tension with a national context self-defined by being in time, at one with time. This untimeliness, which should not be confused with an out-of-timeness, gains new national relevance in a century in which the United States no longer seems to have the monopoly on time.

If "ruin" is a helpful figure in this context, it needs to be spatially and historically situated in order to compare and contrast its pre- and post-Katrina manifestations, or what I prefer to think of as the disjunction between "Katrina time" and an interruptive New Orleans temporality. Indeed, by this comparison we might see post-Katrina New Orleans not as an instance of the ruins of the American century or the return of a traumatic "real," but rather as the enactment of the nation's own death drive that post-9/11 realities only partially sublimated by inaugurating a clearer narrative of insides and outsides. Rather than seeking to put this negativity to work in the service of redemption, this book is interested in preserving the critical functions of New Orleans culture in such a way that it does not become subsumed in a narrative about U.S. decline. Ironically then, a city long imagined as the outer limit or even the negation of national ideology, long associated with death, might offer alternatives to narratives of self-destruction that seem to haunt contemporary projections of U.S. cultural, political, and environmental futures.

Overview

This book explores post-Katrina New Orleans with three temporal vantage points in mind: "American time," or the time of an American Century that seems to have run its course; "Katrina time," or the time of neoliberalism; and "New Orleans time," an interruptive temporality that resists both the fantasy of "American time" and the nightmare of "Katrina time." The book is divided into three parts, each of which centralizes one of these temporal modes while attending to the ways in which they compete with and bleed into the others. While constructions of past, present, and future are in play throughout the book, part I, "American time," is oriented toward the past and explores the ways in which New Orleans has historically been at odds with national conceptions of temporality. Part II, "Katrina time," works largely with the present to explore the ways in which art and political practices in the post-storm city have attempted to resist the short-term market logic that has dominated the so-called recovery. And part III, "New Orleans time," is oriented toward the future, though this is a future that battles with the claims of the past, one that is shot through with historical memory.

My narrative's present spans the ten years between the late summer of 2005 and 2015, taking in key texts and issues that emerged during this period, as well as the conversations that marked the ten-year anniversary of Hurricane Katrina. This exploration of New Orleans is staged from the perspective of an outsider, which in New Orleans is necessarily that of a "tourist" (unless you have been there long enough to be unlovingly described as a "transplant"), and its object will be read through a wide variety of cultural texts: news media, political, fictional, and scholarly narratives, involving written, visual, cinematic and oral sources and practices. Its most immediate body of scholarly coordinates will be the work produced thus far on cultural representations of post-Katrina New Orleans, which involves myriad essays, a 2009 *American Quarterly* special issue,[55] and two collections published in 2010, *Old and New Media after Katrina* edited by Diane Negra and *Culture after the Hurricanes: Rhetoric and Reinvention on the Gulf Coast*, edited by M. B. Hackler.[56] While a number of full-length studies on the significance of Hurricane Katrina emerged very soon after the storm—including Henry Giroux's *Stormy Weather* (2006)[57] and Michael Eric Dyson's *Come Hell or High Water* (2006)[58]—it has taken a decade for monographs that take full account of cultural representations to emerge.[59] Amidst the veritable deluge of books on Katrina that appeared with the tenth anniversary, Bernie Cook's *Flood of Images: Media, Memory, and Hurricane Katrina* (2015),[60] especially in its focus on the documentary format, speaks most directly to the concerns of this work. The aim here is to put discussions of Katrina in a systematic dialogue with relevant political, philosophical, and environmental conversations, as well as reflecting the ways in which this topic and the texts that it has inspired speaks to American studies in a world in which U.S. power is on the wane.

This book is framed by key conceptual concerns that radiate from a number of different directions: the last decade has seen the emergence of several important collections that have attempted to reorient American studies in the new century, the most significant for this book being Russ Castronovo and Susan Gillman's *States of Emergency: The Object of*

American Studies (2009),[61] which treats the development of the discipline in its post-9/11, post-Katrina manifestations. Donald Pease's *The New American Exceptionalism* (2009) is important here given his argument that 9/11 and Katrina have unwittingly enacted the return of a kind of "traumatic real" that has exposed the nation to its own traumatic origins in the twenty-first century. While this is a compelling thesis that carries much weight given the pervasive tendency to view violent events through the prism of trauma, in the rest of the book I elaborate an argument that seeks, with a number of contemporary theorists, to move away from trauma as the predominant framework in which to understand disaster. In particular, Lauren Berlant's insistence on "ordinary crisis" as the context of neoliberal capitalism under-scores the precarious nature of contemporary life much more accurately than does the exceptional logic of trauma.

With Berlant, this book is interested in the "cruel optimism" at the heart of investments in the "American dream" and the queering of time and the critique of the future that goes with this recognition. And yet, as partially outlined above, the rejection of all identity politics and program-matic political agendas is the luxury of those who do not need to involve themselves in messy political struggles against structural inequalities. The queer critique of the future is put under most pressure, I argue, when we encounter narratives of racial and environmental vulnerability and injustice that require the production of alternatives "timelines" that discard neither the past nor the future. Here the work of Wai Chee Dimock, and in par-ticular her sense that American studies needs to look beyond "the short chronology of a young nation," has been formative.[62] In its attempts to push against the collapsed temporality of "Katrina time," this book strains toward timelines that precede New Orleans' status as an American city and indeed precedes the Mississippi valley's physical manipulation by European explorers, in an attempt to reimagine the collective and historical values that might make the future something other than a repetition of the present. It also centralizes Afro-Creole cultural contributions to New Orleans: the cultures that have evolved from the descendants of slaves and free people of color are crucial to the ways in which the city activates memories that not only transcend the United States as a formal national unit but which also transcend its triumphalist ideology as it manifested itself in the twentieth century. New Orleans' status as a "black city," this book argues, is central to its role as a whistleblower vis-à-vis the nation. Black New Orleanians have suffered the most as a result of "Katrina time," and it follows that the cultures they represent are also central to resisting it.

The 2011 collection edited by Cedric Johnson, *The Neoliberal Deluge: Hurricane Katrina, Late Capitalism, and the Remaking of New Orleans*, has been invaluable in terms of thinking about how post-storm New Orleans intersects with and intervenes with these larger trends. The book highlights the particular challenges posed by neoliberalism—and the "horizontal" constellations that come with the dismantling of the state—to progressive academic scholarship that has been committed for so long to identifying and disrupting top-down social arrangements. But what *The Neoliberal Deluge* misses, and what I hope this book will keenly attend to, are the specific ways in which New Orleans, both past and present, potentially runs against the grain in terms of its commitments to public space, as well as its investments in time that are not always already reducible to monetary value. As suggested above, without reifying or romanticizing the city's cultural differences, this book seeks to read these differences as alternatives to a mainstream that disciplines New Orleans as it does elsewhere. For this reason the large body of work on New Orleans culture, history, and geography plays an important role here, in particular Richard Campanella's incomparable and invaluable work on the city's "historical geography."[63]

This book is therefore eclectic in terms of genre, encompassing literature, film, political and journalistic discourse, interviews, tourist practices, and spans a wide variety of disciplines: transnational American studies, in literary and historical guises, critical race theory, environmental studies, disaster studies, urban studies, New Orleans studies. But the methodology deployed here is one developed in cultural studies, whereby the aesthetic and contextual dimensions of cultural texts are consistently considered in relation to questions of power. Race, neoliberalism, and U.S. ideology are the principal frames through which power is explored and understood in this book which centralizes representations of New Orleans produced during the ten years after Katrina.

Part I considers post-Katrina New Orleans in the light of its historical relationship to "American time," as both New Orleans and the United States evolved from the revolutionary period into and beyond the twentieth century. Chapter 1, "New Orleans and Empire," seeks to chart the reputation New Orleans has acquired for being somehow foreign to the national imaginary by tracking its relationships to the modalities of empire and revolution. Through an exploration of New Orleans' links, identifications, and tensions with the Caribbean nation of Haiti, I suggest that the city exposes the multiple paradoxes at work in the larger U.S. embrace of a revolutionary legacy and its rejection of an imperial one. The chapter begins with the figure of Guantánamo Bay, which I argue is a crucial coordinate for mapping post-Katrina New Orleans' relationship with the so-called war on terror, the war on drugs, and the pre-Katrina city's historic connections with Haiti via Cuba and the larger transatlantic slave trade. The chapter traverses the transnational prison-industrial complex and the period between the 2010 Haiti earthquake and the declaration of Haitian independence at the turn of the nineteenth century as a result of the first and only successful slave revolt in history. An exploration of constructions of the Haitian Revolution focuses on Isabel Allende's historical novel, *Island Beneath the Sea* (2009), which explores eighteenth- and nineteenth-century links between the two Caribbean/Latin locations, and which I read as a post-Katrina "magical realist" fictionalization.[64] This chapter establishes the ways in which New Orleans' spatial coordinates—both real and imagined—illuminate and challenge the nation's supposedly anti-imperialist trajectory, while introducing the city's complicated temporal horizons vis-à-vis "American time," which are further elaborated in the next chapter.

Chapter 2, "New Orleans and Americanization," charts the paradoxical process by which New Orleans came to exhibit many key features common to U.S. cities in the twentieth century, while it simultaneously gained a reputation for exoticism, the good times, and an orientation toward the past. The chapter will trace the transformation of New Orleans during the course of the twentieth century from a bustling economic center to a weak, service-based economy dominated by tourism. Through an examination of the evolution of tourist practices in the city and its surroundings, this chapter will show the way in which the overwhelming focus on "history" and "haunting" in New Orleans tourism has long linked the city with often racialized ideas of decline and obsolescence. This link has been exacerbated by the city's association with the time of leisure as opposed to that of work. New Orleans, by the end of the twentieth century, had higher numbers of native-born residents than any other major city in the United States. This attests to the ways in which it has countered trends toward national mobility, with deep local roots that also might be juxtaposed to the global networks that dominate the city's history and economy.

Consequently the city's reputation for leisure has often been coupled with the idea that it is somehow "stagnant"—a characterization that dates back to the beginning of the twentieth century, and which overlooks the myriad ways in which these deep roots have nurtured the unique cultures for which New Orleans is famous. The consequence of these associations is that New Orleans has often seemed to capture trends that are in tension with the idea of relentless progress associated with the march of the

"American Century," while nonetheless encompassing many of the features associated with so-called "urban blight" in the twentieth century. I argue that this peculiar "untimeliness" with regard to the rest of the nation has been exacerbated and complicated since Katrina.

The second part of this book will focus on the post-Katrina present to explore the effects on New Orleans of what I am calling "Katrina time." This part of the book identifies two key and related developments in post-Katrina aesthetic and political practices: the turn to documentary as a key and deeply politicized mode for representing Katrina, and the emphasis on the "right to return" as a central narrative of resistance to what many view as the post-Katrina attempt to dismantle the public sphere.

Chapter 3, "Documenting Katrina," explores the ways in which the production of social documentary in the storm's aftermath has seemingly sought to refute the sensationalist reporting styles that were deployed in much news media coverage of Katrina. Documentary might also be seen as a mode uniquely capable of placing the Katrina story in a larger, continuous narrative of social injustice that refutes understandings of it as an exceptional event. This chapter explores two key examples of post-Katrina documentary, examining their ideological and political coordinates as art and advocacy attempting to illuminate and challenge key aspects of Katrina's neoliberal milieu. I read Tia Lessin's and Carl Deal's acclaimed documentary film *Trouble the Water* (2008), analyzing its temporal assumptions in the context of Lauren Berlant's notion of "cruel optimism," as well as the dilemmas of the left-identified rhetoric of "empowerment" in a social context sold on the right-identified myth of "self-reliance."[65] I then turn to Luisa Dantas's 2011 documentary film, *Land of Opportunity*,[66] arguing that its multilayered approach to storytelling and politics acknowledges the loss of a useable linear narrative for progressive politics, while offering alternatives to what Vincanne Adams terms the "affect economy" of Katrina time.[67] I conclude by briefly looking at Spike Lee's epic documentary films, *When the Levees Broke: A Requiem in Four Acts* (2006) and *If God is Willing and Da Creek Don't Rise* (2011), which together act out Katrina's temporal reach, ambivalently undoing the temptation toward redemption that seems to partially motivate both films. All of these films, I suggest, seek to return viewers to the violently excluded "real" of the storm so distorted by the news media coverage that followed in its wake.

Chapter 4, "Resisting Katrina," focuses on the rhetoric of the "right to return," a slogan that emerged with particular force in post-Katrina organizing that sought to challenge the realities of displacement and gentrification. The chapter begins by looking at the debate about public

housing, the history of which long precedes Katrina, which was in turn
merely used as an excuse to push through what this chapter characterizes
as a racist "neoliberal urban policy" of demolishing the projects in favor
of new, "mixed-income communities." The transfer of public housing into
the hands of private enterprise or nonprofit agencies finds its reflection in
the post-Katrina education reforms, which similarly oversaw the destruction
of a key community asset: the neighborhood school. Again, as with public
housing, African Americans are the principal victims of neoliberal restructuring. The development of a two-tiered charter school system in New
Orleans, like the privatization of public housing, is part of a larger retreat
of the welfare state. While the welfare state is increasingly outsourcing its
work to non-governmental agencies, the penal arm of the state is increasingly being called on to address the problems of grotesque inequality, not
only in prisons but also, and disturbingly, in some schools too. This chapter
assesses the problems posed by increased privatization and militarization to
the practice of protest and dissent—which are increasingly cannibalized by
a neoliberal context insistent on the idea that "there is no alternative." This
can perhaps be most starkly seen in the post-Katrina city by the preference
for horizontal organizing practices that often seek not to make demands
on the state but rather to assert independence from it. Nonetheless, this
chapter concludes with a brief exploration of the various ways in which the
idea of the "right to the city" pervades New Orleans culture, creating not
a unified political movement but a foundation from which the case for the
survival of the public sphere might forcefully be made.

The final part of the book turns to the future, but one mediated by the
temporally complex notion of "New Orleans time." Again it examines key
and related political and aesthetic discourses that circulate around post-Katrina New Orleans as well as its larger regional, national, and transnational
coordinates, this time to explore narratives of survival. Chapter 5, "New
Orleans and Water," explores the way in which the unstable ecology of the
region has rendered it for many "the ground zero of climate change," the
frontline of the environmental justice movement. Using Rebecca Solnit's
and Rebecca Snedeker's *Unfathomable City: A New Orleans Atlas* (2013) as
a starting point, this chapter explores the cultural significance of water in
the Crescent City.[68] Reliance on levees has exacerbated the threat of flooding
these defences seek to contain, creating a false sense of security that ensures
that flooding is experienced as a traumatic interruption as opposed to an
expression of everyday "slow violence." And yet while the reality of the city's
water-logged physical geography and Louisiana's rapidly depleting wetlands
is walled out, the memory of the city's fluid foundations are mirrored back

into an urban environment that routinely reflects on its conditions of pre-carity. Memory loss in relation to environmental agency is counteracted in traditions and practices that repeatedly return to New Orleans' proximity to finitude—to a fluid that both represents life and holds out the possibility of drowning.

These issues, which balance the human need to engineer a safe environment against the reality that vulnerability and indeed water can never be completely banished, are carried into a discussion of the post-Katrina struggle for the Lower Ninth Ward. The chapter explores the way in which this neighborhood has been singled out as a possible site of "footprint shrinkage" in a discussion shadowed by race and class prejudice. And yet, through an analyses of Benh Zeitlin's *Beasts of the Southern Wild* (2012), the chapter also argues that Louisiana's rapid land loss and vulnerability to climate change demand narratives of complicity that exempt nobody from dilemmas opened up by a world increasingly buckling under the weight of "turbo-charged capitalism."[69] I conclude by considering a recent piece of immersive theatre first performed in the swamps of St. Bernard Parish, *Cry You One* (2013), that gestures toward a culture that might begin to register "slow time."[70] This piece explores the ways in which art can help us reimagine our relationship to the "natural" world via exposure to new kinds of temporalities and new ways of materializing memory.

The book's concluding chapter, "New Orleans and the Nation," considers the ways in which Katrina has offered a commentary on the larger experience of U.S. decline. It opens by exploring Chris Hedges's and Joe Sacco's work of graphic journalism, *Days of Destruction, Days of Revolt* (2012), which identifies a series of "national sacrifice zones" in order to explore what it characterizes as the abandonment of the social contract in the contemporary United States. While I argue that this text provides an illuminating window onto the conditions of "Katrina time," I also suggest that the book's mode of representation peculiarly reinforces the logic of abandonment that it charts, particularly with regard to the urban environment. The chapter then turns to David Simon's and Eric Overmyer's television series, *Treme* (2010–2013), in order to explore a narrative that appears to celebrate—as opposed to condemn—the urban setting.[71] And yet *Treme*'s "ode to New Orleans culture" is so invested in a view of the city as exceptional that it ultimately repeats many of the clichéd and stereotyped visions of the city that have also often suggested that it deserves its fate. Where Hedges and Sacco endorse the idea that their quintessential symbol of urban decline, Camden, is "dead," Simon's and Overmyer's collaboration problematically links New Orleans to narratives of self-destruction. The chapter concludes by examining a novel that places New Orleans squarely in the national predicament of neoliberal capital so central to *Days of Destruction, Days of Revolt*, while hanging on to aspects of New Orleans exceptionalism featured in *Treme*. I argue that Moira Crone's *The Not Yet* (2012) thus brings together New Orleans' representative and exceptional features in a narrative that refuses to equate the city with self-annihilation.[72] In this work of speculative fiction, New Orleans becomes the personification of Zygmunt Bauman's "liquid modernity," a framework that runs throughout this chapter as a way of thinking about the transition from "heavy" to "weightless capitalism," from an economic system at least partially invested in rewarding its workers to one that rewards predatory practices and redistributes wealth upwards.[73] I suggest in this chapter that the "Islands of New Orleans" that feature in *The Not Yet* fascinatingly stage an encounter between liquid capital and liquid precarity, wherein the latter anticipates the destruction of the former. I argue that Crone's contribution is a post-Katrina text that imagines the end of "Katrina time" by invoking a temporality that resides on the fringes of her decentered, fragmented "United Authority"—the post-American entity that has superseded the United States.

The Not Yet thus dramatizes this book's argument that post-Katrina New Orleans is prophetic in simultaneously representing a message from the past and a warning for the future. Its promise lies not in the role of neoliberal laboratory but rather in offering an estranging glimpse of what a post-American world might be like.

Part I

American Time

1

New Orleans and Empire

Legacies from the "Age of Revolution"

There is a striking moment in Dave Eggers's post-Katrina narrative *Zeitoun* (2009) when the principal protagonist, incarcerated in "Camp Grey-hound"—a makeshift prison hastily constructed in New Orleans' bus station in the storm's wake—realizes that his surroundings remind him of Guantánamo Bay.[1] This moment provides the opportunity to map, across myriad times and spaces, a genealogy of U.S. empire. This genealogy offers insights into the connections between the contemporary "war on terror" and an older history of U.S. imperial designs and territorial annexation, white supremacy and deep investments in the slave system. Guantánamo Bay as it appears here in Eggers's text conjures a triangular relationship between New Orleans, Cuba and, this chapter argues, Haiti—a nation that has played a surprisingly central role in the imagination of New Orleans on the one hand and U.S. supremacy on the other. That these hands are at one and the same time distinct and indistinct is part of the complexity of the story that binds New Orleans to the United States, as both subject and object of empire.

Just a few days after Katrina George Friedman claimed in a hyper-bolic piece for *The New York Review of Books* that the storm's "geopolitical effect was not, in many ways, distinguishable from a mushroom cloud."[2] His suggestion that Katrina was comparable to a nuclear strike, and that an attack on New Orleans was more significant than an attack on New York or Washington, clearly insinuates 9/11 into our frame for thinking about Katrina. Though not the intention of Friedman's piece, this frame also enables us to reconsider one of the labels that has policed understandings of 9/11: "Ground Zero." Amy Kaplan argues that "like the use of *9/11*, *Ground Zero* is a highly condensed and charged appellation." For Kaplan, the label Ground Zero

> resonates with the often heard claim that the world was radically altered by 9/11, that the world will never be the same, that Americans have lost their former innocence about their safety and invulnerability at home. This way of thinking might be called a narrative of historical exceptionalism, almost an antinarrative, claiming the event to be so unique and unprecedented as to transcend time and defy comparison or historical analysis.[3]

And yet, Kaplan goes on to explain, the history of the term itself belies this narrative of exceptionalism: "It was coined to describe the nuclear strikes on Hiroshima and Nagasaki." If, as Kaplan claims, "the term *Ground Zero* [in the context of 9/11] both evokes and eclipses the prior historical reference," Friedman's suggestion that Katrina bore similarities to a nuclear strike has the opposite effect.[4] His controversial piece quite explicitly meditates on the history of New Orleans as an object of empire, as, in his terms, a "geopolitical prize." Friedman speculates that had the British won the Battle of New Orleans of 1815, "we suspect they wouldn't have given it back. Without New Orleans, the entire Louisiana Purchase would have been valueless to the United States." He goes on to claim that Andrew Jackson's "obsession with Texas had much to do with keeping the Mexicans away from New Orleans." "If the Soviets could destroy one city with a large nuclear device," in Friedman's opinion, it would have been New Orleans. He reaches this surprising conclusion by making the similarly extraordinary claim that "until last Sunday, New Orleans was, in many ways, the pivot of the American economy." This claim is made on the basis that the city sits at the confluence of a river system that made one nineteenth-century commentator claim *"New Orleans is beyond a doubt the most important commercial point on the face of the earth."*[5]

Although today the city still boasts the nation's largest port—based on the volume of cargo it handles—its pre-Katrina reputation as something of an economic backwater motored largely by the tourist trade might make one sceptical about Friedman's insistence on the city's economic centrality. Today the Port of New Orleans is a mechanized one that no longer needs a large population to supply it with labor. This was not the case in the nineteenth century when New Orleans was a boom town as a consequence of its unsurpassed location—environmentally vulnerable but economically indispensable—at the mouth of the Mississippi River. Friedman's commentary on Katrina is helpful because it reminds us of New Orleans' desirability as an object of empire, and prompts an examination of the suppressed narrative that Kaplan detects in relation to 9/11.

This suppressed narrative concerns the fact that, as Marcus Rediker argues, "extraordinary violence has always been central to the making of modern capitalism."[6] And New Orleans, this chapter argues, is a key site in highlighting the myriad ways in which the United States has participated in—and has been a central agent of—this extraordinary violence. According to Rediker, the plantation and the slave ship are "the two main institutions of modern slavery," which in turn underwrite the history of capitalism itself. At the start of the nineteenth century New Orleans, surrounded by sugar and cotton plantations, was a key site on the transatlantic slave trade, and after 1810 it became the center of the U.S. domestic trade in human beings. I would like to take these two institutions, the plantation and the slave ship, which crucially inform the history of New Orleans, as examples of containment on the one hand and mobility on the other. Together, I argue, they form a dialectic of empire that refuses the notion that the one is a sign of oppression whereas the other is indicative of liberation; clearly the imperial path of modern capitalism has relied on a flexible process of drawing boundaries to variously include and exclude peoples and territories, in ways that have secured the flow of money as well as its accumulation. And yet the example of New Orleans evidences that this dialectic is also the path to resistance, both in the form of rooted understandings of belonging and in a freewheeling, transnational flux that in the nineteenth century pitted the city against national trends.

This chapter considers contemporary material that I argue offers echoes of late-eighteenth- and nineteenth-century New Orleans, and which provides us with the opportunity to map New Orleans' central place in the history of U.S. empire and the city's ambiguous status with regard to Americanization. This status positions New Orleans on the periphery, if not as the complete inversion, of what this book is calling "American time" as it developed from the revolutionary period and came to fruition in the mid-twentieth century. The first section explores the contemporary transnational prison-industrial complex, glimpsed in Dave Eggers's post-Katrina text, as an echo of both the plantation and the slave ship. The section suggests that the detention camp at Guantánamo Bay provides the opportunity to begin exploring historical links between New Orleans and Haiti that culminated in the nineteenth century following the first and only successful slave revolt in history. These links are forged in the second section via comparisons between post-Katrina New Orleans and post-earthquake Haiti. The striking similarity between often racist constructions of the victims of both disasters brings into view a biopolitical regime that works both within and beyond U.S. national boundaries to render certain groups of human beings disposable in the context of neoliberal capitalism. These constructions have a history in the virulently racist responses to the Haitian revolution which threatened the entire slave and imperial system on which modern capitalism was built. The final section offers alternative approaches to "writing revolution," focusing on Isabel Allende's 2009 novel *Island Beneath the Sea*. This text might be read as a post-Katrina rendering of the Haitian Revolution which registers its enormous impact on nineteenth-century New Orleans and the legacy of this encounter which survives into the present day: the idea that New Orleans is somehow irrevocably foreign, a city whose Creole culture has partially resisted Americanization. In this sense New Orleans emerges here as a "geopolitical prize" whose contemporary reputation as a "Caribbean city" pays tribute to the myriad ways in which it has resisted colonization by the United States.

Bounding Empire: "Homeland" and the Transnational Prison-Industrial Complex

"Guantánamo Bay" in contemporary rhetoric—and in *Zeitoun*—has become a cipher for the U.S. detention camp that is situated in the U.S. naval base which is stationed at the southeastern end of Cuba.[7] We have to travel back in time to recover Guantánamo Bay as a vast and stunning natural harbor, one that, as Jonathan Hansen writes, "enjoys a front-row seat along the Windward Passage, one of the hemisphere's busiest sea-lanes and an integral link in the circum-Caribbean communication system. The passage takes its name from the breeze that blows in off the Atlantic between Cuba and Haiti, hurtling crews and cargo into the heart of the Caribbean basin." Before becoming a dystopian symbol of U.S. extra-legal authority and shame, the remoteness of this rugged corner of Cuba made it "a land of exile and refuge accommodating marginalized people from within Cuba and across the Caribbean basin."[8]

Given the superior strategic position Guantánamo commands in the western hemisphere, it is unsurprising that, once the United States had given up "the dream of Cuba"—its long-held goal of annexing the entire island that animated U.S. presidents for more than a century after the nation's founding, from Thomas Jefferson onward—it insisted on the Guantánamo lease as a condition of ending its occupation of Cuba. Cuba had seduced successive U.S. presidents for two key reasons: following the Haitian Revolution, Cuba took the former Saint-Domingue's place as the most lucrative colony in the world; it would also secure for the United States control of the Gulf of Mexico, and access to the waterway for what would become the United States's second most important port: New Orleans. Hanging on to Guantánamo thus secured New Orleans and the Mississippi River.

1898 saw similar U.S. interventions in the Philippines, Guam, and Puerto Rico—all of which realized, like Cuba, that liberation from the Spanish, overseen by the United States, did not come without a price.[9] This year also saw the annexation of Hawaii. Niall Ferguson notes in his book, *Colossus: The Rise and Fall of the American Empire* (2004), that where many U.S. historians deny that the United States is an imperial power, they will concede that it did succumb to the temptations of empire for a brief moment at the turn of the twentieth century.[10] Ferguson notes more than a brief moment of U.S. imperial indulgence, however. And I suggest that the unfolding of the history of Guantánamo Bay is a poignant reminder of this continuous history, one that does not vindicate the United States as a basically benevolent empire, as in Ferguson's account, but rather tracks its evolution into a power that has claimed porous borders and granted itself endless exemptions from the rule of law.

Michael Hardt and Antonio Negri's conception of "Empire"—at the center of which is the United States—is one that transcends the model created by European powers with their stark distinctions between center and periphery, and which accretes power by blurring, as opposed to demarcating, territorial boundaries. They write:

> Thomas Jefferson, the authors of the *Federalist*, and the other ideological founders of the United States were all inspired by the ancient imperial model; they believed they were creating on the other side of the Atlantic a new Empire with open, expanding frontiers, where power would be effectively distributed in networks. This imperial idea has survived and matured throughout the history of the United States constitution and has emerged now on a global scale in its fully realized form.[11]

Hardt and Negri also claim that as well as having no spatial limits, Empire's temporal horizons are similarly infinite: "the concept of Empire presents itself not as a historical regime originating in conquest, but rather as an order that effectively suspends history and thereby fixes the existing state of affairs for eternity."[12]

Guantánamo does not fit neatly into Hardt and Negri's own rather totalizing and indeed imperious rhetoric. Nonetheless, it might be seen as a crucial node in the complex network of U.S. imperialism, which has shuttled back and forth between the more traditional, territorial model of empire (the plantation) and the uncircumscribed ambition of economic, political, and cultural imperialism (the slave ship). Guantánamo has seen the unfolding and dissolving of myriad forms of U.S. authority, and this process of reimagining American power currently has no end: as in Hardt and Negri's account of "Empire," Guantánamo is leased to the United States in perpetuity.

The desire on the part of the founding fathers to make empire work for republicanism—against the tide of contemporary theories that the two were incompatible[13]—is illustrative of the fact that the American Revolution was not a revolt against empire. And yet innocence in relation to imperialism has become crucial to American exceptionalist accounts of U.S. history, with the British Empire emerging in this narrative as an organizing symbol of tyranny and un-freedom.[14] Indeed, this apparent contradiction of U.S. imperial innocence is precisely in keeping with the logic of exceptionalism: the United States claims for itself a category apart, one that is unique and strikingly self-authorizing. Guantánamo, described by Anne McClintock as a "historical experiment in supralegal violence," is an obscene example of this state of exception.[15] Guantánamo illuminates like no other symbol the curious status of contemporary U.S. empire in the American imagination: everybody knows it exists—it is hypervisible evidence that the United States detains and tortures people who are more than likely innocent, indefinitely—and yet eyes are peculiarly averted, reluctant to peer through the wire-mesh fences to imagine ourselves into the position of those orange jumpsuits.

McClintock writes of Guantánamo inmates:

> The men are reduced to zombies, unpeopled bodies, dead men walking, bodies as imperial property. This image is hypermodern and yet, alongside it, unbidden, the history of American slavery rises up—imperial déjà vu. When each new prisoner is brought off the plane, his ear muff is lifted and a U.S. marine says in his ear, "You are now the property of the U.S. Marine Corp."

> Called "packages" by the Marines, these men are unpeopled bodies, reduced to subhuman status, mere property of the state.[16]

This "imperial déjà vu" returns us not just to the memory of U.S. domestic slavery and its persistent legacy, but to the new forms of social control over the racialized body that have followed in its wake. As Angela Davis, Michelle Alexander, and others have argued, the contemporary system of mass incarceration that can be witnessed across the United States is more than simply an echo of slavery, an expression of the racialized poverty and social exclusion that is its legacy. What Alexander refers to as "the New Jim Crow" reflects a new set of technologies of racialized control that have arisen in response to late-twentieth-and early-twenty-first-century realities. As Alexander points out in her influential 2010 publication *The New Jim Crow: Mass Incarceration in the Age of Colorblindness*, "more African American adults are under correctional control today—in prison or jail, on probation or parole—than were enslaved in 1850."[17]

Nonetheless, Alexander notes "a profound sense of déjà vu," one that registers the links between this new system and its previous incarnations.[18] As Abdulrahman Zeitoun discovers in Eggers's text—on release from his incarceration in Camp Greyhound followed by several weeks "lost" in a high security prison—the Louisiana State Penitentiary, Angola, often simply referred to as "The Farm," was built on a former slave plantation. Inmates from Angola constructed "Camp Greyhound."[19] Exploitation of the labor of prison inmates, often unwaged and, if paid at all, usually at rates well below the minimum wage, is a common practice in America's prison system. At Angola, where average prison sentences are about ninety years and African Americans make up 80 percent of the population, every physically able prisoner is expected to perform farm labor for 2–20 cents an hour for a minimum of forty hours a week.[20] As Davis explains, prison labor today resembles the convict lease system that operated in the South soon after slavery was abolished, and which guaranteed cheap labor from the pool of newly criminalized emancipated slaves. Black Codes which proliferated in southern states "racialized penality" while linking "it closely with previous regimes of slavery." Thus, according to Davis, "southern criminal justice" emerged "largely as a means of controlling black labor."[21] Louisiana, which boasts the nation's largest prison in the form of Angola, stands at the center of a system in which it is still legal to exploit the labor of prison populations which are overwhelmingly and disproportionately black. Angela Davis told a crowd at Tulane University, New Orleans, in November 2013, that

Louisiana "now rates number one in the nation in terms of its incarcerated population. The United States can claim 25 percent of the world's prison population, both proportionately and absolutely more than any other country in the world. Louisiana claims the highest percentage of incarcerated people in relation to its population than any other state in the nation." This makes New Orleans the epicenter of "the prison capital of the world."[22]

Alexander's contention that the evidently racialized nature of mass incarceration amounts to a "new Jim Crow," though not original, has been the focus of some controversy for a number of reasons. Alexander argues that America's vast prison populations are largely the result of the "war on drugs" declared in the early 1980s before the so-called crack epidemic swept through America's inner-city ghettoes. Some prominent critics, notably James Forman, have suggested that the war on drugs itself garners disproportionate attention from commentators keen to show that contemporary mass incarceration is a new system of racial caste. This critique is important given the fact that, as Forman points out, "drug offenders constitute only a quarter of our nation's prisoners, while violent offenders make up a much larger share: one-half."[23] Forman also notes that prison populations soared immediately following an exponential rise in crime, particularly violent crime.[24] Nonetheless, given that the United States currently imprisons more than two million people at any one time, the one-quarter which is attributable to the drug war remains a significant number. Moreover, drug-related offenses account for a significant proportion of the rise in prison populations—that have more than quadrupled since 1980[25]—as well as being over-represented in Louisiana's state prison system. New Orleans thus emerges as a key site of the war on drugs.

While New Orleans is testimony to the very real harm done to black communities as a result of drug use and drug-related violence, it is, according to Alexander, the criminal justice system that is largely responsible for the economic and social collapse of many African-American neighborhoods across the United States. Punitive laws in relation to crack cocaine—as opposed to powder cocaine, more commonly used by whites—and unchecked racial profiling mean that staggering numbers of young black people, mostly men, are routinely swept off the streets and into the nation's prisons. Often with no legal representation, these people are ushered into a system in which stunningly harsh mandatory minimum sentences pressure people to plead guilty regardless of whether they have actually committed a crime. The notorious "three strikes and you're out" laws—that operate in Louisiana and a number of other states—condemn many to life sentences for nothing more than possession of marijuana.

Alexander shows that the war on drugs, which provides myriad financial incentives to law enforcement agencies that pursue it, has led to the veritable occupation of poor black communities by the police. Because the war on drugs, like the war waged on "terror," is essentially a never-ending project, with too many potential targets to take on, the police have to be selective as to where the war will be waged. As Alexander writes, "the enduring racial isolation of the ghetto poor has made them uniquely vulnerable in the War on Drugs."[26] Mass round-ups in poor black communities, as opposed to white suburbs, gated enclaves or college campuses—where drug activity is just as likely to take place—engenders no political backlash. Indeed, police have been able to argue that it is more effective to target impoverished communities who rely on an "open-air drug market" than those with access to private spaces which are harder to police. Such "reasoning" is supplemented in the South by a police force that, as Leonard Moore has shown in relation to New Orleans, in the postwar period picked up the baton of "white mob activity"—such as that practiced by the Ku Klux Klan—which was "replaced by police violence as a means of restricting black social mobility."[27] In 2012 the *Times-Picayune* reported that in New Orleans, one out of every fourteen black men are behind bars, and one in seven is either in prison, on parole or on probation.[28] In 2013, social justice lawyer William Quigley reported that jail incarceration rates in New Orleans were four times the national average and that African Americans make up 84 percent of the city's prison population.[29]

The war on drugs does of course affect white people who come into its net—roughly 10 percent of those rounded up by the police—but for Alexander, these people are "collateral damage" in a system that is designed to target black people.[30] This is the price, Alexander suggests, of racial caste in an "age of colorblindness" in which racism dare not speak its name. And yet, as Forman notes, the tendency of the "New Jim Crow writers" to overlook the significance of violent crime in incarceration statistics is in itself troubling, as well as pointing to a potentially larger problem with the analogy. Where black people are no more likely to commit drug crimes than whites, and are dramatically over-represented in conviction rates, this is not the case with violent offenses which African Americans are more likely to commit. Thus the drug war serves the Jim Crow analogy better, given that the difference in treatment between blacks and whites "lies in government practice, not in the underlying behavior."[31] As Forman suggests, no serious treatment of mass incarceration can ignore violent crime. Arguably Alexander's thesis overlooks this difficult statistic because her account, though cognizant of poverty, does not take class seriously as a category of analysis that might in turn provide a socioeconomic account of violent crime.

In contrast, Christian Parenti's *Lockdown America* (1999), which preceded Alexander's text by over a decade, paints the rise of mass incarceration as a key moment of class struggle.[32] Parenti, like Alexander, argues that the origins of the "war on crime" agenda issues from the civil disobedience of the 1960s black freedom movement, describing it as "counterinsurgency by other means."[33] Attacking racialized crime has since become a key electoral strategy for U.S. politicians. But Parenti also identifies another, later critical moment in the "criminal justice build up" which immediately preceded the dramatic rise in prison populations. This is the deregulation of capital in the 1970s, and involves the response to the crisis of overproduction and declining profits that closely followed the postwar boom at the end of the 1960s. Neoliberal restructuring represented an attack on labor in the form of deindustrialization and welfare rollback—which doubly afflicted African-American communities, which both relied on and were employed by the public sector in large numbers. Parenti argues that mass incarceration became a way of managing the consequent surplus population that capitalism both requires and is threatened by. For Parenti, the new zero tolerance policies that fostered the expanding prison population represented a "postmodern version of Jim Crow."[34] This is a more slippery understanding of Jim Crow that embraces not just black people but also the "visibly poor." This formulation of the Jim Crow analogy thus allows for the fact that race and class demarcate who falls within the purview of the criminal justice system.

Part of Forman's objection to the Jim Crow analogy is that middle-class blacks are largely free from interference by the criminal justice system and so where the original Jim Crow system targeted *all* black people (in the South), mass incarceration does not. And yet this objection reveals the extent to which Forman's analysis of racism is itself divorced from a consideration of class: it overlooks the fact that Jim Crow itself was designed to subordinate black labor in ways that echoed slavery. It was not until the defeat of Jim Crow and the successes of the Civil Rights movement in the 1960s that a sizable African-American middle class came into being. That this section of the black population—a significant minority—is largely exempt from the criminal justice crackdown does not invalidate the claim that mass incarceration is a new system of racial caste. It shows the ways in which racial caste has always been powerfully articulated through class paradigms that have exploited poor whites as well.

This insight applies to the part of Alexander's thesis that Forman and others argue is the most convincing. Alexander contends that in spite of the great harm done to individuals, families, and communities by disproportionately long prison sentences, the greatest harm results not from "prison time" but rather the "prison label," the invisible world of discrimination that follows felons as they exit the prison and attempt to reenter a society that is now overwhelmingly stacked against them. Excluded from public housing, food stamps, and employment opportunities—many of which explicitly exclude felons who are required on most job applications to declare their status—the route into an illegal economy and back to prison is almost inevitable. The fact that most states bar felons from voting compounds Alexander's claim that this system amounts to a new form of Jim Crow. Indeed, the fact that prison populations like Angola are usually concentrated in white rural communities, and are counted for the purposes of political representation of the given district but are excluded from voting, mimics the plantation system which similarly gave disproportionate political clout to slave-holding states within which the slaves, counted as three-fifths of a human being, were denied the right to vote.[35] This is also one of the many ways in which predominantly black urban communities, like that which resides in New Orleans, are disenfranchised in an electoral context that skews power in favor of white rural voters who are in the numerical minority.

Prior to Katrina, then, New Orleans, with a 67 percent majority black population, was a key site in the war on drugs, notorious for its levels of crime which have long been linked to pernicious stereotypes linking blackness and criminality. The racial "underclass" that Katrina supposedly brought to the surface of national attention has been fundamentally shaped by this new system of racial caste that makes it more likely that a young black man will end up in jail than college. As Alexander shows, this new system of racialized control, while reserving its most brutal effects for those individuals and families directly affected by the "cruel hand" of the criminal justice system, in fact affects all black people living in the United States. All are shadowed by the stereotype of the "black criminal."[36]

The unspoken story of *Zeitoun*, ostensibly set against the backdrop of the so-called war on terror, is the war on drugs, the war on crime in general, and mass incarceration. The book's main plot charts the Katrina experience of a Syrian American who remains behind in New Orleans to look after his property and help his neighbors. His heroic record of rescue missions is violently interrupted by an arrest by state police, who initially appear to suspect him of unstated terrorist activities. His subsequent imprisonment in Camp Greyhound and then at Elayne Hunt Correctional Center, a high security prison, lead to Zeitoun's disillusionment with a national culture and state apparatus that has apparently vilified him on the basis of his ethnic and religious identity. Dave Eggers ostensibly wanted to tell this story to celebrate the "American Muslim hero," a figure that had been eclipsed by post-9/11 Islamaphobia.[37] And yet, though this is Eggers's stated intent, the text invites an alternative reading.

It offers a glimpse into the workings of a criminal justice system whose failings were merely highlighted by the Katrina moment. Rather than converting the reader to the idea that an American Muslim could be a good citizen, I suggest that the Zeitoun family's middle-class respectability, earned via hard work and enterprise, is precisely the obvious object of identification for the kind of readership McSweeney's can anticipate. This is not to deny the poisonous post-9/11 atmosphere for Muslims residing in the United States, and the important work that a text like *Zeitoun* might do in this regard. But it is to suggest that much further beyond the realms of middle-class identification is the criminalized black male whose unnatural relationship with the criminal justice system has been thoroughly naturalized in the middle-class imagination. The story of a Muslim man being branded guilty, apparently on the basis of his identity alone, allows us to consider a much more entrenched symbol of racialized criminality. As Davis points out, the treatment of the black criminal paved the road for the post-9/11 treatment of suspected Muslim terrorists. Those who argued in the immediate aftermath of 9/11 that national "othering" was a game of musical chairs, and that the vilification of Muslims might paradoxically relieve African Americans of their signature pariah status in U.S. society, wholly underestimated the critical role played by the descendants of slaves in defining the bottom rung of U.S. racial hierarchies.[38]

Arguably Eggers's stated project in *Zeitoun* has backfired since the real-life character has been held in jail on domestic battery charges and, latterly, charges that he plotted his wife's murder. Eggers has been taken to task for his portrayal of an unblemished hero and family man whose message seemed to rely on this saintly status. Zeitoun was acquitted of the charges against him in July 2013, but his wife's accusations and his association with violence against women are unlikely to go away.[39] And yet in some ways, the uncomfortable return of Zeitoun's non-fictional complexity only underscores the text's message about the criminal justice system. No one doubts that Zeitoun was innocent in relation to the vague suspicions—he was never charged—that led to his arrest in 2005. And yet in the eyes of many commentators, he is now "guilty" in a deeper sense, which somehow renders his original story less powerful, less shocking and disturbing.[40] Such logic only reinforces that of a system that reverses the "innocent until proven guilty" dictum for subjects branded by race.

Zeitoun also provides a frame through which to trace the links between U.S. prison populations at home and abroad. Where the system of internal colonization of a large segment of the nation's black population might be compared to the plantation, Guantánamo is reminiscent of the slave ship, and the fact that America's "rooted" forms of racism are intimately connected to transnational, "routed" iterations. Indeed, Angela Davis argues that the increasingly privatized U.S. prison industry provides a "scaffolding for global repression" as it is transplanted into other national contexts, creating new markets in the denial of human freedom.[41] And yet as Davis suggests, as with the peculiar spectacle of Guantánamo—hypervisible but somehow at a safe distance—"we have all learned how to forget about prisons . . . we have not learned how to talk about prisons as institutions that collect and hide away the people whom society treats as its refuse."[42]

Again, Guantánamo functions here as a mirror, the purveyor of "imperial déjà vu"—as a place that has historically detained refugees considered "refuse" by the U.S. government. Guantánamo, now a key site in the war on terror, once a key indicator of U.S. territorial ambition, should also be remembered as a central location of black Atlantic oppression. Throughout the twentieth century, Guantánamo was used to detain Haitian refugees, most notoriously in the 1990s when it became what many regard as the first detention camp for victims of HIV/AIDS. Just as the U.S. domestic criminal justice system treats its victims as "detritus," here the "diseased" raced body was consigned to what initially appeared to be indefinite detention without charges, legal representation or trial. The backstory to the construction of the Guantánamo naval base into a zone that stripped Haitians of their legal rights is the stream of refugees fleeing persecution from the U.S.-backed Duvalier regime in the late 1970s and early 1980s. When the U.S. policy of deporting Haitian refugees was condemned by the judgment of a district court in a 1980 ruling—as both immoral and racist—Guantánamo came into view as a conveniently nebulous territory, neither Cuba nor the United States. Here Haitians could be intercepted at sea, taken to Guantánamo, and denied due process. This is in stark contrast to treatment of refugees from communist Cuba, who have routinely been granted asylum in the United States. We will return to the particular history that has reserved unusually virulent forms of U.S. racism for Haitians.[43]

In the same essay that explores the term "Ground Zero," Amy Kaplan charts the emergence of the term "Homeland" as part of the post-9/11 lexicon for demarcating an embattled United States from the various fronts in the so-called war on terror. For Kaplan, Guantánamo is the unarticulated site that guarantees the currency and visibility of these other two terms. She argues that "Homeland" in particular marks the peculiar emergence in U.S. nationalist discourse of a term associated with the rooted "blood, soil, and land" brand of European nationalisms that the nation of immigrants, bound for the future, supposedly left behind. While America's successive systems of racialized control—slavery, Jim Crow, and mass incarceration—testify to the fact that ethnocentrism more than lingered into the history of the New World, the post-9/11 embrace of this apparently Old World rhetoric seems significant. It underscores a previously disavowed imperial logic in which white supremacy has worked internally and externally as a way of policing U.S. boundaries, at once elastic and fixed.

Kaplan suggests though that far from satisfactorily demarcating national boundaries, "the idea of the homeland works by generating a profound sense of insecurity, not only because of the threat of terrorism, but because the homeland, too, proves a fundamentally uncanny place, haunted by prior and future losses, invasions, abandonment."[44] If the United States finds its uncanny double in the dystopian image of the Guantánamo detention camp, then this image in turn found its internal double in the dystopian scenes in post-Katrina New Orleans. Here indefinite detention was translated into "Katrina time," which reflected a criminal justice system no longer concerned with rehabilitation or indeed crime. The following section explores the unfolding of "Katrina time" in New Orleans in the late summer of 2005, and the uncanny echoes that sounded from Haiti five years later. In both instances imperial behavior eclipses the progressive temporality that exceptionalist discourse associates with the United States.

New Orleans, 2005; Port-au-Prince, 2010

In an op-ed piece for the *New York Times* in January 2010, Jonathan Hansen wrote:

> Coinciding with the one-year anniversary of President Obama's unfulfilled pledge to close the American prison at Guantánamo Bay, the disaster in Haiti suggests a new mission for the United States naval base, one that might burnish America's reputation in the world, if not redeem the base itself. . . . Even as the United States works to close the prison, it should use the base for humanitarian intervention.[45]

Hansen's vision of "Guantánamo to the rescue" is well aware of the deeply paradoxical idea that the naval base might form a real refuge to Haitian victims of the earthquake which struck on January 12, 2010, killing over 200,000 people, injuring and rendering homeless many more, and devastating Haiti's capital of Port-au-Prince. And yet the full extent of the irony of this piece had yet to unfold, as the U.S. army took control of Haitian airspace and flooded the country not with aid—which was in some cases diverted by U.S. forces—but with military personnel. For many who lived through Katrina, however, the militarized response to the worst natural disaster in the history of the Americas would have occasioned something like imperial déjà vu. Certainly Abdulrahman Zeitoun could have told the suffering Haitians that a "reimagined Guantánamo" was not the answer.

The story of the disastrous post-Katrina response effort in New Orleans on the part of city, state, and federal authorities is now widely known. The federal government took an incomprehensible five days to reach Louisiana. Meanwhile the places of "last resort," the Superdome and Convention Center, where people who were unable to evacuate were housed, degenerated into unsanitary and dangerous environments in which people lacked access to water, food, and basic sanitation. At this stage the media swooped on the story and stirred up a deeply ambivalent global outcry—that at one and the same time condemned the U.S. government for abandoning its own people and blamed the stranded New Orleanians for the appalling conditions in which they found themselves. When authorities did arrive, their orders were clearly centered on the imperatives of "law and order" as opposed to "search and rescue." There were brief moments of reprieve, like the appearance of General Russel Honoré who memorably ordered his troops to put their guns down. But for the most part, post-Katrina New Orleans was conceptualized as a deeply unstable zone that needed to be contained and secured by U.S. forces and their various, private—unaccountable—offshoots.

As Kathy Zeitoun realizes in Eggers's text, post-storm New Orleans had been flooded with security forces "armed for urban combat": "Kathy added it up. There were at least twenty-eight thousand guns in New Orleans. That would be the low number, counting rifles, handguns, shotguns."[46] Zeitoun's experience at Camp Greyhound was arguably unique for the ways in which it highlighted the collision of post-9/11 and post-Katrina "security" strategies. But his story is nonetheless part of a much larger post-Katrina reality which criminalized the storm victims. As one survivor told Rebecca Solnit, "We ended up in this concentration-like camp with barbed-wire fences and snipers, like we did something wrong."[47] And as Linda Robertson writes, "On September 1, 2005, the State of Louisiana declared war on the survivors in New Orleans," as Governor Kathleen Blanco announced:

> These troops are fresh back from Iraq, well-trained, experienced, battle-tested and under my orders to restore order in the streets. They have M-16s and they are locked and loaded. These troops know how to shot and kill and they are more than willing to do so if necessary and I expect they will.[48]

Blanco's statement responds to the idea that New Orleans had been taken over by marauding gangs. Visions of looters, rapists, and killers took hold of a media imagination typified by this CNN report: "On the dark streets, rampaging gangs take full advantage of the unguarded city. Anyone venturing outside is in danger of being robbed or even shot. It is a state of siege."[49] As with the logic of mass incarceration, much of the perception of post-Katrina crime turned out to be unfounded, the result of a sensationalist media campaign that criminalized the plight of those left to fend for themselves in a drowning city. While some opportunistic looting did occur—indeed, some of the more notorious examples were committed by the police—the vast majority of cases involved people recovering food and water for themselves and their families, in the face of a massive government failure.

Solnit suggests that instances of "elite panic" in the hurricane's aftermath "turned New Orleans into a prison city." This idea might be qualified by the fact that, as suggested above, New Orleans was already a prison city—with an extensive network of city jails surrounded by rural prisons, sometimes ironically referred to as "black suburbs," filled with large segments of the black urban population. This population had already witnessed and suffered as a result of the transition from community to militarized policing of their neighborhoods. As with many aspects of Katrina's aftermath, the storm merely exacerbated and brought to light long-term and slow-burning trends that had already done unimaginable harm to the city's social fabric. The media were able to mobilize a host of stereotypes that had long demonized black urban populations. In addition, commentators were also able to draw on pernicious associations between blackness and "welfare dependency" to castigate poor African Americans for failing to evacuate.[50] This is in spite of the fact that large numbers of poor people in the city, disproportionately black, lacked access to transport to heed the mandatory evacuation order issued by the mayor's office—which came with no kind of assistance. This again reflected a scenario in which federal aid programs had been rolled back in previous decades leaving the poor protected by only the most rudimentary social safety net. As Michael Eric Dyson writes in relation to the racialized and racist responses to the storm, such commentary "battered the victims of Katrina all over again."[51]

These insults were compounded by the fact that, as discussed in the introductory chapter, politicians and media commentators widely adopted the term "refugee" to describe Katrina evacuees from New Orleans. Given the fact that these observers were referring to a group of predominantly black Americans, the understandable reaction from African-American spokespersons was that this was a racist denial of U.S. citizenship.[52] Certainly the label was technically incorrect; according to international law these were not refugees but rather "internally displaced people."[53] The construction of post-Katrina New Orleans as more akin to a "Third World disaster zone" than the United States further removed the evacuees from the realm of public concern.

But arguably, the post-storm city was an uncanny spectacle within the national imaginary because it revealed the fact that Katrina's most vulnerable victims were *already* disrespected and disregarded, already at the bottom of a social hierarchy in a society that ruthlessly discards those no longer considered economically useful. The "refugee" label is instructive for the ways in which it conjures the relationship between evacuees and the state—a body that, quite apart from offering protection, treated these U.S. citizens as enemies, and post-Katrina New Orleans as a front for waging war. It is little wonder that many New Orleanians experienced the arrival of U.S. troops as a foreign invasion. According to Henry Giroux,

> Katrina laid bare the racial and class fault lines that mark an increasingly damaged and withering democracy and reveal the emergence of a new kind of politics—one in which entire populations are now considered disposable, an unnecessary burden on state coffers, and consigned to fend for themselves.[54]

Giroux is here defining a biopolitical order that has moved on from the one described by Michel Foucault, in which modernity itself was marked by a transition from traditional forms of sovereign power—over matters of life and death—to "more disciplinary modes of confinement and control."[55] For Giroux neoliberal postmodernity inaugurates a reality in which the exception becomes the rule, and in which Foucault's prison becomes a metaphor for the militarized state. The "state of emergency" declared in Katrina's aftermath might in this vein be seen as an intensified version of the war that had long been declared on New Orleans' racialized underclass. As Michelle Alexander explains, this underclass was created by the fact that black neighborhoods in the United States were made to bear the brunt of deindustrialization and globalization. [56] As manufacturing jobs were outsourced to foreign workers, usually open to grotesque exploitation as a result of the lack of unions and a minimum wage, it engendered "the economic collapse of inner-city black communities" across America. While white workers suffered too, Alexander shows that African Americans bore the brunt of globalization:

> In 1954, black and white youth unemployment rates in America were equal, with blacks actually having a slightly higher rate of employment in the age group sixteen to nineteen. By 1984, however, the black unemployment rate had nearly quadrupled, while the white rate had increased only marginally.[57]

At least some of these white workers will have been helped by the explosion in the prison industry, which typically offers employment opportunities to white people living in rural areas. Today in New Orleans, unemployment among African-American men stands at around 50 percent.

For Giroux, Katrina unmasks a biopolitical regime that determines the kinds of lives that can be lived, and defines some lives as not worth living. Katrina unveiled some particularly dramatic examples of such a regime: armed police shooting at evacuees trying to cross a bridge into neighboring Gretna; the unpunished murder of possibly hundreds of black men by white vigilantes across the city, and particularly in Algiers. The post-Katrina context was not short of criminal activity, but those responsible for some of the worst crimes walked free.

In contrast, prisoners in the city jails were not only left to drown or drink the sewage-infected water which flooded their locked cells. As Pamela Metzger explains, in a narrative that has much in common with *Zeitoun*, "once evacuated, the OPP [Orleans Parish Prison] prisoners were lost to the known world, just as surely as if they had been among the "disappeared" of a country struggling under a repressive dictatorship."[58] Transported with none of their legal documents, personal papers, or identification, many of these prisoners were left in Louisiana prisons for months after Katrina. Metzger's account shows that the vast majority of these were poor, pre-charge detainees rounded up shortly before Katrina, usually for minor misdemeanors such as drunkenness, traffic violations, blocking the sidewalk (i.e., being homeless). Although the practice violates various legal principles, detainees are not usually granted legal counsel until they have been charged with a crime. This means that poor pre-charge detainees usually lack any legal representation.

As Metzger shows, this is why so many were "doing Katrina time" in a system that openly discriminates against poor defendants.

> Even before Katrina, poor precharge detainees had languished in jail for weeks in a kind of jurisprudential limbo: not charged but not free. After Katrina, poor precharge detainees descended into a Kafa-esque hell: not charged, not free, not known.[59]

As suggested in the introduction, "Katrina time" might be appropriated to name a wider condition that transcends Katrina's temporal horizon, a condition in which so many U.S. citizens were living prior to the storm. This is an unproductive temporality that has no future, a condition that Giroux names "living death,"[60] Alexander names "civic death,"[61] and Orlando Patterson, who was describing slavery, named "social death."[62] This condition was perhaps most disturbingly realized by the bodies that lay on street corners and which floated in the stagnant water and amidst the storm debris for days after Katrina. A number of commentators have compared images of these bodies to lynching photography, which celebrated the disposability of black bodies in the aftermath of the trade that somewhat paradoxically accorded high cash values to the physical lives of slaves. Following Emancipation, the labor of black people became infinitely replaceable. As disproportionately unemployed or incarcerated, the status of poor African Americans as what Giroux describes as "the waste-products of the American Dream" is only intensified.[63] Writing of the distinctions between slavery, Jim Crow and mass incarceration, Alexander suggests that "while marginalization may sound far preferable to exploitation, it may prove to be even more dangerous."[64]

Despite the fact that the national public outcry after Katrina was contradictory and short-lived, it is widely accepted that the criminally inept government response to the disaster was responsible for the steep decline in popularity of George W. Bush, which in turn sealed the fate of the Republican Party in the next general election. When an enormous earthquake devastated Haiti in January 2010, just a year into the Obama presidency, some dubbed the emergency "Obama's Katrina."[65] Reminiscent of "Guantánamo to the rescue," and in similarly oxymoronic vein, Mark Thompson, writing for *Time* just a few days after the disaster struck, suggested that the presence of the U.S. military in post-earthquake Haiti constituted a "compassionate invasion":

> Louisiana became the 18th of the United States back in 1812, but you'd never have known it watching the Federal government's

ham-fisted response to 2005's Hurricane Katrina. The Obama Administration is doing things differently: Haiti, for all intents and purposes, became the 51st state at 4:53 p.m. Tuesday in the wake of its deadly earthquake. If not a state, then at least a ward of the state—the United States—as Washington mobilized national resources to rush urgent aid to Haiti's stricken people.[66]

In the days and weeks after the catastrophe, it was repeatedly suggested that the best solution for Haiti—"the poorest country in the western hemisphere," as media commentators constantly reminded us—might be some form of United States or United Nations protectorate, that could help this ill-fated nation get back on its feet. The ironies of such proposals and this *Time* article are manifold. The ways in which journalists flirted with gross violations of Haiti's sovereignty rides roughshod over Haiti's legacy of successfully revolting against slavery and colonialism to form the first, independent black republic in the New World. Nonetheless, while some objected to the idea that the Haitian earthquake was Obama's Katrina— Haiti was not, contrary to many U.S. actions, a possession of the United States[67]—the label is interesting for what it reveals about the links between post-Katrina New Orleans and post-earthquake Port-au-Prince. Arguably, and contrary to Thompson's suggestion, the Obama administration's reaction to the earthquake was just as damaging as the Bush administration's response to Katrina.

As human rights activist Beverly Bell noted on January 21, 2010, the fact that the United States so rapidly flooded Haiti with troops in the aftermath of the earthquake meant that "more than 1,400 flights of aid and relief workers have been blocked from getting in . . . People are lying on the ground with crushed bones and their response of choice is *guns?*"[68] One major difference between Bush's and Obama's responses to the storm and earthquake, respectively, is that the latter was able to occupy the affected areas rapidly and efficiently. This is not to suggest that the U.S. military did not do any good in post-earthquake Haiti, but it is to suggest that it was first and foremost U.S. security needs, and not the needs of the earthquake victims, that prompted the invasion. The United States has long had a vested interest in portraying Haiti as a needy, if recalcitrant, child, dependent on the benevolence and paternalism of its powerful neighbor.

Prior to the earthquake Haiti was already known as "the republic of NGOs."[69] As Paul Farmer points out, in countries like Haiti the presence of NGOs has initiated this "vicious cycle": "aid bypasses the government because it is weak, and then further weakens the government."[70] The earthquake led to one of the largest humanitarian aid efforts in history, but of the $2 billion in acute relief aid, only 1 percent has gone to the Haitian government. The vast majority has gone to foreign NGOs whose work, according to many experts, has historically done more harm than good in Haiti.[71] This assessment also applies to aid from the U.S. government: historically offered to Haiti in the context of structural adjustment programs, commentators argue that it has wrecked local economies. One notorious example is that of the USAID food program, which in the 1990s dumped huge amounts of rice produced by U.S. farmers onto Haitian markets, killing off local competition and leading to the disastrous consequence that Haiti now relies on food imports to feed its population.[72]

Many now argue that the largest legacy of the U.S. relief effort in Haiti will be the construction of the Caracol Industrial Park near Cap-Hatien, located in the midst of a region formerly off-limits for construction due to environmental protections—much needed in Haiti's deforested landscape. This park will be run by the Korean firm Sae-A, and is billed to create 20,000 jobs, making it the largest employer in Haiti. And yet, as the journalist Jonathan Katz explains, the factory owners will not pay taxes to the Haitian government and will channel all of their profits out of Haiti.[73] While a gated community is being constructed for Korean executives of Sae-A, currently under fire for alleged abuses in a factory in Guatemala, many are predicting that Caracol will become an impoverished slum for garment workers already routinely denied the minimum wage in Haiti.[74] This is perhaps the most prominent example of the ways in which post-earthquake Haiti has magnified the country's long-standing role as a site of "disaster capitalism," an opportunity for the United States and other western countries to further exploit the nation's resources. The ways in which post-storm New Orleans has had to similarly endure "structural adjustment" as a result of a neoliberal reconstruction effort is part of the story that this book charts in subsequent chapters. Here, I would simply like to note that in both cases, disaster exacerbated the exploitative and indeed colonial relations the United States has historically exercised with regard to these two regions, the one officially part of the U.S. but decidedly marginalized and part of a state that is, according to some, treated "like a colony of the federal government";[75] the other officially independent from the United States but decidedly central to its understanding of its strategic interests in the Caribbean.

The ways in which the U.S. military and U.S. aid failed to respect Haitian sovereignty in the aftermath of the earthquake, supported by a media that portrayed Haiti as a child who had long depended on American paternalism, echoed the U.S. occupation of Haiti in the twentieth century.

While U.S. trade "liberalization" policies might be compared to the trope of the slave ship, the moment in 1915 when the United States embodied a traditional imperial force in Haiti might be compared to the trope of the plantation. Certainly many Haitians, some of whom formed an armed resistance to the occupation, thought that the United States planned to return the nation to a plantation system; suspicions of which were seemingly confirmed as the occupation government instituted the practice of forced labor. Revealingly, the Unites States pulled out of Haiti at a moment when the Guantánamo lease was renewed, thus securing U.S. influence in the Caribbean.

Like post-Katrina New Orleans, post-earthquake Port-au-Prince is the site of "imperial déjà vu." Indeed, the levels of devastation in Port-au-Prince can be traced back to the centralization policies of the U.S. occupation, while New Orleans' vulnerability to hurricanes is directly connected to federal policy.[76] Just as the majority of Haitian society has come to view the elite oligarchy and their American allies who run their country as obstacles to their flourishing, New Orleanians discovered a similar truth about their own government following Katrina. Strikingly, while both disaster locations were subject to variants of a colonialist dependency theory on the part of U.S. commentators, they also became the imagined sites of urban unrest. Post-earthquake Port-au-Prince was also overtaken by the racist spectre of marauding looters. As in New Orleans, while some cases of looting did occur, for the most part these images promoted by the global media were fantasmatic. If the coverage of the Haitian earthquake echoes that of Katrina, then imaginaries of Katrina in turn gestured back to Haiti. Writing prior to the earthquake, in 2007, Anna Brickhouse observes:

> In strictly historical terms, one of the most remarkable if unac-
> knowledged aspects of the public discourse generated in the
> immediate aftermath of Katrina was its direct rhetorical inher-
> itance from a more general U.S. discourse on Haiti beginning
> in the nineteenth century.[77]

Brickhouse's immediate reference here is the coverage of the Port-au-Prince fire of 1866 which left 50 percent of the city in ashes and thousands homeless. "The people, instead of helping to stop the progress of the fire," reported the *New York Times*, "either ran about half wild in the streets or tried to rob and plunder."[78] For Brickhouse and a number of others, the origins of this rhetorical economy can be traced back to the U.S. reaction to the Haitian Revolution. This uprising, which successfully overturned the plantation system and the imperial ship on which it was based, challenged the foundations of the entire Atlantic economy, sending fear into the planter class across the U.S. South. To preserve the slave system, it was necessary to distance the American Revolution and its ideals from events in the Caribbean. This fuelled the narrative widely circulated in the U.S. press that the Haitian Revolution was exceptionally violent. As Rachel Cleves writes, "Americans dwelled on images of cannibalism, infanticide, rape, and murder in the Haitian Revolution."[79]

There are myriad historical reasons why echoes of racist rhetoric directed at the Haitian Revolution might resurface in New Orleans 200 years later, criss-crossing the Caribbean Sea and the Gulf of Mexico into post-9/11 New Orleans and, as we have seen here, into the tale of a Syrian-American immigrant. The section that follows explores the literary construction of "black revolution" and the literal and imaginative ways in which Haitian revolutionary impulses have infused New Orleans culture.

Writing Revolution

It was practically and ideologically expedient that the Haitian Revolution be portrayed in the U.S. press as an event that would not be replicated in or recognized by the United States. Despite some initial aid supplied to the rebel leader, Toussaint L'Ouverture, by U.S. merchants and the U.S. Navy, the election of Thomas Jefferson to the presidency in 1802 decisively turned U.S. policy against the emerging republic, a policy that many argue has continued until the present day. It was not until 1862, following the South's secession from the Union and thus at a key moment in the demise of U.S. domestic slavery, that Abraham Lincoln finally recognized what in 1804 had become the Republic of Haiti. And yet the influence of the revolution on the United States was profound. Most historians agree that Napoleon's decision to bequeath Louisiana to the United States for a bargain price in 1803 was a direct result of events in Haiti, which forced him to abandon the idea of an empire in the Americas. The Louisiana Purchase delivered to the United States a vast proportion of its continental empire, including the "geopolitical prize" on the mouth of the Mississippi. And many, including W. E. B. Du Bois, have characterized this priceless transfer of territory as "Haiti's gift to the United States."[80]

New Orleans was in turn to be the recipient of approximately 15,000 exiles from the former slave colony of Saint-Domingue, most of whom came via Cuba, which expelled the refugees in 1809.[81] This influx at least doubled the size of the New Orleans population. These exiles included white slaveholders, their slaves, and a significant proportion of free blacks.[82] As Anna Brickhouse explains, because many of the *gens de coleur libre* who fled Saint-Domingue themselves owned slaves, the mythology of the New Orleans Creoles (of color) is of a class of people who had internalized the aristocratic and slave-owning values of those who oppressed them. And yet, Brickhouse points out that the primary print journalism of Louisiana's nineteenth-century Francophone Creoles, *La Tribune de la Nouvelle Orleans*, paints a very different picture,

> offering a record of francophone radicalism centered on an alter-native discourse of racial politics—one that was not premised primarily on U.S. national identity, but was instead crystallized through a dense set of transatlantic and transamerican historical and literary relations.[83]

Brickhouse focuses on a poem by the New Orleans Francophone Creole Adolphe Duhart, "Pour les Incendiés de Saint Domingue," which stages both historical and contemporary ties between New Orleanians and Haitians suffering in the aftermath of the 1866 fire in Port-au-Prince. Such demonstrations of solidarity with Haitians reappear in mainstream African-American narrative of the twentieth century, which, during the U.S. occupation, revived the spectre of black revolution as a model for race consciousness within the United States. Mary Renda portrays these black-American identifications with Haiti as often profoundly contradictory acts of resistance to a "culture of imperialism" that emerged in the United States after 1915.[84] According to J. Michael Dash, by this point Haiti had emerged "like the Orient" in the U.S. imagination,

> an inexhaustible symbol designed to satisfy material as well as psychological needs. Images of mystery, decadence, romance and adventure are not arbitrary in either case but constitute a special code, a system of antithetical values which establishes radical, ineradicable distinctions between the Subject and the Other, West and East, the United States and Haiti.[85]

As Dash explains, the proximity of the origin stories of both nations—formed in resistance to European rule—made it imperative for the slave-holding nation to project what many have portrayed as the most radical uprising of the eighteenth century as absolutely other. Where C. L. R. James's seminal 1938 study *The Black Jacobins* countered the treatment of the Haitian Revolution as a footnote to its French counterpart by arguing that they were part of the same phenomenon,[86] the American Revolution found in the Haitian uprising its uncanny twin, one that embraced the revolutionary ideals of freedom that were distorted by "the peculiar institution" in the United States. The glaring contradictions of U.S. democracy came alive during the Harlem Renaissance as writers like Zora Neale Hurston, Langston Hughes, and Arna Bontemps looked to Haiti as a symbol of freedom. The work of the latter in particular animated the transamerican trajectory that links Haiti and New Orleans; *Black Thunder* (1936) and *Drums at Dusk* (1939), which dramatize slave uprisings in Virginia and Haiti respectively, show the ways in which events in Saint-Domingue reverberated in acts of resistance in the United States, as well as dramatizing the Louisiana-born writer's exploration of his own Haitian ancestry.[87]

In the aftermath of the 2010 earthquake, Haitian writers called on literary art to enact a similarly decolonizing logic with respect to sensationalized media constructions of "Haitian disaster." Explicitly taking to task the fatalistic tendency to present Haitians as "epic victims," not just of earthquakes, hurricanes, despotic leaders, and poverty, but also of the revolutionary impulse itself—as though abolition and independence are themselves instances of disaster—a number of writers in the collection *Haiti Rising* (2010) evoke Haitian culture and in particular the "Haitian magical real" as crucial weapons of survival. "This nation that people call so poor," writes Michael Le Bris, "has a richness that confounds the poverty."[88]

Evoking a national culture that has been uniquely open to imagining alternative worlds is precisely the project undertaken by Isabel Allende in *Island Beneath the Sea*. This fictionalized account of the revolution made a timely appearance in 2009, so Allende's novel is not, of course, a response to the Haitian earthquake—which occurred after this book was published. But it is, I suggest, a response to Hurricane Katrina. In reviving the "Haitian magical real," Allende's text dramatizes the myriad ways in which this aesthetic was transported to New Orleans. *Island Beneath the Sea* tells the story of the refugees who travelled from Saint-Domingue to Louisiana, where they dramatically accelerated and deepened the region's already pronounced processes of creolization. The novel can thus be read as one of the many books that emerged to defend an apparently unique New Orleans culture from the media storm that so demeaned it in 2005. Just as writers focusing on the Haitian earthquake cannot resist the temptation to evoke the nation's precarious positioning on the "fault lines" of history, its "seismic" revolutionary legacy—in spite of their pleas that the revolutionary legacy not be usurped by a narrative of disaster—Allende's text repeatedly invokes hurricanes constructed by "natural" and "social" worlds alike.[89]

"Hurricane[s] in the Caribbean" are from the start of the novel indicative of the "hostile nature" of Saint-Domingue as it is viewed from the white perspective.[90] This hostility notably encompasses the unsettling presence of vast numbers of slaves, described by Ned Sublette as "the densest concentration of Africans that had ever been assembled."[91] These slaves not only secure the lavish and decadent planter lifestyle, but also threaten this life with the constant murmuring of rebellion, the plague of uprisings that rippled through the colony "like a terrible hurricane."[92] When the wealthy French families finally attempt to escape the "political storm on Saint-Domingue,"[93] their ultimate refuge, New Orleans, emerges as a "city of catastrophes" similarly at the mercy of hurricanes, floods, fires, epidemics, rebellions.[94] In this way Allende's novel imbues Haiti and New Orleans with a shared political ecology similarly infused with the dialectics of disaster and resistance.

Allende's account of the revolution is far from an antiseptic repudiation of the U.S. tendency to portray the long rebellion in Haiti as exceptionally violent. Where the novel simply reports that Port-au-Prince had been burned to the ground, the assault on Le Cap by the rebels is described in vivid detail: "several Negroes were carrying decapitated heads by the hair . . . A woman whose throat had been slit was thrown out a window."[95] "In desperation," reads a particularly lurid and fanciful sequence, "some were jumping into the water and attempting to swim toward the ships, but the sea was boiling with sharks attracted by the scent of blood."[96] And yet the fact that this last image is so clearly evocative of the horror of the Middle Passage—which, as Marcus Rediker observes, has been shadowed by a mythology of bloodthirsty sharks—provides crucial context for the Haitian Revolution, which, like its French counterpart, did by all accounts involve widespread acts of sometimes extreme violence.[97]

Island Beneath the Sea paints the sugar plantations of Saint-Domingue as places of "slow death"[98] which, as Ned Sublette explains, should be viewed as a large factory that absorbed, exhausted and killed vast amounts of human capital. Because sugar cane is so labor-intensive the planters of Saint-Domingue adopted a policy of quite literally working their slaves to death. Unlike cotton plantations where female slaves were accorded a particularly high cash value as "breeders," and torture usually stopped short of endangering the lives of valuable property, sugar plantations more commonly relied on large populations of male slaves who were constantly replaced by new, relatively cheap supplies shipped from Africa. According to John Garrigus, "a successful Caribbean sugar planter . . . was as much a manufacturer as a farmer" and therefore some historians regard Saint-Domingue as a "proto-industrial society in which slaves were not peasants working for a lord, but rather capital assets whose owners carefully measured their productivity and costs of acquisition and maintenance."[99] This is the picture Allende's novel paints, underscoring the point the writer has made in interviews that she wants readers to link these events to modern forms of slavery under a capitalist system.[100] Unsurprisingly, this "death camp of sugar" engendered particularly vicious forms of torture and abuse on the part of the slave-holding class.[101] As the revolution itself shows, this culture of cruelty inspired widespread resistance that encompassed acts of violence deeply implicated in a dense network of religious and magical symbolism.

Island Beneath the Sea has been greeted with critical disappointment due to the feeling that it does not live up to the popular writer's reputation as a magical realist.[102] Certainly this historical novel can be criticized for its tendency to perpetuate rather than scrutinize racial and sexual caricature, and the neatness of the plotting of its family saga. "African blood" seems to play too large a role in determining not only a person's destiny but their ability to dance and their sexual appetites. Typically for this genre, everyone seems to be related. But the novel's treatment of "magic" and the "real" is, I suggest, complex and sophisticated.

Catholicism and Voodoo, both branded "magical" by western Protestantism, form the European and African religious frameworks in Haiti and New Orleans alike. While blending in discomforting ways, in the novel they provide mirror-images of one another that signify both likeness and difference. Hence the deeply Catholic Eugenia becomes the "madwoman of the plantation" partly as a result of her fear of voodoo ceremonies, while Zarité, her slave and the novel's central character, is disturbed by her mistresses religious rituals. Both frameworks threaten rupture from the "real" while providing compelling alternatives to it. Allende's "magical realist" aesthetic in *Island Beneath the Sea* seems to be a direct echo of that envisioned by the Cuban writer Alejo Carpentier, whose prologue to *The Kingdom of This World* (1949), a novel about the Haitian revolution, makes one of the earliest references to the mode that Homi Bhabha argued in the 1990s was "the literary language of the emergent postcolonial world."[103]

Carpentier names the aesthetic that he finds on a visit to Haiti and locates in "the history of all the Americas" the "marvellous real." It manifests in *The Kingdom of This World* in the central event that both he and Allende cast as inspiration for the Haitian Revolution: the (failed) execution of the now legendary Macandal. In the mid-eighteenth century, Macandal, after losing his arm in a sugar mill, escaped to join a community of maroons (runaway slaves) and is now associated with the mass poisoning episode that menaced the slave-holding class and arguably anticipated the uprisings in Saint-Domingue in 1791. Following his capture and at the event of his public execution, just prior to the moment that he is to be burned at the stake, Carpentier's novel reads: "the bonds fell off and the body of the Negro rose in the air, flying overhead, until it plunged into the black waves of the sea of slaves. A single cry filled the square: 'Macandal saved!' " A "pandemonium" ensued, "and the noise and screaming and uproar were such that very few saw that Macandal, held by ten soldiers, had been thrust head first into the fire, and that a flame fed by his burning hair had drowned his last cry."[104] While Macandal's Christ-like resurrection—which in many variants of the story transforms him into a mosquito—is the image that remains in the minds of the slaves, the white perspective is different. This split perspective, these parallel dimensions, is not the archetypal magical real that we find in Gabriel Garcia Marquez or indeed in Allende's critically acclaimed *House of Spirits* (1981). But it is the variant that we find in Allende's account of the Haitian Revolution. And where Carpentier locates "a natural surrealism" in the tropical excess that he contrasts with urban "reason,"[105] Allende carries her variant of the "marvellous real" into the sub-tropical urban milieu of the city of New Orleans.

The world of *Island Beneath the Sea* is one of fragmented realities. Where Eugenia "spends the night tormented by nightmares and the day tormented by reality,"[106] her husband toasts the colony's return to "normal," wondering "what the devil 'normal' meant: whites and blacks, free and slaves, all living sick with fear."[107] Valmorain, in spite of his professed "realism," becomes "tormented by visions." He "detested the island" and "he tricked time by reading and playing cards with Tété," waiting for the inevitable explosion.[108] When the spectre of "a band of Maroons" follows Valmorain to New Orleans, his inner world becomes as unsettling as that of his deceased wife Eugenia.[109] These scenes of extreme anxiety find their realization in the world of the slaves.

In particular, Zarité's inner life, nourished by voodoo symbolism, provides refuge from her daily horrors. As Valmorain rapes her, "her soul flew to a different place. *Erzulie,* loa *of desire, make him finish quickly.*"[110] As her mind blanks out with thirst on the journey from the besieged plantation to Le Cap, "then came the goddess of Erzulie like a powerful burst of wind and mounted Zarité, her servant." At this moment it appears that the trance that overtakes Zarité is the real: the white soldier Etienne Relais witnesses "a woman with her back to him, erect, proud, her arms held out to fly and swaying like a serpent to the rhythm of a secret, glorious dance." And yet moments later, following Zarité's collapse, Relais "saw a mulatta very different from the one dancing along the road, a pitiful young woman covered with filth and sweat, her face contorted, one eye purple, her lips parted with thirst, her feet bleeding through rags."[111] Where the shape-shifting activity of much magical realist writing is rendered concrete, apparent to all onlookers, in *Island Beneath the Sea* it is radically perspectival, just like the resurrection/execution of Macandal in Carpentier's text. It is not that the various dimensions experienced by the characters are any less "real" for them, it is simply that they are not usually recognized across the lines of black and white, slave and master—relations that are themselves rigidly determined by power. In this way Allende evokes the cultural resistance to slavery without implying, as some magical realist texts do, that hierarchies can be overcome by transgressive acts of the imagination. Rather, slavery is repudiated in Saint-Domingue in a sea of blood, one that refuses to romanticize the Haitian Revolution.

Both Allende's and Carpentier's depictions of the revolution are stalked by cycles of captivity, oppression, and violence. As the elderly Ti Noël returns to post-revolutionary Haiti in *The Kingdom of This World*, in awe of "this marvellous world" of "Negro" power, "a heavy blow landed across the old man's back" and he is absorbed back into a system of forced labor and imprisonment. Zarité in *Island Beneath the Sea* is not freed as a consequence of revolution, and almost as soon as she finally gains her freedom in New Orleans, her daughter is imprisoned. In a scene that cannot escape contemporary parallels, Rosette finds herself in a cell in which "only one girl with blond hair, possibly a servant, was not a woman of color."[112] She is incarcerated for an act that is only deemed a crime because of her race. Though she is eventually freed from prison, the physical ordeal ultimately kills her. The legacy of her "prison time" lives on.

And yet the novel does open up tiny spaces of resistance. Where Valmorain, the slave master, "escapes" New Orleans for what he experiences as the freedom of the plantation,[113] Zarité discovers that "New Orleans was the perfect city for her."[114] This place of freewheeling excess is decidedly not free of painful hierarchies, in which white women sublimate their oppression in a patriarchal system by abusing black slaves, while Creoles of color enjoy distinct social advantages by virtue of the fact that they are not "full-blooded" Africans. And yet the melange of people that arrive in a port city, neither a melting pot nor a democratic "gumbo," subverts the rigid black/white binary that New Orleans was soon to learn was the American way. In this context New Orleans still represents a slave ship, but one that, quite literally, allows Zarité to dance in "place Congo." Where the name of

Carpentier's novel insists on *this* world—that of the often cruel and violent marvellous real—Allende's title describes release: "the island beneath the sea," the death that signified a form of freedom for those who endured the Middle Passage, reminiscent of the widespread practice of slave suicide and matricide that recur throughout the novel. This is where Zarité escapes to as she is mounted by Erzule: "then we go galloping together to visit my dead ones on the island beneath the sea."[115] Where Sublette argues that "slaves on a sugar plantation were already *zombi*"[116]—echoing McClintock's description of Guantánamo—Zarité takes on this spectre by in New Orleans embracing the spiritual framework that in Haiti inspired a revolution.

As Sublette suggests, the exodus from Saint Domingue "had a major cultural impact throughout the Antilles."[117] Sublette's own work, *The World that Made New Orleans* (2009), is another post-Katrina defense of a unique New Orleans culture that, before becoming American, was shaped, according to Sublette, by cultural, political, and economic interactions with Cuba and Saint-Domingue. Long before the Haitian Revolution the trafficking of people, goods, music, dance, and religion was a common practice between these three key New World locations. Where Louisiana appealed to Saint-Domingue exiles—it was (culturally if not by this time officially) a French colony, it was a slave-holding region, it had a similar climate that proved conducive to growing sugar cane—it was simultaneously, according to Sublette, undergoing a process of "Cubanization" under Spanish control, one that allowed slaves more space to breathe in an otherwise inhumane system. This process included "the Kongoization of the city, something that also established a continuity with the heavily Kongo black culture of Saint-Domingue."[118] The Spanish allowed slaves to have Sundays off which enabled the development of "the transnational dance" of the *calinda*—otherwise known as a voodoo ceremony—which was itself followed by the beat of an African drum.[119] "In Louisiana as elsewhere," writes Sublette, drums "implied revolt."[120] This, we might argue, is the resistant "magic" that travelled from Haiti to New Orleans and which, according to numerous historians, still shapes contemporary understandings of New Orleans exceptionalism.[121]

Conclusion: A Caribbean City?

When American evangelist Pat Robertson claimed in the aftermath of the Haitian earthquake that the nation was paying for the "pact to the devil" established in the late eighteenth century, he echoed his 2005 assessment that Hurricane Katrina was sent to New Orleans as a result of divine retribution—retribution that other commentators explicitly linked with "devil worship."[122] In 2010 Robertson was referring to the voodoo ceremony that took place in Saint-Domingue in 1791, that many argue inspired the slave uprisings. In 2005 Robertson had the practice of abortion in mind, but many others who constructed the storm as punishment from God focused on the city's reputation as a center for voodoo. Few in contemporary New Orleans observe variants of voodoo that have much close resemblance to that which can be seen in Haiti today. But commentators remarking on the presence of voodoo in New Orleans in this way refer to a culture that at the turn of the nineteenth century already bore many resemblances to Saint-Domingue, resemblances that were to be compounded by the flood of exiles from the embattled colony.[123]

Historian Emily Clark's account of the figure of the "quadroon" in the revolutionary Atlantic world, a figure that occupies a central and problematic place in *Island Beneath the Sea*, provides a microcosm of the debates that surround the perception of New Orleans as, in part, a "Haitian city." Clark shows how this exoticized creature, initially associated with the Caribbean, ultimately made her mark on the imagination of New Orleans. While the appearance of these famed "Creole beauties" caused "quite a stir" in places as central to the American imagination as Philadelphia, Clark shows that this figure was conveniently "sequestered" in the Crescent City, "effectively turning New Orleans into a perpetual colonial space in the national imagination."[124] For Clark, the branding of New Orleans as "foreign" has in other spaces secured a discourse of American exceptionalism—a discourse from which the Crescent City is itself banished. While Clark's fascinating history ostensibly invites us to see through the exceptionalist pretensions of other American sites, and to instead glimpse a more complex reality of racial hierarchy and intermixture, it is hard not to read her text as a plea to release New Orleans from "eternal exclusion from the American mainstream," allowing it the "comfortable berth in the national historical narrative" that it has historically been denied.[125] In a public discussion in New Orleans in 2013, Clark claimed that the migration from Saint-Domingue to New Orleans "has really left an imprint on the way that other people perceive us to be. And that has been a memory that has lingered, for better or worse, for a very long time."[126] Her scholarship is unequivocal on this point: the branding of New Orleans as "foreign" in the national imaginary has had disastrous implications for the city, most notably in 2005.[127]

Certainly it seems that after Katrina New Orleans was singled out for a particularly vicious attack, one that encompassed but went beyond the already poisonous national discourse of black criminality. In some ways *Zeitoun* responds to Clark's call: New Orleans as it is engulfed by Katrina in this text becomes the paradoxical yet quintessential "promised land" for the Syrian-American immigrant. While it is a watery world that Eggers stresses, one which Abdulrahman Zeitoun imaginatively links to his native Syria, New Orleans is nonetheless the site of his American dream: as the text closes and Zeitoun's building business gears up to participate in the recovery effort, "he envisions this city and this country not just as it was, but better, far better":

> Yes, a dark time passed over this land, but now there is some-
> thing like light. Progress is being made. It's slow sometimes,
> so terribly so sometimes, but progress is being made. We have
> removed the rot, we are strengthening the foundations. There is
> much work to do, and we all know what needs to be done.[128]

Here Eggers absorbs the narrative of post-Katrina New Orleans into one of U.S. progress, motored by the national (Protestant) work ethic. He dramatically simplifies the enormous controversies that have surrounded the grotesquely unequal process of reconstruction—"we all know what needs to be done"—characterized as much by demolition as rebuilding. Zeitoun's vision of rebuilding New Orleans is important and provides a crucial counterpoint to the sinister construction of Camp Greyhound. But the reference here to "weeding out the rot" no doubt inadvertently but unavoidably points us toward the "disposable" elements of a neoliberal society.

Those who argue that post-Katrina New Orleans has become the site of a veritable ethnic cleansing of large sections of the city's black population point to a narrative bolstered not only by the war on drugs—one that evolved from the "law and order" agenda which itself was arguably a direct response to the civil disobedience of the Civil Rights era.[129] In New Orleans the racist backlash against a U.S. freedom movement is compounded by the racist backlash against a Haitian freedom movement that was branded a catastrophe by western nations dependent on slavery and empire, and which have made the country pay time and again for its audacious bid to be free. Where in Saint-Domingue the former slaves paid tribute to the indigenous peoples of the island massacred by Europeans by naming their new state "Haiti," the Louisiana swamps similarly became the meeting place for rebellious blacks and Native Americans. As Clyde Woods has argued, in the nineteenth century New Orleans became a center for insurrectionary activity that we might identify today in its Blues tradition.[130] New Orleans, like Haiti though in less dramatic ways, has also been made to pay for its transgressions.

The culture of excess with which New Orleans is associated in the popular imagination encompasses "sin and sex" in a racist brew, but to claim that we must reject the narrative of the city's difference in the U.S. context—its status as a "Caribbean city"—is also to reject a transgressive embrace of freedom that flies in the face of key national trends. It is to reject the ambiguous space between the plantation and the slave ship that has allowed a unique black culture to flourish despite brutal racial repression. The following chapter explores the ways in which this endangered, resistant Caribbean culture has been subjected to the processes of Americanization and branded other in relation to its mythology of progress. This otherness has, in turn, been commodified by the tourist trade: in moves that have sold the city's "foreignness" to U.S. consumers often blind to the lurid mirror it has offered them. Chapter 2 wrestles with this lurid mirror and the subversion of a neoliberal "Katrina time" that I argue lies hidden behind it.

2

New Orleans and Americanization

"Progress," "Decline," and
Tourism in the Twentieth Century

One of the most memorable images to emerge from Jesmyn Ward's recent memoir, *Men We Reaped* (2013), which I suggest powerfully exemplifies the futureless landscape of "Katrina time," is that of a stationary—or direction-less—car. New Orleans looms in the background of Ward's text, which itself unfolds on the Mississippi Gulf Coast, connected to the Crescent City via a network of interstate highways and local roads. *Men We Reaped* tells the backstory to the social catastrophe revealed by Katrina: it tells the story of five young men known to Ward—her friends, her cousin and, at the book's heart, her brother—who died between 2001 and 2004.[1] Victims of racialized poverty, deindustrialization, and (the war on) drugs, these men are sacrificed to a globalized economic system for which they no longer represent productive labor or future potential. In an interview in November 2013, Ward suggested that the car, a highly compromised symbol which still represents freedom on some levels, provides a refuge, a place of connection for young people—a function once performed by the church for an older generation of African Americans.[2] This secular refuge represents a pause, a moment of reprieve, in a deeply unforgiving social reality constructed by a relentless national ideology of progress that has ceased to work for vast numbers of U.S. citizens.

The car is of course a powerful sign of this destructive ideology that reached its zenith in the mid-twentieth century. The failure of this particular narrative of progress was all too evident in Katrina's immediate aftermath. Car ownership emerged as a key indicator not just of social mobility but of physical survival: New Orleanians who did not own or have access to a car, the city's large and disproportionately black population residing well below the poverty line, were left stranded in the city. Many drowned. While this was interpreted by some as a shocking sign of government neglect, others viewed these stranded and racialized populations as marked by social stasis: locked in place as a result of a pathological dependence on an increasingly fantasmatic welfare system. When, in the days and weeks after the levees failed, the survivors were eventually herded out of the city like cattle—or, as some observed, slaves[3]—it became clear that these same people were the most at risk of being denied the right to return to their homes. Where the previous chapter deployed the tropes of the plantation and the slave ship to think about issues of capture and transportation, this chapter turns to a series of vehicles to think about the related experiences of displacement and home, social mobility and social decline. The car, the streetcar, the train, the bus, the bulldozer. The role played by these vehicles in New Orleans—in the twentieth century and beyond—traces the relationship between the city and Americanization, through a story that tracks New Orleans' identification with the ideologies of progress and decline, as well as the rise of a tourist industry that would cash in on both.

This story is still one of empire in that it charts the uneasy incorporation of New Orleans into the post-Louisiana Purchase United States. The crucial role played by road construction, by quite literally connecting the city to the rest of the nation, and by racial segregation—which imposed a binary model of U.S. race relations on a Creole culture formerly defined by at least three tiers—shows that this is a narrative about mapping and conquering space. But the accent here is placed on time. As Thomas Allen has convincingly argued, nineteenth-century constructions of nation were not simply about westward expansion into the vast territories opened up by the Louisiana Purchase. They were crucially engaged in the construction of a coherent "republic in time."[4]

The emergence of the clock not only enabled the development of mass production, but it also opened up the possibility of standard time that extended, by the end of the nineteenth century with the "closure" of the frontier, from East to West, North to South. The clock thus contributed to the creation of a middle class that would gain that ultimate luxury—time free from labor—along with a disposable income that might buy a railroad ticket or, in the twentieth century, enable them to purchase a car. It also opened up a nation to be explored in this new-found leisure time. New Orleans increasingly became a key destination for intrepid American travellers who, first by train and then in the privatized comfort of their cars, came to discover that in the context of the fledgling tourist industry, time is never really "free."

As visitors increasingly flowed into the city in the twentieth century, residents flowed out. The combination of freeway construction and desegregation meant that New Orleans followed the pattern of many U.S. cities in the latter part of the twentieth century by being shaped by white flight to the newly accessible suburbs, and the consequent loss of a tax base. Ironically, the experience of urban decline was screened for tourists who were instead treated to nostalgic spectacles of lost worlds and causes safely located in the past.

As Barbara Eckstein has shown, in the aftermath of 9/11 when U.S. travellers were avoiding air travel, New Orleans was promoted by the *New York Times* and a number of other publications as a safe destination, offering "unfamiliar sites without the need of a passport." While the city has long been portrayed as an exotic tourist destination offering "foreign" experiences within the United States,[5] its post-9/11 representations in national newspapers carefully domesticate this picture. As Eckstein writes, "here, in the literature of travel, the cultures and the horticulture of Africa, the Mediterranean, the Caribbean, and the Spanish American isthmus have seeped into the city without any threat."[6] Yet this image of New Orleans, as a sedentary place of rest for a traumatized nation, one that offers the salve of a romanticized and idealized past in the face of an increasingly ominous future, has been transformed in Katrina's wake. Though the storm has considerably reduced the size of the city's population—notably in Orleans Parish, which has lost a significant proportion of its African-American population—it has also occasioned an influx of newcomers, many of whom came to help rebuild the city and decided to stay. These transplants are typically young white professionals whose arrival has been branded a "brain gain" by analysts who see these newcomers as an economic boost to a city that has arguably been re-capitalized after the storm, and which weathered the economic downturn remarkably well.[7]

The Louisiana Humanities Center gave historical context for these new arrivals in a series of public talks in the fall of 2013. Influxes of French, Haitian, German, and Irish immigrants defined the city's early history. It was only later that the city became identified with the native-born, a demographic that famously made up 77 percent of the city's population in the 2000 census.[8] This was the forum for Emily Clark to voice her reservations about New Orleans being overly identified with the foreign legacy of the refugees from Saint-Domingue in the nineteenth century—as discussed in the previous chapter. The spirit of these talks seemed to communicate the idea that the post-Katrina population transfers had something to do with progress, and New Orleans' status as an American city. While concern was expressed for the estimated 100,000 African Americans who have been unable to return to New Orleans since Katrina, the Arrivals series constituted a reminder to those who have spoken out against gentrification that the city's population has not historically been a static one.[9]

Concern about particular groups of people is an urgent echo of a debate about cultural loss which has plagued the Crescent City since the nineteenth century—a debate that has in fact too often pitched "culture" and "residents" against one another, as though they are distinct entities. New Orleanians have long feared that external influences, largely perpetuated by the tourist trade, will drive out the city's perceived cultural distinctions, subjecting them to what is often perceived as the homogenous, standard time of Americanization. This chapter explores these anxieties by tracking the city's various mutations through time and space. The first section sets the scene for the twentieth-century city by charting New Orleans' evolution from Nouvelle Orleans to "The City that Care Forgot," exploring the ways in which the city gradually evolved to become a playground for American tourists, a refuge and an escape from the "work-time discipline" of the American Century, the productive rigor of "American time." The second section explores the increasing centrality of a commodified blackness that emerged in the city's dominant tourist narratives in the latter part of the twentieth century. It highlights the peculiar silences and evasions in this discourse by exploring a particularly whitewashed manifestation of this tendency: the plantation tour. While the leisured space of the antebellum plantation has been promoted as "time out" from a fractious social reality defined by desegregation and identity politics, the third section glances in the direction of Attica Locke's 2013 novel *The Cutting Season* (2012), which reveals the contradictions of this spectacle, showing the ways in which the present consistently interrupts the plantation tour's idealized constructions of the past. This final section turns to the post-Katrina context to further the argument that the city's unique cultural heritage is not one that is fixed in the past but is ongoing, if embattled, in the present. It argues that in spite of the tourist industry's commodification and commercialization of much that is distinctive in New Orleans culture, in spite of the post-storm gentrification and privatization of city spaces, the city still incubates vestiges of a culture that pay tribute to notions of time that transcend market values. This alternative temporality offers what might be characterized as an un-American antidote to the pervasive idea that "time is money."

From Nouvelle Orleans to "The City that Care Forgot"

In January 1819, shortly after his arrival in New Orleans, the English architect Benjamin Latrobe noted in his journal that "Americans are pouring in daily . . . In a few Years therefore, this will be an American town." He went on to explain in this entry that "at present, the most prominent, and to the Americans the most offensive feature of the French habits, is the manner in which they spend Sunday." While Latrobe notes some Catholic religious observance, he, like many commentators of the time, was struck by the Creole habit of dancing on the Sabbath. Possibly his most revealing journal entry on this topic came in February of that same year, where Latrobe recounts witnessing a Sunday afternoon meeting at Congo Square. "All those who were engaged in the business seemed to be *blacks*." For Latrobe, this display of music and dancing is distasteful: "The allowed amusements of Sunday, have, it seems, perpetuated here, those of Africa among its inhabitants. I have never seen any thing more brutally savage, and at the same time dull and stupid than this whole exhibition."[10]

Latrobe's reaction to the spectacle of hundreds of black slaves gathering on the Sabbath at Congo Square, a practice that was in time erased by American slavery, exemplifies the cultural clash that took place in post-Louisiana Purchase New Orleans. It demonstrates the distance the city was to travel in the American imagination, from the center of an apparently dissolute and floundering French colony that failed to effectively enforce the color line or the Sabbath, to a strategically and commercially crucial port city, to a destination of mass tourism. The scenes on offer to nineteenth-century observers in Congo Square would in the twentieth century be resurrected to service a consumer economy and tourist appetite nostalgic for a sense of "authenticity" alien to a postmodern age, and seemingly available on the site now widely constructed as the "birthplace of Jazz."[11]

As Ned Sublette notes of Latrobe's account, "it appears that both ends of Louisiana's musical African duality—banjo-playing Senegambia and drumming Kongo were making music together that day in 1819, as they had previously done in Saint-Domingue."[12] Most historians agree that the influx of refugees from Saint-Domingue via Cuba assured the survival of New Orleans' Francophone Creole culture for at least two generations beyond the Louisiana Purchase, in spite of the fact that New Orleans symbolically demonstrated its new American credentials by defeating the British in 1815. The figure of Benjamin Latrobe himself embodied the challenge posed by the American influx to the city. Latrobe's first project in the United States was to design and build a penitentiary. His career also involved road construction. The strategies of containment and control represented by both prisons and roads would make their mark on the New Orleans landscape. But what Latrobe is widely known for is his influence on the shape of pivotal American cities: Philadelphia, Baltimore and, crucially, Washington DC. A personal friend of Thomas Jefferson, Latrobe's neoclassical outlook dovetailed with the president's and played an important role in perpetuating the Greek revival style that is now so identified with U.S. democracy (and which can be seen across the affluent areas of Uptown New Orleans). Though Jefferson himself is a vivid illustration of the deeply contradictory nature of this creed, these contradictions—of a slave-owning republic committed to both empire and liberty—are the foundations of American modernity and its ideology of "progress." When Latrobe arrived in New Orleans to reform the city's waterworks that had condemned residents to successive waves of yellow fever, he represented the forces of modernization. Latrobe was to die of yellow fever himself three years later, a tragically ironic symbol of the fact that the city, during the period that Sublette describes as its "great Caribbean moment,"[13] was not yet ready for the changes he represented.

Although to construct the cultural clash after 1803 as one between Francophone Creoles and Americans is reductive and essentializing, rendering homogeneous what were in fact two very heterogeneous groupings, this binary does capture a symbolic clash that had real import at the time and which has played a central role in the construction of public memory around this important chapter in New Orleans history. The Creoles did of course include a significant Spanish element, and their ranks spanned the vast distances between aristocrat and slave, with many shades of freedom and unfreedom in between. The Creole elites, whose attachments to French language and culture rendered them anachronistic in the American city, viewed the new arrivals as uncouth "Kaintucks," but as Joseph Tregle has shown, the majority of antebellum American arrivals to New Orleans came not from the southern frontier but from the northeastern seaboard.[14]

For the newcomers it was Louisiana itself that required civilizing. The Spanish and French had cultivated forms of slavery that, while brutal, allowed the slaves to indulge in leisure time and thus partially preserve their original African cultures. More radically, these slave systems had allowed slaves to earn money during their time off which could then be used to purchase their freedom. As John Hope Franklin suggests, "the very existence of a free black population was a threat to the institution of slavery."[15] This racially anarchic culture—or so it seemed to the Americans—was also, "by the time of Louisiana's statehood [1812] . . . a center of what one could accurately call organized crime."[16] As Sublette explains, the U.S. ban on the foreign importation of slaves coincided with a boom in the sugar industry across the Antilles and particularly in Cuba and Louisiana as a result of the demise of Saint-Domingue. To meet the seemingly insatiable demand for slave labor, privateers like Jean Lafitte intercepted slave ships bound for Cuba to supply Louisiana planters and the booming slave trade in New Orleans itself. Sublette explains that New Orleans received the last wave of Africans to the United States in the 1810s, a fact that partially accounts for New Orleans' reputation as North America's "most African city."[17] Sublette also contends that the practice of privateering in Louisiana, that included the trafficking of many goods as well as slaves and which was widely associated with the refugees from Saint-Domingue, was an act of defiance against Anglo-American power—which proved, for a time, powerless to police the illicit trade that went on very openly in markets in and around New Orleans.

Another factor behind the maintenance of Creole traditions in the Crescent City was the separation of New Orleans into three distinct municipalities in 1836, two of which were largely Creole and one of which was identified as "American." By the time the city was "opened up" in 1852, the world of the Domingan privateers was a distant memory and Louisiana planters were dependent on the domestic slave trade whereby slaves from the Upper South supplied the Deep South. As Sublette explains, by this point it was apparent that many plantation owners were quite consciously "breeding slaves" to meet the demand that had resulted from what was, following the Louisiana Purchase and the absorption of the region's sugar plantations, a massive expansion in American slavery.[18] Moreover, free people of color from the North, like Solomon Northup,[19] were being kidnapped and brought to New Orleans. Where Louisiana was once a French penal colony, it was now an American one.

Most scholarship concurs that a crucial aspect of the Americanization of New Orleans was the imposition of a binary racial divide on a culture that had previously combined racial subjugation with significant acts of blurring the color line. When the city was reunited in the mid-nineteenth century, both white and free Creoles of color experienced significant social decline as the English language and racial segregation were increasingly imposed. For white-identified Creoles, white supremacy and the retrospective invention of a racially pure bloodline emerged as socially advantageous survival strategies in the new American context. While blacks experienced a brief but significant reprieve during the post-Civil War Reconstruction period, the white backlash in New Orleans was particularly severe, and the city soon became a bastion of Jim Crow. It is no coincidence that the infamous "separate but equal" Supreme Court decision turned on events in the Crescent City. Homer Plessy is testimony to the dying world of the Francophone Creoles. His grandfather was a white French refugee from Saint-Domingue who came to New Orleans and married a free woman of color. Plessy, who could pass for white, deliberately violated the recently enacted Separate Car Law in 1892 as part of a civil rights campaign by the Comité des Citoyens. The result was the landmark 1896 Supreme Court ruling that provided the legal underpinning of Jim Crow across the South, and confirmed that the progress brought by Emancipation was a deeply qualified freedom that arguably represented regression for those classified as free blacks under the slave system. The ruling effectively thwarted the social mobility of blacks in the South for over half a century, underscoring the fact that Americanization did not represent progress for Louisiana's black population.[20]

In the meantime, as the world of the Francophone Creoles declined in the post-Louisiana Purchase city, New Orleans was booming. The era of the steamboat meant that by 1840, New Orleans was the third largest city in the nation, "a bizarre and cosmopolitan outpost in the American South,"[21] and levels of immigration and port activity were second only to New York. The rapid expansion of American cities at this time represented yet another contradiction of Jeffersonian democracy, which was envisioned as a nation of farmers continuously expanding into the western frontier opened up by the Louisiana Purchase. As Thomas Allen has argued, American studies scholars who have focused on the idea that the U.S. empire was premised on expansion in space have neglected the crucial role played by temporality in the imagination of the "empire of liberty." Six years before coining the term "Manifest Destiny,"[22] John O'Sullivan wrote a piece entitled "The Great Nation of Futurity" which defined America as the empire of the future. Allen shows that Jefferson similarly adopted O'Sullivan's position; focusing on a utopian future was a useful evasion of the issue of territorial expansion that was for Jefferson a necessary evil, making space for the population growth that he both feared and saw as essential to the developing republic.[23] And yet urbanization was another solution to both population growth and to an increasingly time-bound culture that, contrary to Jefferson's agrarian idyll, favored industry and commerce over and above agriculture.

As Allen shows, Monticello, Jefferson's elaborately modelled home in Virginia, embodies these early and contradictory visions of U.S. democracy. Monticello, a slave plantation in Jefferson's time, also prominently featured the clock—a device that Jefferson directly identified both with the federal government and the U.S. constitution.[24] The combination of slavery and a key sign of modernity and technological progress points to a compatibility between the two systems that those who romanticize slavery as an essentially agrarian and paternalistic system deny. While Monticello's neoclassical design is indicative of the optimism at the heart of U.S. identifications not with the imperial powers of Old Europe but with ancient Rome, it also belies a commonly voiced fear of the time that imperial power inevitably veers into corruption, tyranny, and decline—as was of course the case with ancient Rome.[25] America's rapidly expanding cities became key sites of anxiety for those who subscribed to a narrative of U.S. declension, and New York City in particular emerged at the end of the nineteenth century as a symbol of contracting space and moral decline, in an age when westward expansion was no longer an option. Indeed, as early as the 1830s, Thomas Cole's series "The Course of Empire," a sequence of paintings tracing the stages of civilization, featured an image of "The Consummation of Empire" seemingly modelled not only on ancient Rome but on modern New York.[26]

This was an empire that by the end of the nineteenth century was imagined not spatially but rather temporally, in an increasingly marketized culture enabled by rigorous timekeeping. It would be ironic if New Orleans, that other "other" American city, identified in its early history with the time of leisure, corruption, and decadence, had itself became a bastion of such an ideology. But in fact its path diverged significantly from that of New York. As Richard Campanella explains in a timeline that prefaces his authoritative overview of New Orleans' historical geography, *Bienville's Dilemma* (2008), it is clear that by the "late 1800s–early 1900s," "New Orleans, founded for its river/sea position and overly dependent on waterborne transportation, is ill-prepared for [the] modern era."[27] As railroad transportation becomes the norm, New Orleans is overtaken by other expanding metropolitan areas like Chicago.

As Anthony Stanonis's account of the rise of New Orleans' tourist industry shows, at the turn of the twentieth century, the city was still at a crossroads, not yet ready to embrace its fate as an anachronism in the context of what came to be imagined as the "American Century."[28] Observers had since the eighteenth century been shocked by the city's apparent transgressiveness, particularly in relation to Puritan mores, to the point that by the end of the nineteenth century, it had accumulated a host of related sobriquets: "Great Southern Babylon," "Necropolis of the South," and "Sodom and Gomorrah."[29] These associations with sex and death intimated a temporality bound by gratification in the present, release and finitude: with little relationship to the future. This is precisely the temporality that attends the epithet which pursued New Orleans into the twentieth century and which hovers over it still: "The City that Care Forgot." And it was this reputation that city boosters in the early part of the twentieth century were eager to displace.

In 1922 city official Andre Lafarge presented the New Orleans flag to mayor of Orleans, France, in a public ceremony. He claimed:

> Strewn with golden lilies, the red, the white and the blue of our flag will forever stand as the perpetuation of the founding, growth and development of our city. Your colors are ours, your ideals and traditions are likewise ours. We are proud of our flag, because it reminds us of old France and of young America.

As Stanonis comments on this part of Lafarge's speech, "emphasis remained on development out of French ways. A youthful America promised growth and prosperity."[30] In line with this vision, throughout the 1920s New Orleans' Association of Commerce repeatedly pursued policies that would actively thwart the city's nascent tourist trade. Eager to associate the city with industry and commerce and not leisure, these businessmen argued for an expanded Central Business District that would push leisure activities beyond the city limits. The Mississippi Gulf Coast was vigorously promoted as New Orleans' playground, with some concessions made to lakeside recreation within the city. Most notably, many business interests called for the demolition of what is now the city's premier playspace, the historic French Quarter—an ethnic slum which, it was argued, was retarding the growth of downtown.[31]

The sites (and sights) required by tourism tend to fix the urban landscape in place, whereas the Association of Commerce imagined what they promoted as the nation's second port as a growing, functional, work-oriented city. As Stanonis observes, for the business community for much of the 1920s, "progress trumped preservation."[32] Thus ironically, two forces in the city's urban political scene that have for many decades been at loggerheads, the preservation movement and the tourist industry, were initially united in the desire to reify New Orleans' past against the city's powerful business elites whose eyes were on the future.

And yet when the Convention and Tourist Bureau, the publicity arm of the Association of Commerce, unveiled their new city slogan in 1922— "New Orleans—America's Most Interesting City"—in the hope that they could "relegate to the scrap heap the familiar descriptions of New Orleans as the "City that Care Forgot" and the "Paris of America,"[33] they did so amidst mixed messages. While part of the idea was to shift New Orleans' reputation as a place of vice and pleasure in order to make it more invest-ment-friendly, the new slogan still focused on the city's distinctive status vis-á-vis the nation. Moreover, it was perhaps the most significant slogan to appear in a contradictory list: "New Orleans: The South's Greatest City," "New Orleans: City of Romance," and, interestingly, "New Orleans: City of Progress." As Kevin Fox Gotham outlines, the same body also produced stories about the city titled "Historic New Orleans," "Port of New Orleans," and "Modern New Orleans."[34]

By the 1930s, it was the "romantic," historical New Orleans that had won out against the city of modern progress. Stanonis describes a 1932 ad campaign that appeared in *National Geographic* and a number of Midwestern cities, sponsored by the Association of Commerce, which was attempting to thwart the Washington Bicentennial celebration and the Chicago Century of Progress Exposition by instead luring visitors to the Crescent City.

> One ad pictured the St. Louis Cathedral framed by the floral gardens in Jackson Square. A small article underneath claimed: "The charm of the Vieux Carre (French Quarter) is undimmed by mortal worries or the modern city's haste. This is your thrifty trip abroad." Another ad depicted the French Quarter and declared, "Romance of France just a day away."[35]

These adverts suggest that by the 1930s the city's boosters had given in to New Orleans' reputation as a city somehow antithetical to modern American life, and were hoping to cash in on its exotic appeal. But exotic only in care-ful measures. Echoing tourist promotional literature issued during the First World War and anticipating post-9/11 messaging, these descriptions show that New Orleans was no longer a pleasure capital just for male transients; indeed its gritty reputation for "sin, sex and alcohol" had here been trans-muted into "charming" and "romantic" qualities suitable for all the family.

Stanonis identifies two key factors behind this ultimate embrace of the tourist industry: the rise of the automobile and the Great Depression. While post-Civil War railroad travel allowed for a tourist district centered on downtown and the French Quarter, stimulated by the 1884 Louisiana World Exposition and New Orleans' growing reputation as a convention city, Stanonis argues that it was the car that enabled mass tourism. "Auto-mobiles liberated growing numbers of Americans from train schedules and iron rails."[36] They also revolutionized the way Americans could spend their leisure time. While the road improvement and construction efforts that fol-lowed the Federal Highway Act of 1921 were ostensibly aimed at boosting trade, they "grew into efforts to satisfy motorists' hunger for adventure."[37] Studies show that the growth in automobile ownership was hardly dented by the Great Depression, and city boosters realized that in the absence of a healthy economy within which industry and commerce could flourish, the leisure industry, which provided much needed respite from the dire social and economic context of the 1930s, might save the city.

Yet while cars themselves enabled the rise of a suburban consumer nation and precipitated the unexpected death of many downtowns across the United States, the impact of the car was atypical and paradoxical in New Orleans. The draining of the city's backswamp in the twentieth century allowed for massive lakewards development, as did road construction, which in turn stimulated the expansion of the suburban parishes. By mid-century New Orleans was and in many ways still is a car culture. But visitors arriving in New Orleans by car were eager to get out of their vehicles and experience what was to become a novelty in urban America: a walkable city—or at least a walkable French Quarter. To visit the city's famous Garden District or other historic Uptown neighborhoods huddled along the natural levee created by the Mississippi River, tourists could—and still can—ride the St. Charles Streetcar, the city's oldest running line. The appeal of the New Orleans streetcar is precisely that it is a relic: as Barbara Eckstein explains, New Orleans, like other U.S. cities shaped by General Motors, destroyed much of its very efficient public transit system including its extensive network of electrified streetcar lines.[38] Arguably, like much in the New Orleans landscape, the iconic status of the streetcar is partially the direct result of the fact that the city very nearly destroyed them completely. The same might be said of Francophone Creole culture. The streetcar and the city's French past both constitute signs of obsolescence and decline in the context of a teleological narrative of modern American progress that privileges the car as a key indicator of mobility, the ability to conquer both space and time. In this context New Orleans is called in to stand for all that is not modern, progressive, and mobile. It is a "doomed southern city"[39] that is willing—in very un-Southern and un-American ways—to celebrate and even revel in this fate.

Much the same might be said of Congo Square, the legacy of which has been bulldozed into the ground before being resurrected, commodified and sold as a relic of the city's past. The section that follows explores the location of Congo Square on the dividing line between the affluent French Quarter and the black neighborhood of Tremé, charting the way in which the one has constituted the other. I also turn in this next section to what might be considered the metaphorical counterpoint to the nineteenth-century scenes at Congo Square: the plantation. While these "death camps of sugar"[40] represent the reverse of the sometimes ecstatic scenes of Congo Square, modern tourism has constructed plantations not as the site of brutalized labor but as yet another romantic symbol of obsolescence for a modern culture that has moved on. Plantation bus tours that begin in New Orleans might often steer silently past Louis Armstrong Park and the site of Congo Square to move through the Louisiana swamps into a whitewashed history that renders African-American culture almost entirely invisible.

"America's Most Romantic City": Selling Slavery, Erasing Race

Tremé, founded on the subdivided land of Claude Tremé's former plantation, was one of a number of New Orleans' Creole faubourgs—developed beyond the ramparts of the original city—to accommodate the wave of refugees from Saint-Domingue following 1809. While the original city itself was seen by many at this time as unsanitary and undesirable, Tremé's "back of town" location away from the river and toward the swamps highlighted its decidedly inferior status in relation to what became known as the French Quarter, despite the proximity of the two areas marked by the shared boundary of the now liminal zone of North Rampart Street. Tremé incorporates the site of Congo Square, which in turn hovers over the French Quarter and marks the neighborhood's centrality to the city's African traditions—traditions that extend back into a 200-year history during which blacks made up the majority of the New Orleans population. As Michael Crutcher writes, "the French Quarter may be the city's showpiece and playground, but Tremé is its soul." While this status as New Orleans' "soul" has been increasingly recognized since the 1990s and into the post-Katrina present, Tremé is deeply marked by its history as "one of the city's pariah neighborhoods."[41] This paradoxical status in turn illustrates the way in which Tremé in particular and black New Orleans in general has been constructed to serve what Lynnell Thomas argues is the tourist industry's carefully balanced racial dialectic of "disaster and desire."[42]

Thomas contends that as the twentieth century progressed, "the city's promotion of black cultural consumption produced a 'desire' for 'blackness' at the same time that this 'blackness' was used to signify the 'disaster' of black emancipation and desegregation." This dialectic:

> Acknowledges and celebrates black cultural contributions while simultaneously insisting upon black social and cultural inferiority

and indicting African Americans for perceived postbellum and post-civil-rights-era social ills of poverty, crime, immorality, educational inadequacy, and political corruption.[43]

Tremé is home not only to Congo Square but also to Storyville, the jazz funeral, Homer Plessy, gun violence, and police brutality. Though it began its life as a racially mixed residential area, its status as "America's oldest African-American neighborhood" derives from the fact that it has incubated much of the city's musical and parading traditions, as well as being a hotbed for Afro-Creole radicalism in the nineteenth century in ways that anticipated the modern Civil Rights movement. That it suffered severe urban decline in the 1970s and '80s along the lines of many other black inner-city neighborhoods means that Tremé plays a deeply ambivalent role in the imaginary of the contemporary tourist industry, which has attempted to export, package, and sell its cultural products while screening its actual physical presence from the tourist view.

Anglo-American attitudes toward the Tremé have only relatively recently gained such nuance. Soon after it was established Tremé became a center of power for property-owning free people of color, many of whom— contrary to deliberately engineered stereotypes that have wanted to construct free people of color as conservative race traitors[44]—subscribed to radically egalitarian French revolutionary principles that presented a direct challenge to the foundations of the entire Atlantic economy. Tremé was home to the nation's first black daily paper, *La Tribune de la Nouvelle Orleans* mentioned in the previous chapter, and also saw the formation of the Comité des Citoyens, a civil rights organization that aided Homer Plessy. The American rebuff to Plessy's challenge coincided with the renaming of what was only ever informally known as Congo Square after a confederate soldier. The insult of "Beauregard Square" was belatedly addressed in 2011 when the city officially named the site "Congo Square." By this time much of the legacy that Congo Square stands for had been quite literally demolished.

As Crutcher explains, after the 1919 fire that burned the New Orleans Opera House to the ground—marking the "symbolic end of Old World French Creole public institutions in New Orleans"—the city authorities identified the need for a new large meeting place that would enable New Orleans to host conventions. This important moment on the path to mass tourism coincided with an era of so-called "slum clearance" across the United States. Consequently, "instead of building the new auditorium on the French Opera House site, a commission chose a location to the rear of the French Quarter, in Faubourg Tremé."[45] The new Municipal Auditorium, with its neoclassical architecture and "whites only" facilities, required the demolition of one square block of Tremé and the displacement of countless residents. Following its opening in 1930, the neighborhood again came under the spotlight as a site for public housing. In the early 1940s, after the stimulus of the U.S. Housing Act of 1937, two public housing projects appeared in Tremé, Lafitte and Iberville. Iberville alone razed nine blocks on the site of the former Storyville, the city's fabled vice district that had transported the sexual economy of the plantation into an urban environment,[46] and in so doing saw the early samplings of what in the first part of the twentieth century was viewed as a degraded and morally suspect form of music: "jass" or jazz.

By the time Tremé was again under the predatory eye of city authorities in the post-World War Two period, this time with an expanded civic center in mind, "slum clearance" had been euphemistically transformed into "urban renewal." This involved the removal of 122 families, 121 of which were non-white.[47] The Theatre for the Performing Arts eventually appeared in the early 1970s but much of the project stalled. In the meantime, the Tremé community had come under assault from the destruction that followed in the wake of the 1956 Interstate Highway Act. The construction of Interstate 10 spanned from 1961 to 1969. This went through the cultural and business heart of Tremé's Claiborne corridor. While the elevated expressway led to the demolition of 170 residences and 50 businesses, it suffocated many more, effectively killing off Claiborne as a thriving business district and its large neutral ground that was, among other things, the scene of black Mardi Gras, a much-loved children's playground, and home to 500 oak trees. A 1961 *Times-Picayune* editorial remarked that while the wounds from this level of destruction would take many years to heal, the construction of I-10 was "indispensable to general progress."[48] It would ease traffic congestion in other, more valued parts of the city.

As Crutcher suggests, "the decline of New Orleans's French Quarter and subsequent efforts to save it have been linked to the destruction of large sections of neighboring Faubourg Tremé."[49] While I-10 was under construction, French Quarter residents and preservationists were winning their battle against a riverfront expressway that would have blocked access to the Mississippi. The revival of the French Quarter as a well-groomed theater for the past—and indeed the theme of decline—meant that Tremé was made to bear the scars of so-called "modern progress." In so doing Tremé shared the fate of many black inner-city neighborhoods across America that were throughout the twentieth century demolished in the name of "revitalization" and often geographically isolated for the purposes of freeway

construction. What distinguishes the New Orleans story is that while federal
and state policies were rapidly destroying the physical and communal sites
that fostered jazz, the form was experiencing something of a revival, both
at the grassroots and at the tourist industry level. One of the many ironies
of this particular story is that the stalled civic center project that had seen
the destruction of much of Tremé ultimately became the site of a park that
pays lip-service at least to the legacy of New Orleans' most famous jazz
musician, Louis Armstrong.

That plans for Armstrong Park have themselves faltered on various privatization schemes mean that for much of its life its gates have been locked,
and when they have opened the park has become a site of fear, anxiously
presided over by various police patrols. Before and in the years immediately after Katrina, Armstrong Park loomed forbiddingly over the dividing
line that separates the French Quarter from Tremé, an urban menace that
tourists are consistently warned against visiting. The threat of race dictates
that "black Tremé" is the space against which the Quarter has defined itself.
In this scenario Armstrong's legacy is siphoned off, carried over the park
fence and into the supposedly safe spaces of the French Quarter where it
is cocooned in the light of its past and separated from the supposedly dis-
reputable neighborhoods that nurtured it. In the early part of the twentieth
century jazz musicians left New Orleans for cities like New York: New
Orleans' deeply racist, segregated culture which denigrated jazz held no
future for them. The founding of Preservation Hall in 1961 represented a
genuine attempt to rescue New Orleans jazz from oblivion in an increasingly
crass tourist-oriented French Quarter, but its enormous success capitalized
on postwar U.S. nostalgia for an "authentic" past, one that threatened to
isolate jazz not only from its neighborhood roots but from the present.[50]

This was the context for the peculiar domestication of an art form
initially identified in the white racist imagination with a sexualized blackness
that carried the threat of interracial sex. Though blackness has become an
important ingredient in the sale of jazz in New Orleans, it has been shorn
of its everyday context, transported out of an environment where the damage of racist oppression is clearly in evidence. In this sense, as in Thomas's
formulation, racial "desire" is separated from racial "disaster," though the
two continue to coexist in discomfortingly close proximity. And it is in this
vein that the appreciation of jazz takes place alongside tourist experiences
originally created as "whites only" affairs, whether it be the exclusive, elitist
masked ball modelled on those run by the viciously racist and segregationist
old-line Mardi Gras krewes,[51] or the indulgence in the supposed "charm"
of the plantation home. This latter pursuit, like the incubation of jazz,

relies on a hazy, de-politicized nostalgia for days gone by, but unlike the fetishization of New Orleans jazz, it eschews a desire for "blackness" and is instead haunted by the "disaster" of Emancipation.

On arrival in the French Quarter tourists are bombarded by literature encouraging them to participate in the many tours on offer and that supposedly enable visitors to access the city's rich history. Haunted History Tours, Jazz Walking Tours, and New Orleans City Tours—often now including a "Katrina" add-on—are the most common New Orleans-based attractions. Quite in contrast to the visions of early city boosters, who imagined the Mississippi Gulf Coast as an "escape" from the urban environment, the two most popular tours out of New Orleans are billed as providing crucial context for the city itself. The Swamp Tours offer a window onto New Orleans' well-known watery location and precarious ecological and environmental context, where the Plantation Tours provide insight into the supposedly "genteel" qualities of New Orleans culture, crucial to which is an orientation toward "leisure." Worlds away from the edgy experience of Bourbon Street or the sensual pleasures the industry, in careful measures, has tended to associate with jazz, the plantation home symbolizes the lost world of a southern aristocracy whose legacy has only been partially polluted by the uncomfortable fact that their wealth and status rested on often industrialized levels of slave labor. Where commentators like Andrei Codrescu—and many more—have liked to associate New Orleans itself with the fallen image of Blanche DuBois,[52] the corrupted southern belle, the plantation home seemingly offers the tourist a less complicated *Gone with the Wind*-brand of southern nostalgia.

Of the many restored plantation homes dotted along the River Road between New Orleans and Baton Rouge, Oak Alley is arguably the most iconic and the most popular. While the female guides who greet visitors in extravagant period costume have in more recent years been joined by reconstructed slave quarters—a concession to the increasing popularity of heritage tourism—these quarters are not part of the standard tour, and neither does their shadow darken the generally upbeat portrait of life in the family home. The focus is narrowly on interiors: the style of the furniture, the lace trimmings, the architectural tricks that allow for maximum breeze in the long summer months. The scripted tour that I heard in both 2011 and 2013 did also offer visitors the image of slaves fanning guests at the dining room table, and the admission that Jacques and Selena, the antebellum owners, acquired the plantation "along with 57 slaves"; but this admission is immediately followed by the words: "and they began to build their dream home." It is this latter aspect of the home that is accented on the tour, one that encompasses an appeal to late-twentieth- and early-twenty-first-century consumerism and an obsession with adorning the home—even if you have a guide not afraid to go off script and elaborate on the "long overdue" inclusion of the slave experience on the tour, as I did on my second visit.[53]

As the owner of Oak Alley, Zeb Mayhew, explained to a journalist, while "he is mindful of the surge of interest in slavery," "Oak Alley visitors, for the most part, are looking for a 'Gone with the Wind' brand of fantasy. 'They come for hoopskirts, the grandeur and the elegance. That's a part of the story, and maybe a better part of the story, for us to tell.' "[54] In this vein, visitors are invited to sip a Mint Julep on the veranda to recreate the ambience of "southern leisure." It is without question the case that tourists, white and black (though the majority of tourists in New Orleans are white, particularly those who choose to indulge in the plantation tour), are asked to identify with the slave-holding class. The families who lived here are humanized through various anecdotes—some of which reveal, we are told, a "tragic history"—yet we are not privy to the multiple tragedies unfolding in the fields beyond the sanctified site of the house and its immediate surroundings.[55] Nor are we invited to view the plantation as a site of work. Black heritage tourism riding on the back of the Civil Rights movement has led to some nuances in the stories these tours tell,[56] perhaps most notably at the Whitney Plantation, which in 2014 opened the nation's first museum exclusively dedicated to the institution of slavery. But for the most part, the history of the brutal exploitation of black labor is still screened from the tourist view—as is the embattled site of Tremé. Instead there lingers an uncomfortable investment in this other "tragic history," the Lost Cause of the antebellum South that was not to be an American future.

This latter point is an important horizon of the plantation tour and has a particular twist in Louisiana. In the context of the "desire" for the lost world of the southern plantation Emancipation is indeed a "disaster." And yet paradoxically it is the myth of racial harmony in the present that enables what might otherwise be considered a dangerous and regressive racist fantasy. The story of slavery in Louisiana is particularly useful in this regard. Nostalgia for the Lost Cause is compounded by the fact of the decline of the region's Francophone Creoles. The very concept of "Creole" and its flexible etymological genealogy can be appropriated as a vehicle through which people of all races and political stripes might identify with the inhabitants of the plantation home. This strategy is particularly evident at the Laura Plantation, explicitly marketed as "a creole plantation."

Guides at the Laura Plantation pride themselves on their "realistic" portrait of slavery, in contrast to the other tours (when I visited in 2013, Oak Alley was raised as a point of contrast, in spite of the recent addition there of a slave exhibit). The plantation is one of just a handful that includes the original slave cabins which are typically part of the standard tour (at least those I participated in during 2011 and 2013). As Jessica Adams points out, while Laura Plantation has not converted the slave quarters into toilets or storage rooms as have some of the plantations along River Road, they have not been well kept or lovingly restored as has the home itself.[57] Nonetheless, the story of French and Spanish slavery, and particularly the legacy of more open interracial relations, is important to the story told at Laura Plantation.

This is particularly pronounced in *Reconstructing Creole* (2007), a documentary made about Laura Plantation following a destructive fire there in 2004.[58] The various talking heads deployed to tell the story make up a multiracial cast. While some of the contributors of color express ambivalence about the plantation and its legacy, they conclude that, for better or for worse, this history is nonetheless theirs. And not just as descendants of slaves. As one black interviewee laughingly notes, he can trace his family ancestry back to a slave owner. Indeed, the film includes a family reunion wherein the plantation's assistant manager finds the black Creole wing of his family from which the "white" side of the family "had to dissociate from . . . otherwise perhaps someone who doesn't know the family very closely may think that *we're* black." While this is a rather uneasy description of the racial polarization that occurred during Americanization, the message the audience is meant to glean from it is clear. As Laura Plantation curator Joseph Dunn affirms, in Louisiana "we're all one big happy family."

Most significantly, Laura herself is called into service as a figure of both racial and national unity.[59] She bridges what is constructed as a quirky and racially promiscuous French past with a progressive American future. The film tells the story of her own rapprochement with an estranged black brother (interestingly named "Touissant"), who she bravely acknowledges in the presence of shocked onlookers. This scene is the culmination of a narrative in which Laura is shown to be repeatedly distressed by the facts of slavery. And while her great grandmother shows what is portrayed as comic "disdain for Americans," by the time Laura comes of age she aspires to be American. We are told at the film's conclusion that "though she dreamed of becoming a modern American women," Laura remained a Creole in spirit. As a transitional assimilationist figure squeamish about slavery, Laura represents the twinned inevitability of Americanization and Emancipation. Her marriage to an American and subsequent departure for St Louis—after only ten years spent running the plantation—deposit Laura safely on the side of "progress," which is precisely what takes the sting out of the plantation past, rendering its veritable celebration a "harmless" exercise in historical preservation.

An act of historical renovation frames the film. An interracial group of workers come together to restore the Laura Plantation home after the fire while reminiscing about the highly skilled slaves—of mostly Senegambian origin, as Gwendolyn Midlo Hall's groundbreaking research has shown[60]— who would have built the original structure. And yet despite these references to slavery, as Jessica Adams points out, "plantations have become popular tourist destinations among whites because 'historic house' or 'unique architecture' or 'romantic' comes to mind before the image of slavery does. And when it does, it will have been filtered through architecture and romance and perhaps not seem so disturbing any more."[61] Indeed, historical preservation was the impulse behind early attempts to "save" the physical structures of the plantation home, many of which were "rescued" and restored in the early part of the twentieth century as sites of "national interest." Just as the post-Reconstruction period enabled a rapprochement between estranged sides in the Civil War, the reintegration of the South back into the Union, the plantation home, itself so symbolic of the rift, paradoxically becomes a shared site of national heritage for a reunited American family.

A strikingly similar paradox attends jazz, which is now routinely made to stand in as a metaphor for a multiracial American democracy.[62] In spite of the fact that its emergence might be seen as part of the African-American resistance to U.S. oppression, the jazz metaphor now supposedly symbolizes the fluidity, spontaneity, and hybridity of a multicultural United States and its political system. Interestingly, a documentary made in part to expose the uncomfortable truths which ground this uncritical celebration of jazz and its racialized history, *Faubourg Tremé: The Untold Story of Black New Orleans* (2008),[63] is, like *Reconstructing Creole*, framed around the uniting symbol of historical renovation. Both films, though not structured around the post-Katrina present, take it in and offer poignant images of rebuilding that in turn provide fascinating commentaries on the destruction wrought by the storm.

Though largely shot before Katrina, *Faubourg Tremé* explores a number of the disasters that have afflicted Tremé's black community and concludes that past lessons might offer ways of coping with this latest disaster. The film offers a panacea to the storm debris in the form of rebuilding:

as producer, narrator, and central protagonist Lolis Eric Elie recounts, he bought his house in Tremé in the 1990s because prices in the area were relatively low. His decision to historically renovate the house had in turn nurtured a deep investment in the area and a commitment to its history. What the film does not say is that for many, the latest disaster to have befallen the Tremé community is gentrification, a process exacerbated by Katrina but kick-started in the 1990s as a result of the "rent gap" between Tremé and immediately surrounding neighborhoods like the French Quarter. Historical renovation is a key indicator of gentrification: it is the process that out-prices long-time residents who are then forced to move elsewhere. Historical renovators either become absentee landlords or move in themselves, often altering the character of neighborhoods by, for example, objecting to the noise created by a neighborhood's music and performance traditions—traditions that may have attracted the gentrifier to the area in the first place.[64]

This latter aspect of gentrification is certainly not an attitude borne by Lolis Eric Elie. But the key scenes of historical renovation that frame his film bolster the "architectural fetishism" that Crutcher argues is central to the mechanisms of neighborhood displacement. While Elie's film is clearly interested in remembering the skilled Creole and African-American craftsmen who built these homes, this act of remembrance is problematically silent on the subject of gentrification. The result is that, like the fixation on the plantation home, this is a narrow celebration of culture that fails to consider the people that populate the landscape in the present. In post-Katrina New Orleans, where the needs of tourists are so often prioritized above residents, low-income individuals and families are caught between the destructive "progress" of the wrecking ball and the insidious implications of historical renovation.

"Do You Know What it Means to Miss New Orleans?": Tourism and Culture after Katrina

Attica Locke's 2012 novel *The Cutting Season* is a post-Katrina rendering of the plantation home, one that reframes this primal national site as fundamentally *un*homely. Based on Oak Alley Plantation, Locke's fictive Belle Vie during the course of the narrative unearths its dead in ways that uncannily expose the "nostalgia" of the contemporary tourist industry to earlier, seemingly obsolete meanings of that word. As Jessica Adams suggests in relation to her work on the post-slavery plantation,

> "Wounds of returning" is the literal translation of "nostalgia," a word that, John Frow writes, was "originally defined in the seventeenth century in terms of a set of physical symptoms associated with acute homesickness" and later "came to be closely connected with the 'specific depression of intellectuals,' melancholia. By the nineteenth century it had been extended to describe a general condition of estrangement, a state of ontological homelessness that became one of the period's key metaphors for the condition of modernity." In everyday usage, nostalgia has come to signify the longing to return to a past that probably never existed and to places that have changed irrevocably. But "wounds of returning" suggests something more complicated—that the past itself may return, inflicting new wounds and reopening old ones.[65]

This is precisely the temporality of *The Cutting Season*, in which the past gradually encroaches upon and eventually overwhelms the present. The narrative excavates the remains of Jason, an ex-slave who remained on the plantation after Emancipation, and whose claim to some of the land—under the 1862 Homestead Act—was seemingly thwarted when he disappeared under suspicious circumstances. Meanwhile, in the present, the descendants of Jason and those likely responsible for his death reenact a version of this drama in the present: a Hispanic worker in the neighboring cane field, an enterprise that is itself an updated, corporate version of the slave system, is murdered for "trespassing" on the plantation grounds. Though Ines's murderer is in fact a member of the "plantation owning class"—that stole the land from its black workers—for most of the narrative it is a black man who languishes in prison for the white man's crime.[66]

And yet these "wounds of returning"—of bodies marked by racial violence—dislodge the neat boundary between past and present on which the contemporary notion of nostalgia peddled by plantation tourism relies. In so doing I suggest the novel poses a challenge to Louisiana's dominant tourist narratives so neatly established in the latter part of the twentieth century by sequestering the past, rendering them fundamentally unhomely in the twenty-first century. As Belle Vie becomes the scene of murder and fear—a threat that was always, the novel suggests, lurking in the twisted forms of the plantation's live oaks—New Orleans itself, abandoned by the principal protagonist in Katrina's aftermath, comes into view as the site of nostalgia. In this way Locke's novel reverses the relationship between New Orleans and the plantation that has persisted at least since the 1947 publication of *A Streetcar Named Desire*. Where in that text New Orleans functioned as a gritty negation of Blanche's fantasy of the plantation home, Belle Reve, in Locke's novel the plantation is burdened with the violence of the "real" and New Orleans itself is the lost object.

"Do you know what it means to miss New Orleans?" is one of the tourist industry's most effective post-Katrina marketing slogans, even as the industry takes a central role in effacing the cultural legacies to which the phrase pays lip-service. Though the storm and subsequent flooding did enormous damage to the city's infrastructure and residential neighborhoods, the interpretation of that damage has been pivotal to the vital question of who is able to return and rebuild and who is not. Central to the New Orleans economy, tourist industry interests have had a privileged seat at the interpreters' table. Although the city's edgy reputation as a "sin city" is not unconnected to neighborhoods associated with crime, concerns about safety have long challenged the tourist industry's ability to simultaneously promote New Orleans as a family destination. The same balancing act is required for gentrifying neighborhoods—attracting those who seek "the drama of 'the urban'" but insulation from any real sense of danger. This is the paradox that Christian Parenti identifies in *Lockdown America* (1999) as driving the policing of the "themepark metropolis": zero tolerance policies lurk in suspicious proximity to middle-class bohemia.[67]

The post-Katrina razing of the Lafitte and Iberville housing projects in Tremé, along with a number of other projects in other areas of the city, removes these symbols of perceived urban blight from the view of wary visitors and new residents.[68] The assault on New Orleans' public housing will be explored in chapter four; here the significance lies in the ways in which black New Orleans continues to bear the brunt of a human-induced disaster only exacerbated by Katrina. As Rachel Carrico argues, immediately after Katrina "advocacy arguments for restoring New Orleans' local, black *culture* existed within a material reality where few adequate resources were made available to protect, assist, and support the city's African American *residents*."[69] This separation between culture and residents is, as I have tried to show in this chapter, a move on which the tourist industry has long relied. Carrico elaborates: "Katrina's aftermath did not feature the first battle, but was arguably the most severe in a long history of defending New Orleans against a band of thieves."[70]

If the absence of a solid referent is the very condition of nostalgia, then the post-Katrina transformation of the city, like the near-destruction of the streetcar and the bulldozing of its jazz history, might be seen as a prerequisite for the marketing of the city as a site of loss. Indeed this commodified nostalgia in turn paves over New Orleans' own "wounds of returning" so vividly materialized by Katrina. Arguably the sight of drowned black bodies floating in the city streets brought onlookers far too close for comfort to the underside of a New Orleans culture that the tourist industry had carefully domesticated and held at bay. While soaring murder rates in the city throughout the 1980s lent New Orleans' famous above-ground cemeteries an air of menace that was perhaps more "authentic" than most thrill-seekers were hoping for, the bodies that followed in Katrina's wake confronted spectators with the abandoned "real" behind the façade of New Orleans tourism. Here the "disaster" of Thomas's touristic dialectic brushes discomfortingly close to a social disaster of another kind; one that cannot be contained by a racist vision of a pathologized African-American culture. Thomas convincingly argues that the racialized tourist narrative that rose to prominence in the latter part of the twentieth century paved the way for Katrina as well as providing the dominant frame through which images of the city and its black residents were filtered.[71] And yet as she also acknowledges, Katrina preempted some "unscripted" moments that for a while at least disrupted the narrative of mainstream New Orleans tourism.[72]

The first tourist attractions to draw directly from the experience of the storm exposed visitors to scenes devoid of human inhabitants. Like other variants of disaster tourism, the Katrina bus tours invited visitors to gaze at scenes of destruction—devastated houses, empty and abandoned lots, storm debris that remained for years after Katrina. These peculiarly de-populated landscapes are presented as sites of loss, with little indication of the ongoing human struggles to save them. Ten years after the storm, most tour companies have absorbed the Katrina tour into their standard City Tours, according those areas that still evidence widespread destruction—primarily large swathes of the Lower Ninth Ward—an almost permanent status as sites of disaster.

Writing in 2007, J. Mark Souther wonders whether "the devastation left by the flooding has, to an extent, reordered tourists' spatial understanding of New Orleans":

> Months after Katrina, tour buses groaned through eerily quiet streets as passengers gawked at the brown watermarks, blue tarps, and orange spray-painted rescue signs that now took their place alongside the more familiar iron balconies, gas lamps, and porticos. While disaster tours may do as much to sate voyeuristic appetites as heighten social awareness, a growing penchant for "voluntourism" promises to bring more than the expected social activists into contact with the city beyond the French Quarter.[73]

Writing seven years later, Thomas suggests that the expanding map of New Orleans after Katrina was a temporary phenomenon that has since seen the reassertion of older, more familiar tourist narratives of the city. What may endure for longer is the growing "voluntourism" that Souther suggests the bus tours anticipate. While the typical Katrina tourist is a voyeur who remains detached from the scenes of devastation she is exposed to, the "voluntourist," though well-meant, arguably takes too much interest in the areas beyond the tourist hub that have not previously made it onto tourist maps of the city. Tourism has long acted in New Orleans as an agent of gentrification in the historic neighborhoods that line the Mississippi River, a trend that had begun to seep into Tremé during the decade preceding Katrina. These processes have always been a paradoxical effect of the industry, further distancing what is sold as "culture" in New Orleans from the people who created it. Residents and city boosters alike have for decades been anxious that the city will consequently lose its sense of "authentic" distinctiveness—becoming a Disneyfied simulacra of its former self, in turn resembling so many other tourist destinations across the United States. But as an attraction of an altogether different kind, Katrina has opened the floodgates, as it were, to newcomers who are radically reshaping what it might mean to miss New Orleans.

As Richard Campanella explains in "Gentrification and its Discontents," Katrina opened New Orleans to two distinct waves of gentrifiers. The first wave came in the form of thousands of urbanists, environmentalists, social workers, and volunteers who "took leave from their graduate studies and nascent careers and headed South to be a part of something important." Campanella suggests that most of these newcomers had left New Orleans by 2009, once initial recovery money had run its course, but that in this same period a new wave—larger this time and with more staying power—began to arrive as a result of the city's relatively robust economic climate at a time of national recession. Campanella estimates that this wave numbers about 15,000 to 20,000 and continues to grow. Made up of new media-entrepreneurs, Teach for America recruits or contributors to the city's booming cultural economy, these newcomers, along with those of the first wave who stayed, are in large part responsible for the idea that New Orleans, once a shrinking, reputedly "stagnant" city, is now a growing, economically dynamic and mobile city with a future.[74] Where the influx of newcomers from Saint-Domingue 200 years previously had shored up a declining Creole culture against the seemingly inevitable process of Americanization, the post-Katrina influx arguably wound the metaphorical clock in the opposite direction. Apparently bringing with them the forces of change and Americanization, some say they are effacing the very "foreignness" that the nineteenth-century arrivals ensured would remain central to New Orleans' reputation.[75]

For some post-Katrina transplants, this charge is painfully ironic; as Campanella suggests, "they lament their role in ousting the very vessels of localism they came to savor, but also take pride in their spirited civic engagement and rescue of architectural treasures." Carrico tackles these dilemmas on a different level in her reflexive piece, the narrative of which interlaces her own trajectory as a post-Katrina transplant with that of a fictionalized "Good Thief." This thief has arrived in New Orleans as a result of a "romanticized attraction to America's Creole Soul," but she is doomed to experience "Creole soul without the Creoles . . . otherness without the others," to parade down the city streets as a "spiritless body" precisely because her own physical presence has displaced the bodies of black New Orleanians.[76] While these accounts of gentrification are symptomatic rather than causal, attending to individual motivation for relocating as opposed to the larger shifts in capital that determine trends—and which will be explored in chapter 4—they offer important insights into the way perspectives on New Orleans culture have shifted post-Katrina.

Meanwhile, redevelopment projects on the Iberville site—which will transform the project into a mixed-income development, replacing only one-third of the previously existing public housing units—were during 2013 subject to delay due to the discovery of human remains. As in Locke's novel, inconvenient bone matter—which preserves well in the aqueous conditions of Louisiana soil—interrupts the march of modernization by returning us to prior casualties. Where in *The Cutting Season* it is the plantation home itself that is billed for demolition in favor of an extension of the modern-day sugar cane factory, New Orleans after Katrina has similarly been subjected to new iterations of "progress" that have challenged the city's orientation toward the past. One of the fascinating aspects of Locke's narrative is that the African-American protagonists employed at Belle Vie, many of whom act in the plantation's set-piece for tourists—which circulates around happy slaves and benevolent masters—are angry at the closure of the tourist attraction. Though they recognize that the charade they are paid to engage in is an insulting travesty of slave history, there is a sense that the demolition of the plantation entails an abandonment of their roots which, however distorted, are nonetheless preserved by tourism. In this way *The Cutting Season* partially supports Kevin Fox Gotham's contention in relation to the New Orleans context that while you can distinguish "bottom-up" and "top-down" narratives, they are all permeated by a "touristic culture." For Gotham, "tourism may offer positive functions in enhancing the resources available for local people and groups to create new definitions of place character and transform meanings of authenticity."[77]

And yet in *The Cutting Season* the appearance of human remains similarly thwarts tourism by confronting nostalgia with matter. Jason's bones and Donovan's alternative plantation drama—that includes those bones in its narrative arc—are rejected on the grounds that they are not marketable. In this way tourism itself is shown to be part of modernity's creative destruction of tradition, buildings, and bodies—its relationship with the past is purely commercial. In spite of its dubious interventions into public memory, it is part of the "progress train" that experimental theatre-maker Nick Slie argues is eroding New Orleans' relationship with the past in the post-Katrina period. At a conference dedicated to examining Katrina's legacy at Tulane University in November 2013, Slie, referring to the post-storm newcomers, claimed that "a lot of people are now in New Orleans living ahistorical lives," opting to "jump right on the progress train" rather than tuning in to the "deep one hundred year history of people's families, where they came from."[78] Slie's rhetoric protests what he and many others decry as a new, "glossy" New Orleans, wherein the city's deep-rooted cultures, already threatened by an increasingly Disneyfied tourist industry that is adopting the upscale attractions that can be found all over the United States, are under threat from a new kind of visitor, one that doesn't even pretend to celebrate the city's past, or indeed intend to leave. As Campanella explains, although many post-Katrina transplants pay lip-service to New Orleans culture, they tend to be "much more secular, less fertile, more liberal, and less parochial than native-born New Orleanians. They see local conservatism as a problem calling for enlightenment rather than an opinion to be respected, and view the importation of national and global values as imperative to a sustainable and equitable recovery."[79] And yet like Jason's bones, there is something deeply resistant about the discourse into which "transplants" must insert themselves: that of the New Orleanian native. This fascinating figure has a similarly intimate connection with the soil, and has also risen to the surface in a post-Katrina present that has threatened it with erasure.

Carol Bebelle, founder and director of Central City's Ashé Cultural Arts Center, suggested in an interview that New Orleans culture needs to be thought of as an indigenous, African Caribbean culture, closer culturally to the Reservation than any other cultural grouping in the United States. In order to illustrate the reverence for tradition and family in black New Orleans culture, she refers to mantelpieces overflowing with family photographs and claims that these are versions of African "ancestor alters," which have survived the Middle Passage and slavery into twenty-first-century New

Orleans. Bebelle claims that black New Orleanians live with a heightened awareness of death, both because their lives are punctuated by storms and because "we walk around in the world with boats floating above us in our heads." These "visible reminders of mortality . . . strengthen the bonds of cultural connection." The key to these connections for Bebelle is ritual: not just the weekly gatherings of second line parades which celebrate the community—and reclaim streets maligned both by crime and by rhetoric about crime; equally important are daily meetings on the bus, on the street, the everyday interactions that cement what Bebelle characterizes as a culture of care. "We're not a community in which people are just driven by work, or just driven by play."[80] These represent values that transcend the marketplace, challenging both the Protestant work ethic that has resulted in forced and exploitative labor, and a consumer culture that has ruthlessly commercialized the very idea of "leisure."

Of course the narrative of the New Orleanian native is not solely an African-American one; indeed, Campanella makes the fascinating suggestion that the discourse of nativity is so powerful in New Orleans that it rivals race as a category of social analysis.[81] But in the post-Katrina context it is impossible to avoid the conclusion that it is black native New Orleanians who have been the victims of a ruthless "reimagining" of the city which does not include its poorest inhabitants. The slogan "roots run deep here" could be found across the city's many demolition sites that threatened its former black residents with permanent displacement. In Katrina's aftermath many stories told of the dispersal of some of the most close-knit communities in the United States, several generations of one family living in the same block, individuals who hardly ever left their ward let alone New Orleans itself. While it is important to recognize that a crucial ingredient to this lack of mobility is poverty and social deprivation, conditions that should not be romanticized, it is equally important to see that this enormously powerful sense of place at work in the discourse of nativity is a weapon of resistance to the very conditions that keep people in place. One of the ironies of the post-Katrina media storm was that the image of New Orleans was at least temporarily transformed from a tourist mecca celebrating black culture to a symbol of racialized urban poverty and blight; this new narrative in turn wrote over the strong attachments many black New Orleanians have to their home, and was used to support the insidious logic of displacement: that many would be better off elsewhere.[82]

In his famous meditation on the experience of modernity, *All That is Solid Melts into Air* (1982), Marshall Berman concludes by reflecting on the "expressway world" pioneered by Robert Moses, that ploughed through his childhood neighborhood of the Bronx in the 1950s. Similar to the destruction of Tremé's Clairborne Avenue, the new expressway "cut through" the "heart" of the neighborhood and "made the Bronx, above all, a place to get out of."[83] Berman suggests that ironically, while the city has arguably been *the* site of modernity, the coming of the expressway, a key development in twentieth-century modernity, has in turn rendered the modern city obsolete. The city is an obstacle to the expressway. Both New York City and New Orleans have to a large extent resisted the logic of the expressway, despite localized instances of destruction and suburbanization. For different reasons, both are oriented toward an inner core in ways that subvert the LA-style sprawl that has decentered so many U.S. cities. But when Berman speculates on what might have happened had the Bronx been saved from the wrecking ball, he suggests something that jars significantly with the New Orleans context:

> How many of us would still be in the Bronx today, caring for it and fighting for it as our own? Some of us, no doubt, but I suspect not so many, and in any case—it hurts to say it—not me. For the Bronx of my youth was possessed, inspired, by the great modern dream of mobility.[84]

For Berman this pull toward the hope of a better life is inexorable: "we had no way to resist the wheels that drove the American dream, because it was driving us ourselves—even though we knew the wheels might break us." For complex reasons the reaction to social deprivation in New Orleans in the postwar period was different; it was not overtaken by "the desperate energy of this vision, the frenzied economic and psychic pressure to move up and out."[85] Instead, New Orleans was embraced by many of its residents, and particularly its deep-rooted black population, as an alternative to "a state of ontological homelessness" that in the nineteenth century was the definition of "nostalgia" and "one of the period's key metaphors for the condition of modernity."[86] In this sense aspects of New Orleans culture—in spite of the predominance of the tourist industry and the processes of modernization that the industry only rhetorically downplays—resist a modern culture that experiences the past only as nostalgia.

As plans for the demolition of 1–10 have emerged in the post-Katrina period—plans that belatedly admit that the expressway's construction through the heart of Tremé was a mistake—a similar resistance has surfaced in response to this latest rendition of "progress." The narrative of nativity in New Orleans celebrates a sense of "being in place" that resists the radical social engineering engendered by the tourist industry, the car, or indeed capitalist modernity's prior iterations in the form of the plantation and the slave ship.

Conclusion: Walking in New Orleans

As Solomon Northup moves from freedom into slavery in *12 Years a Slave* (1853), he experiences his journey as a descent into the "sickly regions of Louisiana."[87] Though he does not actually arrive in New Orleans on a steamboat—which he initially boards, with his fellow captives, to Richmond, Virginia, followed by a "brig" to Louisiana—Steve McQueen's film version fuses the two waterborne journeys into one, with the camera dwelling on the red paddle wheel of the steamboat. Now an icon of the New Orleans tourist industry, the paddle wheel here is infused with a sense of menace, recalling the path of the Middle Passage as well as the memory that the Crescent City was contemplated with dread by slaves who saw it as a route into ever worse forms of slavery. This 2013 rendition of the nineteenth-century slave narrative returns its viewers to the image of New Orleans not as a playground for the American imagination, a place to experience the sensorium of a carefully commodified black culture of leisure, but rather as a place determined by the brutal logic of forced labor. The sight of damaged and mutilated black bodies welcome visitors to the Port of New Orleans, by this time the South's largest slave market, bodies that are then conveyed to the plantation—a place that in McQueen's film, in spite of the shocking scenes of sadism and violence, is dominated by work. These scenes of work released in 2013 repudiate not only a leisure industry fixated on a romanticized past but also commentators in 2005 who, on contemplating the damaged black bodies that once again floated on the streets of New Orleans, clung to the deeply racist conceit that links blackness to "shiftlessness." The film reminds us that stereotypes about black lethargy are directly linked to slavery, both as justification for the "peculiar institution"—black people will only work if forced—and as a way of sublimating the reality of the system itself.[88]

Writing about impoverished black communities in pre-Katrina New Orleans in the *New York Times* in 2005, David Brooks followed this racist logic to its conclusion:

> In those cultural zones, many people dropped out of high school, so it seemed normal to drop out of high school. Many teenage girls had babies, so it seemed normal to become a teenage mother. It was hard for men to get stable jobs, so it was not abnormal for them to commit crimes and hop from one relationship to another. Many people lacked marketable social skills, so it was hard for young people to learn these skills from parents, neighbors and peers.

If we just put up new buildings and allow the same people to move back into their old neighborhoods, then urban New Orleans will become just as rundown and dysfunctional as before.[89]

Interestingly, Brooks diagnosed Haiti's cultural pathologies in a similar way in 2010:

Haiti, like most of the world's poorest nations, suffers from a complex web of progress-resistant cultural influences. There is the influence of the voodoo religion, which spreads the message that life is capricious and planning futile. There are high levels of social mistrust. Responsibility is often not internalized. Child-rearing practices often involve neglect in the early years and harsh retribution when kids hit 9 or 10.

We're all supposed to politely respect each other's cultures. But some cultures are more progress-resistant than others, and a horrible tragedy was just exacerbated by one of them.[90]

What Brooks does not say is the fact that both Haiti and New Orleans have been the victims not just of natural disasters but of disastrous American-authored notions of progress. And that in spite of this, they *have* both proved "progress-resistant" in the sense that both locations have powerfully resisted the linear and uncritical model of U.S. progress that Brooks champions. Where Haiti successfully revolted against slavery and empire, the foundations of western modernity and "progress," New Orleans as a city has, more modestly, resisted comprehensive "Americanization," and the marks of this resistance still show.

In John Kennedy Toole's *A Confederacy of Dunces* (1980), Ignatius Reilly, bloated and hilarious as he may be, exhibits a powerful critique of work, a critique that the novel consistently associates with the New Orleans context. Ignatius, in the process of "writing a lengthy indictment against our century," wonders if the faulty miniature baseball machine he likes to play in the Penny Arcade is being repaired: "was it possible to repair the machine in New Orleans? Probably so. However, it might have to be sent to someplace like Milwaukee or Chicago or some other city whose name Ignatius associated with efficient repair shops and permanently smoking factories."[91] Though some have argued that the novel's portrait of New Orleans via the figure of Ignatius Reilly is unflattering, he is unquestionably a figure of resistance in relation to the ideologies at the heart of the "American Century." Significantly, Ignatius suffers from car sickness, which becomes particularly acute during his first and only trip out of New Orleans.

New York functions as a counterpoint in the novel, which is opened by two epigraphs which together suggest that, while bound by the same national horizon, New York and New Orleans are worlds apart. Andrei Codrescu makes a related point when he argues that where New York is America's most "timebound" city, New Orleans is "timeless." Certainly New Orleans seems to partially resist the reality Codrescu ascribes to New York: "chopped to pieces as it is by the guillotine hands of global-economy time."[92] And yet, as the New Orleans tourist industry has made abundantly clear, the notion of "timelessness" is wide open to commodification and recuperation by market values, values which ride roughshod over the very real histories that undergird present realities. The rituals that both Ignatius and Carol Bebelle, in very different ways, associate with New Orleans, while eschewing the logic of "time-keeping" central to the capitalist economy, should not be seen as frozen in time; rather they allude to other kinds of time. Ignatius, although he superficially invites us to view New Orleans as a stagnant city, is engaged in ongoing struggle against what is essentially the "progress" of modern capitalism. For Bebelle the time of ritual, of social bonding, explicitly transcends the time of the market, but this transcendence is dialectical: it concerns active resistance to the forces of commercialization and privatization that threaten to engulf New Orleans in the post-Katrina present.

Resistance to what I am characterizing in this book as "Katrina time" is, I argue, very much at work in the 2013 film adaptation of *12 Years a Slave*. While the film refutes the messaging of the contemporary New Orleans tourist industry, it also marks the whole of the United States as slave territory, with flashbacks to New York State showing free blacks coexisting with slaves—as indeed they did in New Orleans—and slaves being held just a stone's throw from the Capitol building in Washington DC. These portraits of what is clearly a national oppression are temporally unstable, not just via the use of flashbacks which splice scenes of freedom with those of slavery; it also depicts a slave narrative that to an extent reverses the genre's typical progressive trajectory, from slavery to freedom, and instead shows Solomon Northup's descent into slavery, a descent that is also crucially shown to be a captivity narrative. Here the film not only resists the establishment tendency to draw the slave narrative and the larger black freedom movement into a teleological trajectory of the emancipatory logic of America's progressive unfolding. The film's anti-progressive trajectory implicates contemporary viewers by inviting us to splice the flashbacks to the North with our own present realities: it takes us, with Solomon, into and then out of the slave system, depositing us back in the scene of Northup's middle-class home in the North, free but not unscathed. Northup's home resides precariously close to those living in a state of unfreedom, and actively embraces the commodity fetishism of contemporary capitalism. This ostensibly historical drama readily bleeds into contemporary history, replotting the nation's geography and disrupting fictions that seek to fix the past in place. As the film shuttles between the "free" North and the slave South, the past and the present, it carries with it "wounds of returning" that seem to leap over the optimism of the twentieth century and particularly the post-1945 period, arriving uncomfortably and belatedly into a disenchanted twenty-first century context.

As David Brooks' rhetoric shows, the euphemism that defined twentieth-century attitudes toward obsolescence—"urban renewal," "revitalization"—has been replaced by a starker language that no longer includes the socially marginal as objects of "improvement." What follows seeks to navigate a path into the unstable post-Katrina present, into those lives and neighborhoods rendered disposable in the language of neoliberal opportunity. The next part of the book turns to those residents upon whom the tourist industry has always been parasitic: simultaneously appropriating and commodifying their cultural contributions while removing them from their streets and neighborhoods as obstructions to the business of profit. Tourism emerged in the twentieth century as a way for New Orleans to survive in an American Century to which it was arguably ill-suited; and yet its major contribution to the city's dramatically unequal distribution of wealth was vividly on display after Katrina. The post-storm privatization trends— explored in chapter 4—take their cue from an industry that has long drawn as many aspects of daily life in the city into its commercial net. The next chapter explores the attempts to document the plight of New Orleanians who suffered the most as a result of Katrina, and chapter 4 turns to the social movements that have arisen to challenge the status quo. The larger story of this section of the book is one of cultural and political resistance, resistance that draws on a rich history partially charted in this chapter—in which the city has struggled against U.S. norms.

Rather than reworking the image of the car as the very opposite of the progress it was meant to symbolize, as in Jesmyn Ward's tale of pre-Katrina disaster with which this chapter opened, here I would like to offer the image of walking as one way to envision the interruptive nature of "New Orleans time." Walking here is not imagined in opposition to car ownership—which is not only desirable in a hot and humid city in which heavy rain is a common occurrence, but which in Katrina's aftermath became an indicator of survival. Rather, walking is envisaged as a choice, associated with leisure rather than work. As Jane Jacobs has shown in relation to New York, walking, as an activity intrinsic to the mixture that defines the modern city, is anathema to the logic of the expressway, the Robert Moses-style planning that views pedestrians and indeed residents as obsolete.[93] Though New Orleans is partially a car culture, its residents are proud of the idea that it could also be seen as a walkable city, just as they are vocal about the city's differences from the rest of the United States in spite of the many similarities. And indeed the city's traditions, from which tourism steals but which are not reducible to tourism, flaunt the act of walking, and indeed dancing, on the city streets. Walking, unlike the experience of being in a car, is defined by neither stasis nor speed: it is mobile while maintaining an intimate connection to place. New Orleans' parading traditions defy the racialized anti-urbanism that was central to the "American Century" of the postwar years. They might be compared to the instances of "sonic maroonage" that Ned Sublette identifies as part of the legacy of Congo Square: both a flight from and an act of survival within a national culture that has demeaned the city, its streets, and the people that call them home.

Part II

Katrina Time

3

Documenting Katrina

The Return of the "Real"

Wendy and Lucy (2008), directed by Kelly Reichardt, opens with the rusty clatter of the railways, visually and audibly alluding to the sense of anachronism that overshadows the narrative's tentative glance toward the future.[1] The sounds of trains creaking along their tracks follow the camera to a lone figure walking with her dog in the woods, the blurry shapes periodically obscured by trees, branches, and shadow. It is only several scenes on that it becomes apparent that this film is a stalled road movie, as Wendy is woken by law enforcement in her parked car to the discovery that the engine won't start. According to Reichardt, her film is "very post-Katrina."[2] As Reichardt explained in conversation with fellow director Gus Van Sant:

> The seeds of *Wendy and Lucy* happened shortly after Hurricane Katrina, after hearing talk about people pulling themselves up by their bootstraps, and hearing the presumption that people's lives were so precarious due to some laziness on their part. Jon [Raymond] and I were musing on the idea of having no net—let's say your bootstraps floated away—how do you get out of your situation totally on your own without help from the government?[3]

Set in small-town Oregon, *Wendy and Lucy* seems to chart the fate of a representative of what Lauren Berlant has identified as the "precariat," an ever-growing group of U.S. citizens for whom the American dream has stopped functioning as an enabling fiction. In the film's opening scenes we discover that Wendy is heading for the new frontier of Alaska, hesitantly reaching out for opportunities that seem to have eluded her on the U.S. mainland. As the film progresses and Wendy's problems deepen, culminating in the loss of her car—which is only good for scrap—and her dog, the journey to Alaska seems increasingly improbable, another scrambled dream in what the viewer imagines is a mounting list of failures. In this way Wendy acts out Berlant's definition of "cruel optimism" by remaining invested, if only tentatively, in a life plan that seems to be her undoing.[4]

As Reichardt acknowledges, the racial identity of her protagonist means that in a really difficult situation, she would likely "get help" from onlookers if not the government, whereas those unable to call on white privilege might well not. Though Reichardt claims to have been influenced by Italian neorealism, Wendy does not fit the description of disposable life that Reichardt evokes as part of that genre: people deemed "no use to society—maybe they're too old or poor so they're a blight—they're like stray dogs."[5] But she teeters on the edge, hinting toward the "attrition of a fantasy" of the "good life" that according to Berlant affects growing numbers of Americans facing social and economic decline. As Berlant explained in 2011, "the current recession congeals decades of class bifurcation, downward mobility, and environmental, political, and social brittleness that have increased progressively since the Reagan era."[6]

Wendy and Lucy is thus part of a "cinema of precarity," its plotless trajectory signifying an impasse in Berlant's sense, "a thick moment of ongoingness," of treading water, "a middle without boundaries, edges, a shape."[7] This lack of temporal structure that forecloses on a vision of the future evokes what I have been calling in this book "Katrina time," a term appropriated from the legal context where it was indicative of the limbo many pre-charge detainees in New Orleans' prisons found themselves in the aftermath of the storm. I am attempting here to stretch this term in order to consider Katrina's larger and long-term implications, just as Reichardt's filmic rendition of the "post-Katrina" displaces the storm's immediate geography in order to expand our sense not only of what "Katrina" might mean but who should feel affected by it. And yet Reichardt's decision to set *Wendy and Lucy* in a rural location in Oregon—that could feasibly be anywhere in the United States—with a white actress playing the central protagonist also underscores the dilemmas of decontextualization. What she loosely casts as a fictionalized "Katrina" arguably enables a logic that rides roughshod over the specificities of those lives most comprehensively devastated by Katrina—metaphorically displacing those Katrina survivors who have been subject to violent acts of physical displacement. The very scene of a lone protagonist at the center of a road movie—even a stalled one—

fails to do justice to the fact that so many of the Katrina "diaspora" were embedded within dense social networks that were in turn defined by deep attachments to a particular place. Many of these people manifestly did not wish to leave New Orleans, despite its lack of economic opportunities. In this sense *Wendy and Lucy* does not capture the "post-Katrina" predicament that faced particularly working class and poor African Americans—whose lives were most comprehensively uprooted, disoriented, and in some cases destroyed by Katrina. Though admirably calling its viewers to the kind of empathic leap so missing from much news commentary immediately follow-ing the storm, the ethical dilemmas thrown up by *Wendy and Lucy* possibly provide a clue as to why it is that so much post-Katrina representation, and particularly that which has been at the center of critical attention, has taken the form of social documentary that has centralized the experiences and voices of Katrina survivors themselves—particularly New Orleanians.

The first part of this book charted the ways in which African-American communities in New Orleans have been made to bear the scars of mod-ernization, of the city's transformations from a French colonial backwater to an American destination of mass tourism. It explored the fact that the fetishization of New Orleans culture has often gone hand-in-hand with the demonization of those who produce that culture, a trend that has only been exacerbated since Katrina. The second part of this book explores the ways in which artists and activists since Katrina have responded to these processes accelerated by the storm, processes that have highlighted New Orleans' longstanding status as an object of the U.S. imperial gaze. This chapter explores two key examples of post-Katrina documentary, examining their ideological and political coordinates as art and advocacy attempting to illuminate and challenge key aspects of Katrina's neoliberal milieu. The next chapter shifts emphasis to consider more direct acts of resistance to the logics unleashed by Katrina, but similarly identifies modes of storytelling as some of the most effective means of resisting "Katrina time." Together they explore the interconnections between aesthetic and political responses to the post-Katrina present; as both challenges to and in some cases manifestations of "Katrina time"—a temporal category that, I hope, is elaborated here in such a way that does not lose sight of the singular case study from which I am drawing.

The first part of this chapter explores the centrality of social docu-mentary in post-Katrina representation, holding up 9/11 fictionalization as a point of contrast. The second reads Tia Lessin's and Carl Deal's acclaimed documentary film *Trouble the Water* (2008), analyzing its temporal assump-tions in the context of Berlant's notion of "cruel optimism," as well as the dilemmas of the left-identified rhetoric of "empowerment" in a social context sold on the right-identified myth of "self-reliance."[8] The third section turns to Luisa Dantas's 2010 documentary film, *Land of Opportunity*, arguing that its multilayered approach to storytelling and politics acknowledges the loss of a useable linear narrative for progressive politics, while offering alternatives to what Vincanne Adams terms the "affect economy" of disaster capitalism.[9] I conclude by briefly looking at Spike Lee's epic documentary films, *When the Levees Broke: A Requiem in Four Acts* (2006) and *If God is Willing and Da Creek Don't Rise* (2011), which together act out Katrina's temporal reach, ambivalently undoing the temptation toward redemption that seems to partially motivate both films.[10] All of these films, I suggest, seek to return viewers to the violently excluded "real" of the storm so distorted by the news media coverage that followed in its wake.

"Not as Seen on TV"

In the aftermath of 9/11, TV viewers were subjected to endlessly repeated footage showing the planes crashing into the World Trade Center, and the subsequent crumbling of the Twin Towers.[11] According to some commentators, viewers who had not witnessed events in New York firsthand were traumatized by watching the news.[12] As media discourse in the United States congealed around George W. Bush's "you're either with us or you're with the terrorists" logic, many artists and writers increasingly saw their role as providing an antidote—if not to the orgy of national flag-waving, at least to the desensitization that might paradoxically follow the endless repetition of traumatic images. Newspapers were increasingly carrying collections of hastily penned short stories fictively reframing 9/11 for a public imagination hypnotized by the event's defining image. Prominent U.S. writers like Don DeLillo and John Updike stepped up to the challenge posed by the British writer Ian McEwan, issued as early as September 15, 2001, in the *Guardian* newspaper: "Imagining what it is like to be someone other than yourself is at the core of our humanity. It is the essence of compassion, and it is the beginning of morality."[13] McEwan's post-9/11 statement was not specifically a call to fiction, and neither was it an indictment of the media portrayal of 9/11. Rather it was a challenge directed at the "failure of imagination" that McEwan saw at the heart of the attacks themselves, a call to empathy. While McEwan's position has often been characterized as reactionary, symptomatic of the binary logic that poisoned much post-9/11 discourse with an unapologetic chauvinism, DeLillo, and especially Updike, self-consciously attempted to fictionalize the mind of the Islamist, the figure that has emerged in the twenty-first century as the "other" of the western imagination.[14] What is fascinating in the twists and turns of the emergence of the "9/11 novel" is that within days of the attacks, fiction was established as an important site for negotiating the meaning of that day in September. This seems not to have been the case with Katrina.

Despite some interesting novelistic results, both *Terrorist* (2006) and *Falling Man* (2007) have been widely dismissed, along with a host of 9/11 fictions, as themselves "failures of the imagination." Many literary critics have argued that prominent U.S. writers have been guilty of perpetuating essentially the same myth as that which predominated in political and media discourse: of a traumatized nation that needs to retreat into itself in order to negate the "other," non-American world that stalks the 9/11 moment.[15] Centering on ahistorical and apolitical stories of individual trauma, these fictions "domesticate" the crisis and fail to interrogate the notions of differ-ence, otherness, and strangeness that might begin to address the incredible post-9/11 rallying cry: "Why do they hate us?" As Pakistani writer Kami-la Shamsie put it in a 2012 article titled "Storytellers of Empire," "your soldiers will come to our lands, but your novelists won't."[16] This apparent unwillingness to venture beyond physical or psychic barriers of the nation represent, according to these critics, a wilful ignorance in relation to U.S. transgressions in the arena of foreign policy, and the maintenance of the national story of innocence that keeps the subject of the 9/11 attackers and the worlds that hover behind them "taboo" in the American imagination. These calls for a more globalized, empathic twenty-first-century U.S. litera-ture challenge the ethical and political foundations of fictions that seemingly refuse to peer outward.

This is not the place to assess the veracity of these attacks on U.S. literary constructions of 9/11, although it does seem that these texts have been singled out for particularly fierce treatment, with little thought to the ways in which an examination of the neuroses of middle-class Amer-ican domestic life might shed light on the problem of national insularity. But the suggestion that the only place for the U.S. novel to look to—in order to confront an image that might contradict its sanctimonious claim to innocence—is an external other seems to miss the powerful internal challenges posed by events like Hurricane Katrina. And in fact, while there have of course been numerous "Katrina novels" and likely many more will appear in the future,[17] what is striking when surveying the field of cultural representations of Katrina is that documentary has emerged as the choice mode for meditating on this event. This is not to discount the myriad novels, short stories, feature films, and TV dramas that in various ways narrate "Katrina" (not to mention poetry, visual art, and art installations that don't necessarily narrate the storm but might reflect on it via abstraction). Rather it is to suggest that anxieties about the distorting lenses offered by the initial news media coverage of the storm and its fallout—discussed in detail in chapter 1—have led to countless documentary projects that have attempted to directly compete with and counter these accounts in the same, nonfictional space.

Where critics of the media response to 9/11 have on the whole condemned not the representation of facts but rather the perpetuation of a particular mood, critiques of the coverage of Katrina routinely involve both substance and style. Where 9/11 fictions to an extent have provided narrative for visual imagery so powerful that it seems to transcend any story we might tell about it, post-Katrina documentary has tended to offer direct counternarrative to the sensationalized and often racist stories that circulated in the late summer of 2005. These stories routinely involved depictions of inner city life in general and New Orleans in particular grotesquely distorted by racist stereotypes. Challenging these stories was particularly important given that, as a number of critics have argued, Katrina was experienced by the vast majority of people as a media event.[18] The vast outpourings of firsthand accounts, oral history projects, biographies, photography projects, and documentary films can be seen in this vein as a kind of corrective to media discourse that seemed to threaten New Orleans with forms of loss just as surely as had Katrina. Post-Katrina documentary might thus be seen as a form of retrieval, an act of cultural rescue in an ideological context seemingly intent on providing evidence that, if New Orleans was to be rebuilt—and that assumption was questioned—it would not, as David Brooks (as cited in the previous chapter) asserted in the *New York Times*, be restored as it was prior to the storm.[19] Where the tourist industry has typically "preserved" New Orleans culture at the expense of residents, this genre of documentary, I suggest, has turned to New Orleanians as the excluded "real" of the Katrina story—the authentic voices that a tourist industry so enamoured by "authenticity" has tended to elide. In this way it has responded directly to the messaging of numerous New Orleans residents: one of the many slogans that cropped up all over the city on abandoned lots and spray-painted onto destroyed houses was "Not as seen on TV."

Where literary heavyweights moved onto the fictional terrain seemingly opened up by 9/11, well-known artists like Spike Lee and Dave Eggers sought not to create a feature film or a novel in Katrina's wake, but rather to capture the storm's "raw material." While this material was collated more rapidly for the fact that it arguably required less of a gestation period than does the novel, its temporal net is, I argue, much wider than that addressed by the early post-9/11 novel. This possibly reflects a recognition that the storm's reach transcends the rupture/recovery model inherent to simplistic accounts of trauma circulated in 9/11's wake—accounts that the early 9/11 novel tended to grapple with if they did not necessarily reproduce. Where the complexities signified by "9/11" have been captured in a deceptively simplistic designation—a single date—Katrina's temporal sequence is immediately confounding, sewing together the national and transnational horizons at work in New Orleans and the disaster itself. The storm's temporality, or "Katrina time" as I have termed it, poses fundamental challenges to the future, circumscribed as it is by the short-sightedness of market logic. And yet the narrative of Katrina is so often articulated in the terms of a U.S.-identified narrative of progress, as well as a mythology of regress problematically associated with New Orleans. These temporal complexities are at work, sometimes self-consciously, sometimes not, in many post-Katrina documentaries.

Zeitoun (2009), Dave Eggers's post-Katrina biography discussed in chapter 1, itself emerged from a collection of firsthand accounts of Katrina produced by McSweeney's, *Voices from the Storm* (2008).[20] *Times-Picayune* journalist Chris Rose brought together over a year's worth of his reportage from the post-storm city in *1 Dead in Attic: After Katrina* (2007).[21] Dan Baum's *Nine Lives: Death and Life in New Orleans* (2009) evidences the long-term commitment to the city at work in so many of the post-Katrina documentary projects.[22] It charts nine lives over a period of forty years, years bracketed by two major storms (Hurricanes Betsy in 1965 and Katrina in 2005). Baum's work covering Katrina in New Orleans for the *New Yorker* led to the realization that the obsession with the disaster threatened to write over the much more compelling story of the people who live in the city. Josh Neufeld's 2009 graphic exploration of Katrina, *A.D. New Orleans After the Deluge*, similarly presents nonfictional accounts of Katrina.[23] Even Spike Lee's acclaimed *When the Levees Broke*, which appeared as early as 2006, offered four hours of film edited down from many more hours of interviews, demonstrating an investment of time in New Orleans lacking from the fleeting and transitory post-storm media reporting that Lee's film directly challenges.[24] Lee's investment in the Katrina story and New Orleans itself was reemphasized in 2010 when he released a second four-hour epic, *If God is Willing and Da Creek Don't Rise*, which explicitly works through its own inability to find closure in the face of the disaster's ongoingness.

This list captures only a fraction of the vast numbers of book projects and films that have been curated in the name of bearing witness to lives and experiences perceived to be endangered, and which might otherwise be lost to the cultural record. It doesn't even touch on the myriad exhibitions, digital portals, and photography projects that have harrowingly visualized the storm's destruction. Purely visual material is beyond the scope of this chapter simply because here I am interested in analyzing documentary projects that have self-consciously provided a narrative for those images by variously appropriating the voices of the storm's victims. The photographs of Robert Polidori and other collections like his stunningly convey the ways in which Katrina defamiliarized the built environment.[25] But with regard to the people that might have once inhabited the scenes that appear at one and the same time as blight and art object, they are stubbornly, sometimes disturbingly, silent. Spike Lee's Katrina films, along with the other two discussed below, *Trouble the Water* and *Land of Opportunity*, make use of photographs, but these stills are embedded within larger narratives that are overtly political and at times polemical. More than other forms of documentary, film directly subverts the TV screen of the storm's immediate aftermath. Obliquely but nonetheless unquestionably, they advocate on behalf of the voices they showcase. In this sense they are related to, if not entirely subsumed by, a long and not entirely comfortable tradition of documenting the dispossessed in the name of social justice.

In the United States this tradition arguably emerged with the work of photographers like Jacob Riis and Lewis Hine who, in the late-nineteenth and early-twentieth centuries, captured the dehumanizing conditions of New York City's immigrant slums and labor conditions across the United States. While Riis's work is recognized as having been instrumental in improving conditions for the poor, and Hine's work influenced the development of child labor laws in the United States, their photographs have more recently been identified as in some senses dehumanizing themselves.[26] Though Riis wielded his camera as a tool of social reform, his self-declared method showed little respect for the dignity of his subjects. Riis's own words characterize his entry into the slums as an invasion: "our party carried terror wherever it went . . . The flashlight of those days was contained in cartridges fired from a revolver . . . it was not to be wondered at if the tenants bolted through windows and down fire-escapes wherever we went."[27] The averted gaze of early documentary photography was transformed by the arrival of moving pictures and the emergence of documentary film. Early works by the influential British filmmaker and theorist John Grierson—credited with coining the term "documentary"—established the idea that the documentary film was both a "creative treatment of actuality" and an instrument of public use.[28] But this instrument now provided a forum in which the disadvantaged could speak directly to the camera.

An early pioneering British offering, clearly inspired by Grierson's work, was *Housing Problems* (1935). As Bill Nichols explains, *Housing Problems*

> gave slum dwellers the opportunity to speak for themselves, in a synchronous sound interview format set within their own homes. The words of actual workers appeared on British screens for the first time, a sensational achievement in the days long before television or reality TV. But they appeared as if they came with hat in hand, to explain their miserable living conditions politely in the hopes that someone else would agree to do something about it. . . . There was less militancy than supplication. The stage was set for a politics of charitable benevolence.

The politics of charitable benevolence belied a more problematic fact; as Nichols explains, "*Housing Problems* had the Gas Light and Coke Company as a sponsor since government slum clearance, the proposed 'solution' to the workers' plight, served the company's own interests of ultimately increasing gas consumption."[29] The use of documentary as propaganda for both state and corporate interests signals the fact that the "creativity" of documentary filmmaking crucially involves ideology as a key constituent of aesthetics.

Writing in 1980, Brian Winston claims that "each successive generation of socially concerned filmmakers since the war has found in housing and education, labor and nutrition, health and welfare, an unflagging source material. For the most prestigious publicly funded documentarist as well as the least effective of local news teams, the victim of society is ready and waiting to be the media's 'victim' too."[30] This source material, along with critiques of the criminal justice system and police brutality, is similarly the stuff of post-Katrina documentary filmmaking, in which "housing problems" loom particularly large. Unlike *Housing Problems*, the documentaries discussed below were not funded by corporations with a stake in slum clearance, but rather advocate against what some have characterized as this latest round of "Negro removal" in post-Katrina New Orleans. Nonetheless, the understandable desire to provide a counternarrative to problematic news media commentary needs to be considered in the context of the knotty ethical issues that surround dramatizing real human subjects, as well as an understanding of post-Katrina documentary in a larger cultural context of what David Shields terms "reality hunger." This hunger has arguably fuelled the rise in the last few decades of feature-length documentary films rivalling Hollywood movies at the box office. As Shield suggests,

> Living as we perforce do in a manufactured and artificial world, we yearn for the "real," semblances of the real. We want to pose something nonfictional against all the fabrication—autobiographical frissons or framed or filmed or caught moments that, in their seeming unrehearsedness, possess at least the possibility of breaking through the clutter.[31]

Trouble the Water as "Cruel Optimism"

Tia Lessin's and Carl Deal's *Trouble the Water* promises just this: to break through the clutter of a duplicitous media discourse characteristic of a slippery postmodern age, in order to tell it "how it really is."[32] "Truth" emerges in this film primarily in the shape of Kimberly Rivers Roberts, whose own spontaneous footage of the unravelling of Katrina as experienced by her, her husband, and friends in the Lower Ninth Ward is the springboard for the larger film in which Kim plays a starring role. As we discover in the opening scenes of *Trouble the Water*, Kim has seen the potential of her Katrina home movie: she declares in footage that appears to show her quite literally selling her film, "all the footage I've seen on TV. . . nobody got what I got." This is emphasized throughout the first hour of *Trouble the Water*, which splices Kim's film with news commentary; the one ironically commenting on the other, offering alternative ways of understanding the storm. The third layer of film is the outer frame, the movie that encapsulates Kim's movie, forming yet another level of commentary. Thus at one point, footage of a calm dialogue between Kim and her companions with some ineffectual soldiers guarding a naval base in the Ninth Ward is followed by a Fox News report excitedly declaring: "this city that has fallen into near chaos has thousands of national guard units rush to try to restore some semblance of order." In turning the gaze back on Kim, the third layer of the film emphasizes that it is Kim—along with her husband Scott and their friend Brian and other residents like them—who is, in some senses and contrary to this Fox report, charged with redeeming the city. Kim becomes, I suggest, the point of optimism around which the narrative circulates. And yet this optimism is considerably compromised by the film's social, economic, and ideological contexts.

As Jane Elliott suggests, the film we are watching is the result of Kim's promotion of her film in the early scenes, which hint in the direction of "a transaction, possibly financial, that took place between a Katrina evacuee, a poor African-American woman from New Orleans, and a couple of documentary filmmakers from New York." Kim's video footage covering the immediate events of Hurricane Katrina is framed by a larger story about Kim and her husband Scott, filmed over two years and produced by Lessin and Deal. As Elliott suggests, "in a through-the-looking-glass version of what Naomi Klein terms 'disaster capitalism,' Roberts attempts to capitalize on her own hurricane experience." But she does so at the cost of her artistic independence. In following "neoliberal capital's injunction to make profit from risk," Kim's story in *Trouble the Water* dramatizes the various ways in which her anticipated tale of uplift is circumscribed not just by the socioeconomic conditions revealed and exacerbated by Katrina, but, obliquely and discomfortingly, by the context of the film's production itself.[33] Where Kim describes her original film in its real-time narration as a "documentary," now she has the chance, she tells someone on the phone, to be part of a "*real* documentary" that has emerged as the result of a chance meeting with the filmmakers from New York.

In pointing out the relations of power that shadow the film's conditions of production, Elliott argues that her aim

> is not to impugn the documentary ethics of Lessin and Deal . . . That the existence of *Trouble the Water* arises from this transaction is less a fault than the central means by which form mirrors content in the film: *Trouble the Water* both arises from and materially embodies a transaction based on Kimberly Roberts' self-entrepreneurship, and the film is fundamentally about what it means to live in a neoliberal world in which such individual enterprise is offered as the only personal avenue of transformation or uplift.[34]

While the first hour of *Trouble the Water* slides back and forward in time, hovering over the devastation wrought by Katrina and excavating the details of Kim and Scott's experience of it, the narrative nonetheless strains toward linearity. Clues as to where we might be going are provided at the film's opening. The audio accompaniment to the opening credits and the early shots of Kim and Scott is a sound collage of news commentary announcing the post-Katrina dispersal, the scattering of what many now estimate is upward of one million people from the Gulf Coast and particularly from the New Orleans area, to all corners of the United States. One reporter announces that this is the largest migration in the United States since the dustbowl of the 1930s. It is on this wave of what one publication terms "the Great Katrina migration" that the first two-thirds of the narrative arc of *Trouble the Water* rides.[35] The movement is decisively away from New Orleans. As Brian tells the soldiers guarding the naval base, "we got war on the streets, right here in Louisiana, right here in New Orleans streets." "That's the reason why I'm leaving man," Scott adds, "I don't want to see no more."

The first stage in this development appears to be the sense of empowerment afforded to Kim and Scott by the storm itself. *Trouble the Water* levels a devastating critique of government failures in Katrina's wake, but paradoxically this is the context which allows Kim and Scott to discover survival and nurturing skills unknown to them in their previous lives. In looking out for so many friends and family members, and in overcoming previous hostilities to pool resources in the face of Katrina, Kim and Scott exhibit the kind of citizen engagement Rebecca Solnit describes in *A Paradise Built in Hell: The Extraordinary Communities that Arise in Disaster* (2009).[36] For Elliott, their role as "life preservers" in Katrina's immediate aftermath is an extreme example of the "requirements of neoliberal citizenship," which demands that "those who have been systematically denied both boots and straps" demonstrate "their fitness for survival precisely by employing the few scavenged and substandard resources to which they have been allowed access."[37] Nonetheless, Kim and Scott are clearly excited by their chance to embody the imperatives of what Elliott terms "self-responsibilization."

In the run-up to Hurricane Rita, Scott announces: "I'm starting my life over, I'm going to see how it is to do it right from the beginning." Similarly deploying the conceit of the "blank slate," Kim claims, "I'm already at the bottom, all I can do is go up . . . I'm trying to better my life." Kim, Scott, and Brian's journey to Memphis marks the high point of the narrative, the moment at which Katrina's "silver lining" most fully emerges, with Kim exclaiming "thanks Katrina!" This narrative of mobility and progress is not only enabled by Katrina but is specifically linked to the destruction of New Orleans—both literally and imaginatively. As Kim explains, "I see it now, I couldn't see it when I was inside the city. Now I'm on the outside looking in [shakes her head] I don't want to be part of that anymore." Her assertion that fear can stop you from achieving "great heights," from "soaring," "all because you were afraid to step out," seems to refer to the fear of leaving home—especially relevant for Scott, who has never left Louisiana—and fades into the redemptive notes of the title song.

In their sense that opportunities afforded by Katrina lie decisively outside New Orleans, Kim and Scott again quite strikingly offer the mirror-image of the disaster capitalism that flooded New Orleans after the storm. As I explore in more detail in the following chapter, post-Katrina profiteering seized on the myth that particularly poor African-American New Orleanians would find a better life elsewhere—in the process leaving behind what was often prime real estate long viewed with predatory eyes by the city's developers. In this discourse we see the emergence of two distinct imaginaries of New Orleans, the one a pre-storm dystopia harboring unimaginable levels of concentrated poverty, drug abuse, and crime; the culmination of the inner-city nightmare. The other a glossy "new New Orleans" pictured as an oasis of mixed-income neighborhoods and economic success. Kim and Scott are victims of the propaganda in that they initially embrace the vision of their city as itself a disaster, hoping to become the success stories that appeared on a number of adverts across television networks, showing Katrina evacuees from New Orleans happily building lives elsewhere, whole-heartedly welcomed into their new communities. While these stories as reported in the news were sometimes colored by the suggestion that these host communities were concerned that the new influx from the Crescent City would bring with them increased levels of crime, few noted any misgivings on the part of the evacuees themselves. As an article published in the *The Christian Science Monitor* soon after the storm—and littered with statements like "thank God for the change!"—suggests, these success stories were not simply about promoting the interests of developers intent on making a profit out of New Orleans.[38] They might also be seen as part of a post-Katrina process of national healing, whereby the harm done to storm survivors by both government and the media is negated by the welcoming actions of good citizens all over the United States.

And yet this story that is suggestive of another chapter in the narrative of the Crescent City's "Americanization"—where the "old New Orleans" is assimilated into the rest of the nation while the "new New Orleans" is constructed by outside business interests in the name of "progress"—is not, ultimately, Kim and Scott's story. Following the scenes that depict arrival in Memphis and Kim's rendition of her song "Amazing"—undoubtedly the high point of a narrative where the sense of hope and possibility is most apparent—we then see Kim and Scott, presumably some time later (indicated by changed appearances and new hairstyles) return to their home town. On sighting an army truck rumble through the Lower Ninth Ward ten months after the storm, Kim wryly comments "still treating us third world." Demonstrating, perhaps, that the location of their return lies outside the orbit of the "American dream" that seemed to so animate their journey out of Louisiana. Indeed, the meaning of the slogan on Scott's T-shirt that the camera dwells on as he journeys to Memphis—"success . . . the only option"—with its overtones of capitalist individualism, is transformed by the return to New Orleans. While Scott gives an economic rationale for their return, Kim claims "it was just too hard to start all over in a strange place, basically. . . . This our home, our food, our neighbors," she says as she waves people down on the street, invoking a wide kin network; people might not be able to help her out with money here, Kim claims, but they can all offer conversation. The final scenes in the film depicting Kim's involvement in political protest against various "housing issues" in the post-Katrina city underscore the way that a philosophy of individualism gives way to a collectivist ethos in the final phase of the film.

In the context of the film's closing twist, "success . . . the only option," becomes an instance of Berlant's cruel optimism, a post-Katrina narrative of the "good life" spun by an opportunistic market-oriented recovery to purge the city of some of its poorest inhabitants. But what must be stressed when drawing on Berlant's theory or Reichardt's "post-Katrina" film is that while increasing numbers of people may be affected by these cruel outcomes, some people are much more vulnerable than others. Kim's class and racial identity means that she is far more likely than Wendy to embark on a good life quest doomed to failure. When Berlant suggests that the surveillance state means that everyday life for *everybody* has become "an audition for citizenship, with every potential 'passer-by a culprit,' "[39] this needs to be qualified by a nod toward the color of prison populations. Berlant's point that the taken-for-granted rights of the citizen appear to have dissolved in the post-political landscape of neoliberalism is important; but as the media coverage of Hurricane Katrina showed, and indeed as Kim's audition for citizenship through the lens of *Trouble the Water* suggests, the relationship between the camera and African-American bodies remains especially troubling.

Elliott argues that *Trouble the Water* exemplifies the dilemmas of the language of empowerment in "a climate in which doing everything for oneself is the very form of domination."[40] The constraints placed on contemporary politics is encapsulated in a comment made by Scott or Brian (it is not clear which) toward the beginning of the film: "I had a dream that I was going get me some transportation, no matter what it took, to get my people out of New Orleans." *Trouble the Water* dramatizes the shrinking of Martin Luther King's collective dream—in a world that still deals out collective punishment to those deemed inferior, but which refuses to acknowledge the political demands of specific groups, peddling the myth of individual equality before the law. Kim and Scott's return to the city that is here imagined as the "Egypt" of the biblical imagination repudiates this logic by embracing a place they associate with community as opposed to commerce. But in fact, and despite Kim's involvement in political action at the end of the film, she and Scott are not "failed neoliberal subjects" in Elliott's lexicon. Kim and Scott Roberts *are* able to capitalize on Katrina; their involvement in *Trouble the Water* enables them to found Born Hustler Records as a vehicle for promoting Kim's music under the rap moniker Black Kold Madina. Most notably, the film itself successfully promotes her career as a rap artist. While one documentary critic summed up the uneasy ethics of documentary filmmaking in the statement, "They're going to put me in the movies . . . they're going to make a big star put of me"[41]—a promise routinely broken in an industry that has often failed to reward those trapped within aesthetic and ideological conceits not of their making—this is precisely what *Trouble the Water* does, particularly for Kim. The film's Oscar nomination, relentlessly advertised by *Trouble the Water*'s publicists, suggested that the proper destination for its subjects was in fact Hollywood.

While we can be pleased that Kim and Scott Roberts were able to materially benefit from their involvement in *Trouble the Water*, the film itself exploits their talents, even if in the name of "social pedagogy." Elliott argues that Kim's performance of "Amazing" is the one moment in the film that allows her to talk back to her interpreters: "I don't need you to tell me I'm amazing." It is the moment where Kim openly rejects the film as a form of pleading sympathy, or as an audition for citizenship. And it is the moment in which the viewer, if not already sold on Kim and her story, is likely to conclude that she and her story are, indeed, amazing. But we are left with the uncomfortable sense that something precious has been commodified, a sense only confirmed when we follow the "take action" tab on *Trouble the Water*'s website to discover that the first of a list of eight actions is "buy the DVD." In fact only three of these actions do not involve promoting the film in some way.[42] This is not to suggest that *Trouble the Water* is a purely commercial enterprise; but its faith in itself as a teaching tool seems to swamp and eclipse the larger political contexts to which its narrative so eloquently speaks.

Land of Opportunity and the "Affect Economy"

If *Trouble the Water* strains toward a linear narrative of progress even as it critiques this trajectory, posing to some extent as an end in itself within the complicated terrain of post-Katrina politics, the next documentary I consider offers the reverse. Luisa Dantas's *Land of Opportunity* encompasses not just a film and a website promoting the film[43] but also an interactive online site that explodes linearity and puts pressure on the boundary between advocacy and storytelling, art and politics.[44] Its tag line which is also a warning, "happening to a city near you," underscores the film's activist roots. The deeply politicized stories the *Land of Opportunity* project tells unravel the national dream that sits at the heart of its title. The project works on New Orleans as a microcosm of the nation, a "land" of disaster capitalism which itself is only a slightly exaggerated echo of the travesty of the American dream to be witnessed across the United States. And yet this documentary film and online project tempts the viewer with its own promise of opportunities. The engaged subjects that the film follows point us in the direction of renewed possibilities for democratic citizenship, while the interactive website provides us with tools with which to imagine an enlarged public sphere. In this way Dantas's project glimpses an alternative to the "affect economy" that has arguably driven New Orleans' privatized "recovery."

The "affect economy" is a term deployed by Vincanne Adams, whose book, *Markets of Sorrows, Labors of Faith: New Orleans in the Wake of Katrina* (2013), explores what happens when a government outsources recovery assistance to profit-making entities, charitable organizations, and unpaid volunteer labor. Adams's book explores the disaster of the aftermath, the disaster of a market-driven recovery that exposes victims to what she terms the "inefficiencies of profit." Against conventional market wisdom that likes to envision government institutions as themselves lumbering bureaucracies, Adams turns to pivotal post-Katrina programs like Road Home to show that the corporation contracted by the government to disburse recovery dollars, ICF International, was clearly financially better off hanging on to the much-needed funds for as long as possible. It paid to be inefficient, leading to delays that did unimaginable harm to those desperate to rebuild their lives. As Adams commonsensically comments, "some situations, like recovering from disaster, simply require unfettered, unrestrained giving and streams of funding that favor the victim over the company that distributes funding."[45] The corollary of the "inefficiencies of profit" is the equally unreliable "affect economy." As Adams explains, in relying on charitable organizations to do so much of the work that might otherwise have fallen to the government, "the production of affect" becomes critical:

> Affect here is both produced by the disaster and multiplied by a slow and obstacle-ridden recovery, but it has also become a site

of productivity in the new political economy in which the work of charity plays a huge role. The affective surplus aroused by disaster commands a sense of purpose and ethical goodness among those who volunteer and a sense of not only gratitude but also restored faith in society on the part of those who receive help.[46]

While churches in particular proved themselves to be the most effective first responders to Katrina, those who have argued that this arrangement should become part of official disaster recovery plans not only let the government off the hook.[47] They also surrender the idea that recovery assistance is a right of citizenship, allowing it to be rearticulated as a "moral good" embodied by the charities themselves. *Markets of Sorrows, Labors of Faith*, itself driven by extensive ethnographical material and firsthand accounts, flags up its own complicity with an affect economy that relies on generating sympathy for disaster victims, a tendency shared with much post-Katrina documentary filmmaking. Certainly *Trouble the Water*, though illuminating the larger systemic failures highlighted by Katrina, is captivated by the plight of its individual subjects, which in turn wins over the viewer to their cause: we *feel* for them, thus we wish them well. *Land of Opportunity* is not immune to this logic. But, like Adams's book, it self-consciously seeks to expose the insidious process whereby everyday life becomes an audition for citizenship, a plea for help in an affect economy that dissolves rights and substitutes emotions for politics.

Land of Opportunity follows seven subjects over a period of about five years. Unlike Lessin and Deal, who inadvertently stumbled upon their Katrina story in a chance meeting with Kim and Scott Roberts, Luisa Dantas knew that she wanted to make a story about post-Katrina New Orleans, and she relocated there to do so. She explains that her five studies were chosen deliberately to avoid clichés about New Orleans.[48] Where *Trouble the Water* features subjects who emerge as exceptional individuals as a way of reflecting on the larger context, *Land of Opportunity* goes in search of representatives figures. This is not to say that Dantas's subjects don't stand out—some of them do—but that the film centralizes individuals who represent the spectrum of experiences that make up post-Katrina rebuilding and recovery: a planner, a homeowner from the middle-class neighborhood of Gentilly, an organizer from the Lower Ninth Ward; public housing residents and activists, a young displaced New Orleanian, and immigrant workers from Brazil seeking employment opportunities in the rebuilding efforts. This multilayered approach to storytelling undercuts the temptation of linear narration that stalks the tale of any individual life, encouraging the viewer to make both vertical and horizontal links across and between these stories.

What emerges is a patchwork of often competing visions for rebuilding the city that anticipate a demoralizingly slow and disorganized recovery process. A series of opening stills that tell an abridged version of New Orleans' cultural history absorb images of disaster, including Katrina, into its narrative arc. Footage starts on New Year's Eve 2006, with the first post-Katrina glimmer of electric lights returning to the Lower Ninth Ward. Vanessa Gueringer, a Ninth Ward resident-turned-organizer optimistically anticipates "moving forward," but this spirit is undermined by the planning meeting featured next that sees residents overwhelmed by alternative plans for the city in a process that we now know was more about appearances than genuine neighborhood consultation. The distance between residents and planners is demonstrated by Andres Duany, the charismatic founder of New Urbanism whose plans found their way into both post-Katrina New Orleans and post-earthquake Haiti. Duany's evident enthusiasm for New Orleans' uniqueness is articulated solely through building codes, as though the city's "character" is expressed in architecture alone. Once we meet Tr'vel Lyons, the youngest protagonist in *Land of Opportunity*, who is graduating from middle school in Los Angeles, his clear sense that California holds more opportunities for him than New Orleans appears to be justified. "Katrina, you did something," he asserts, echoing Kim in *Trouble the Water* and sounding the multifaceted rhetoric of opportunity that pervades the film.

Kawana Jasper and her mother, Sharon, know this rhetoric well. Facing the prospect of the demolition of their home, the St. Bernard housing project, Kawana comments on a recovery process that spells dispossession for those most in need: "they're trying to make it more for tourists—they're trying to make it like Las Vegas, where all the rich people stay within the city limits, and the poor people, poverty stricken people, live on the outskirts." The opportunities gentrification offers developers receive a different inflection in the experiences of Elza B., who we first see amongst a group of immigrant workers in the Superdome, being told not to steal and that surveillance cameras are on them: there will be no "second chances." While cleaning a toilet, Elza explains that her dream is really an American one: she wants to buy a home for her family back in Brazil. The stories of Elza and Marcio P., also an immigrant from Brazil, are the starkest renditions of cruel optimism in *Land of Opportunity*. They both risk losing their families at home to a desperate investment in a country that taxes their pay but bars them from enjoying the benefits that should accrue from that taxation.

While the film sees Marcio return to Brazil with almost no savings, to a marriage that he can't save, Elza stays on, apparently still fuelled by a good life fantasy that seems to be totally unmoored to her life in America.

This is a fantasy that is more clearly within Al Aubrey's grasp. A homeowner in Gentilly, he and his family languish in a FEMA (Federal Emergency Management Agency) trailer for three years, waiting on the authorities to demolish and remove their destroyed home to make way for a new one: "so we can be normal like everyone else in America . . . we can build a house, let us do it!" By depicting a cross-section of people afflicted by the so-called recovery, Dantas's film exemplifies Berlant's thesis that attachments to good life fantasies are increasingly cruel even for those formerly protected by relative privilege; while *Land of Opportunity* nonetheless quietly insists on a socioeconomic hierarchy that results in vast disparities in terms of life chances and the capacity to recover from natural disaster laid on top of and compounded by the disaster of capitalism itself.

Al Aubrey is far from existing at the top of the food chain, but his relative privilege vis-à-vis others in the film means that his story is a good indicator of how painful the protracted recovery was for everybody. Like subjects in Vincanne Adams's book, Aubrey expresses "the sort of self-responsibility that neoliberalism idealizes,"[49] and thus while he is frustrated that the authorities have not helped him move on, his evident depression—more pronounced than that which afflicts anybody else in the film—is suggestive of an internalized sense of failure. Adams documents the widespread depression and high levels of suicide in the post-storm city, showing what happens to those abandoned to the market and their own self-blame. Her book, like Dantas's film, highlights the ways in which the storm exacerbated social inequalities—she cites the demolition of public housing as the clearest example of the vulnerability of impoverished African Americans, but also shows that even black homeowners were often disadvantaged compared with their white counterparts. To obtain their mortgages, black buyers routinely had to go through unconventional channels, often leaving them without the documentation required by Road Home to prove that they owned the titles to their properties. This in part accounts for the fact that African Americans were disproportionately bypassed by Road Home money.[50] Yet Adams, like Berlant, is insistent that vulnerability is no longer a preserve for those on the bottom of the social hierarchy:

> Instead of the working or laboring classes bearing the brunt of exploitation today, it is now ordinary citizens from all social classes who are made vulnerable by an economy that generates surplus

wealth by inserting everything into the profit market, including social services of caregiving, relief, and humanitarian aid.[51]

And in fact, where Aubrey is partly saved from frustration by his garden, other protagonists in the film—some, as renters, with less to materially fall back on than him—find political routes for expression that liberate them from personal accounts of failure by enabling them to identify structural and systemic rationales for stalled recovery efforts. Sharon and Kawana Jasper emerge as leaders in the movement to save public housing. Vanessa Gueringer tirelessly works as an ACORN organizer, campaigning to bring back the Lower Ninth Ward.

These newfound forms of agency do not entirely escape the dilemmas of "neoliberal empowerment" evident in *Trouble the Water*. Where Sharon and Kawana's fight to save public housing is met with the cruel spectacle of the demolition of St. Bernard, Vanessa in particular labors under a marketized recovery plan that, as Adams explains, seeks to turn disaster victims into entrepreneurs. Returning residents "who could not make themselves visible [to corporations managing the recovery] as fiscal opportunities" were "overlooked in the slow march toward recovery."[52] As Vanessa finds out, this logic extended to specific neighborhoods. While the Unified New Orleans Plan was introduced as an alternative to the much maligned and debunked Bring New Orleans Back Commission (discussed in chapter 5), the new plan placed the burden on residents, mostly untutored in the art of urban planning, to prove that their neighborhoods were viable. If the Lower Ninth Ward was to defeat plans that reimagined New Orleans without it, residents would have to come up with their own alternative "plan" that would in turn attract funds. While many scenes show Vanessa thriving within this new, "do-it-yourself" context, at other times she is clearly overwhelmed by it. In a scene midway through the film, following a sequence showing the battles that ensued after the condemnation of the public housing projects, we see Vanessa sitting round a table in a crowded, noisy room, fielding a difficult and frustrated dialogue. "If we don't take hold of the process these people put in place, they're just going to step on you," she tells the group. Her sense that their voices must be heard in this process is taken back to the bottom line, when the planner advising the group sums up the situation: "we've got to get a plan that we all agree to, and then we've got to go after money." These scenes that turn everyday residents into urban planners are on the one hand moments of successful citizen engagement and apparent direct democracy. And yet as Vanessa's weary aside suggests, engagement doesn't necessarily lead to results, and often entails exhaustion:

"there's just so much to be doing—it's really depressing sometimes." The logic here is again that rebuilding is not a right: it must be fought for within a competitive marketplace designed to protect not people but profits. "It's a lot to be dealing with," says Vanessa, "aside from trying to put your house together . . . fighting everybody to survive. It's *insane.*"

Vanessa's new political disposition is essentially responsive to a context beyond her control: to a process that demands that neighborhoods speak up or die. Interestingly this chaotic, competitive market-based approach itself apparently eschews linear narration. It opens up a maze of transactions and exchanges that rewards the highest bidder—so still respecting economic hierarchies—while remaining opaque to ordinary citizens who are invited into the process as spectators only. As Sharon Jasper declares at the end of a council meeting supposedly tabled to listen to the concerns of public housing residents, and which votes unanimously for demolition, "this is a one-man show." And yet at least Sharon is able to identify power within the context of a movement that, as the camera constantly underscores, argues that "housing is a human right." This banner is visualized throughout *Land of Opportunity*, challenging a recovery context that asks returning residents to take nothing for granted.

That said, *Land of Opportunity* apparently deliberately offers no coherent political vision. While early footage was used in various advocacy campaigns—around housing and the rights of immigrant workers—the finished film refuses one totalizing vision in favor of telling stories that brush up against one another, realizing very particular worlds, the dreams of which are thwarted in different and sometimes contradictory ways. The progressive unfolding of what this book has been calling "American time" is dismissed as irony in the film's title, while the narrative represents the cruel impasse of "Katrina time," the time of disaster capitalism. And yet the models of agency featured in the film are not simply dead-ends. They offer models for active engagement with a world that is much more fully explored in *Land of Opportunity*'s interactive website.

This is a multilayered experimental web platform dedicated to exploring "post-crisis community (re)building in America." It is organized around a discrete series of themes—among them, "Who has the right to return?," "Community/Commodity," "Exclusion/Engagement"—which themselves branch off into seemingly endless possibilities. The website's top layer of content is video clips, some taken from unedited footage from the film itself, others lent by related film projects. As each film is viewed, further suggested web content pops up along the bottom of the screen, and when each film is complete the user can transition to another theme suggested by the site. The project seeks to empower the user by encouraging them to "dig deeper" and "connect the dots." Navigation of this site is perhaps reminiscent of Vanessa's experience of the chaotic post-Katrina planning process—overwhelming—similarly asking the ordinary citizen to take on the work of the documentarist where New Orleanians were asked to be planners. But here the invitation is both genuine and public (even if the literal experience of using the Internet is in some senses "private"). Where returning New Orleans residents were invited to involve themselves in the new public-private arrangements that quietly disenfranchise citizens via a shift toward the private sphere, users of this website are conscripted to take on the task of what Jonathan Kahana characterizes as "intelligence work."

Kahana borrows the term from Walter Lippmann, who argued in the 1920s that the "invisible system of government" of the modern state was so "intricate . . . elusive, concealed, [and] opaque" that it required "intelligence work" on the part of expert individuals who would then make "visible the operations of groups and institutions to themselves and their publics," thus making "possible more hospitable environments for social and political action."[53] According to Kahana, Lippmann's notion of "intelligence work" shaped John Grierson's conception of social documentary cinema while doing research in the United States in the 1940s. Where Grierson's sense of documentary "as a corrective social agency" has led to didactic works of state propaganda, it has also informed more democratic renderings of the genre. The Land of Opportunity interactive site takes full advantage of new opportunities for documentary opened up by the internet, whereby the "citizen-viewer" of traditional documentary film is replaced by the less passive "citizen-user."

In a gesture back to the film, the effectiveness of the interactive site also seems to hinge upon identification with those facing post-crisis situations. In presenting us with a bewildering range of alternative visions, diagnoses, and interpretations, the site places us, as I have suggested, in the position of Vanessa, the returned resident forced to actively chart a path to recovery in the absence of any coordinated government plan. While the Internet's invitation to "choose" (to click on particular links) ostensibly mimics the ideology of choice peddled by the market, it also allows us to go "back," enabling us to move forward in different directions, and thus accepting a simultaneity of experience that resolutely, frustratingly defies a singular vision. This is yet another example of the way in which what was initially envisaged as the liberatory terrain of cyberspace becomes the more mundane but useful analogue of offline experience. In this vein the Land of Opportunity project offers no answers or solutions, offering us instead a wealth of information with which to wrestle. Crucially though, unlike Vanessa, the returned resident, who faces a non-negotiable time pressure to prove the viability of her neighborhood or accept defeat, this pressure is lifted on the interactive site. There is *time* to wrestle with this information, to chart alternative paths, to imagine different kinds of futures. In this vein the site refuses the "affect economy," by opening up pockets of time within which users encounter Katrina survivors in the process of coming to awareness of the constellations of forces stacked against their own lives, and who in turn challenge us not to feel but to think, critically.

Conclusion: Documenting Katrina Time

In contrast, Spike Lee's epic documentary made for HBO, *When the Levees Broke: A Requiem in Four Acts* (2006), rides on the wave of popular anger against the Bush administration. As Kahana explains, HBO's connections to TimeWarner gave Lee "priceless" access to "the archival resources of CNN," which Lee makes extensive use of in his film.[54] Lee's film is structured around a large number of talking heads, ranging from key political and cultural figures to ordinary storm victims, most of whom are New Orleans residents. Footage of these figures is on the whole taken from poised and captivating studio interview material, juxtaposed with media reporting that both does the work of communicating key events and which is in turn undermined by contradictory evidence advanced by interviewees. Thus like *Trouble the Water* and *Land of Opportunity*, Lee works against transparent notions of truth on which government institutions and private corporations alike rely to per-petuate dominant discourses that secure their hegemonic status. Yet unlike the spontaneity of the fly-on-the-wall style of much of *Trouble the Water*, or the understatement of *Land of Opportunity*, *Levees* circulates around a specific confrontation, if not a singular message or polemic. And that is the confrontation between people and a state that has manifestly failed.

In this sense Lee's film embodies the paradoxes that Kahana suggests face U.S. documentary film in an age that has seen "the decisive aban-donment of New Deal principles of government and social welfare." For Kahana argues that "the American welfare state was partly defined by the documentary forms that made it seem necessary." Consequently "a different documentary ideology accompanies the waning of this political imaginary." Kahana suggests that in contrast to the image of a benevolent welfare state, post-9/11 documentary filmmaking has to reckon with a "spectral form of the state" that "flickers up in shocking images to remind us of the state's last prerogative, what Weber called its monopoly on violence, both physical and symbolic."[55] Post-Katrina New Orleans was not short on images of the hollowed-out security state brutalizing its own citizens, and Lee's film is attentive to these. But *Levees* also pursues deeply flawed embodiments of the inept state: George W. Bush (along with his stunningly insensitive mother), Michael Brown, the embattled and incompetent director of FEMA, an aloof Condoleezza Rice, intent on shopping while New Orleans drowned. Paradoxically and in all likelihood inadvertently, the narrative of the inept state makes the case for the retreat of the state, even though state disinvestment was precisely the root of the problems revealed by Hurricane Katrina. This is the dilemma similarly at the heart of Rebecca Solnit's treatment of Katrina in *A Paradise Built in Hell*, elaborated in the introduction—a narrative that similarly underlines the heroism of everyday people versus bad (big?) government.[56]

When Lee returned to New Orleans in 2010 his desire to make a film about the rebirth of a city became mired in the ongoing disaster of Katrina. The New Orleans Saints' seemingly symbolic victory in the Superbowl was decisively eclipsed by the Deepwater Horizon oil rig explosion that led to the catastrophic "BP spill" in the Gulf of Mexico. Even without this latest disaster, Lee's second trip to the Crescent City confronts him with a catalogue of post-Katrina injustices: the demolition of public housing, the closure of Charity Hospital, controversy around the new charter schools, rising levels of police brutality amidst a mental health emergency. Consequently Lee's second four-hour documentary film, *If God is Willing and Da Creek Don't Rise*, is considerably more complex, if on some levels less narratologically and aesthetically powerful. Kanye West's brave and now infamous post-Katrina statement, "George Bush doesn't care about black people," featured in *Levees*, no longer succeeds as short-hand for a story of racial injustice that goes far beyond the differences between Republicans and Democrats, Bush and Obama. Villains from the Bush administration are variously resurrected in this second film, but this move is complicated by the fact that Obama had been in office since January 2009. Obama is praised for his response to the earthquake in Haiti and condemned for not getting angry enough at BP. The lack of a clear target makes for a diffuse narrative that has no systematic critique of what it constructs as the "gangsterism" of a wealthy elite. As such *If God is Willing* performs its own contradictions vis-á-vis the state: that it at one and the same time condemns for its negligent absence and violent presence, with no real vision of what its role ought to be. The public-private arrangements that oversaw the protracted recovery are present in the film but not elucidated by a filmmaker perhaps too steeped in the entrepreneurial ideology that has shaped New Orleans' post-Katrina disaster to identify its deeply problematic workings. Thus Brad Pitt emerges as the saviour of the Lower Ninth Ward while Sean Penn's advocacy in Port-au-Prince after the 2010 earthquake puts him in an apparently more powerful position than the country's president—who explicitly insists, in an interview that takes place against the backdrop of the collapsed palace, that earthquake recovery money has gone not to the Haitian government but to international organizations. These celebrities emerge as the "good guys" to be contrasted with the new villains uncovered by this film, notably the hapless Tony Hayward, the British CEO of BP. Populist anger at the latter fails to "connect the dots" to reveal a narrative that links him to Pitt and Penn via new neoliberal arrangements that have seen the government exit the business of regulating finance, safety standards, and delivering humanitarian assistance.

What is compelling and impressive about Lee's second Katrina documentary is the fact that despite its desire to present a story of redemptive closure, it absolutely refuses to do so in the face of contrary evidence. What we get is a story that is much less polished and formulaic than the one in *Levees* precisely because it feels improvised, as though the narrative has gone fascinatingly, sometimes radically, off-script. Five minutes into the start of *If God is Willing* we are offered an upbeat sequence on New Orleans hosting the Super Bowl, featuring, among others, Condoleezza Rice, claiming that "this is a terrific chance for New Orleans to really come together and to show that the city's back." The fact that this sequence is preceded by images of death and destruction—that reach back to 2005 but which extend into the narrative present of 2010—casts an ironic shadow over Rice's comments, which are rendered shallow and ill-judged. The opening of the film with a poem performed by Phyllis Montana LeBlanc, one of the stars from *Levees*, rebukes the superficial declarations of rebirth inaugurated by the Saints' victory (however satisfying that victory was). LeBlanc's piece absorbs Katrina into a larger net of social justice issues: housing, healthcare, police brutality. This move is reinforced by the historian Douglas Brinkley, who suggests that "Katrina is part of a continuum" of disasters to befall New Orleans, while public housing activist Endesha Juakali puts it like this: "we need to focus on struggle and not entertainment . . . we're on a plantation right now and I'm trying to run away." Here Juakali references a struggle that might confront the dead-end of "Katrina time," a time of abandonment in which past injustices are inscribed via new iterations of exploitation.

In this way Lee's second Katrina film explores what Vincanne Adams characterizes as "prolonged trauma" and what Berlant terms "crisis ordinariness." Berlant deliberately adopts the notion of "ordinary crisis" in order to move away from the "rupture/recovery" model of simplistic accounts of trauma that cling to a state of normalcy to which one might one day return. Arguably *Levees*, like much 9/11 discourse, was driven by a notion of Katrina as trauma. In this model New Orleans' unique cultural character was mobilized as both a rationale for rebuilding and as the city's "normal" that might one day be recovered. Though *Levees* is careful to acknowledge the ways in which Katrina exacerbated already existing trends concerning racial inequalities and injustices, it is also clearly a celebration of the Crescent City itself. This is a narrative that does not equate New Orleans with disaster. Interestingly, the dystopian city of *If God is Willing* is more suggestive of this conflation. But it is equally insistent in underscoring the extraordinary desire of residents to return to New Orleans no matter what. In this Lee's second documentary in particular performs the return of the "real": its focus is not on a tourist mecca but on residents with deep attachments to a place that has labored under a national, political, and economic system that sometimes makes it look and feel more like Port-au-Prince than other places in the United States.

And yet as Kahana suggests, Lee's Katrina documentaries, like *Trouble the Water* and *Land of Opportunity*, work by analogy, one that "both depends upon and displaces the particular value of the individual case, affirming its value in the name of an abstract principle."[57] Unlike free-wheeling fictional analogies like *Wendy and Lucy*, these documentaries are solidly grounded in the material realities of post-Katrina New Orleans. But their stories simultaneously suggest that at the heart of this unique event that befell this unique city, there is a lesson from which we should all take note. In this context a rebuilding New Orleans becomes not a glossy model for twenty-first-century America but rather a case study in the disaster of capitalism itself—a disaster to which the U.S. government is rapidly abandoning its citizens. The fact that New Orleans was abandoned some time ago—indeed it can be argued that it has never been fully embraced as an American city—makes it a fascinating case study in counternarrative. Forms of place-based resistance to the "neoliberal deluge"[58] that followed in Katrina's wake will be explored in the following chapter, before the final part of this book moves to consider the implications of what I have been calling "New Orleans time."

4

Resisting Katrina

The Right to Return

On January 15, 2007, Martin Luther King Day, residents of St. Bernard public housing project broke into their apartments in a symbolic and physical show of defiance against federal, state, and city authorities intent on denying their right to return home. This act of civil disobedience violated what Martin Luther King, Jr., would have regarded as unjust laws, laying claim to public assets that authorities were plundering on behalf of private interests. The act of breaking the locks that had shut residents out of the projects since Katrina appropriated and reversed stereotypes of black criminality—stereotypes that had been mobilized as rationales for demolishing these vexed symbols of a rapidly retreating welfare state. In reclaiming their homes, these resident-activists, mostly black women heading up families and representing dense social networks reaching back decades, challenged the narratives of welfare dependency that have so shaped the racist imaginary of working class and poor African-American females. Instead, they asserted themselves as political agents.

Fast forward to mid-2008. The condemned projects were being torn down while post-Katrina homeless encampments swelled all over the city. Thousands of predominantly African-American children, women, and men were forced to inhabit makeshift tents, abandoned and destroyed buildings or to huddle onto the Claiborne Avenue neutral ground sheltered by the notorious overpass. Meanwhile, the New Orleans Police Department were finding ways to formalize the crime of being homeless in a "property owners' republic":[1]

A pack of Kool cigarettes, a can of Budweiser and a box of Boston Baked Beans sat on the dashboard of an unlocked car with the windows rolled down at 1732 Canal St. Somewhere nearby two New Orleans Police Department officers watched and waited for someone to reach into the bait car and snatch the items. They wouldn't have to wait long, as the police parked the car just one block away from a homeless encampment under the Claiborne Avenue overpass, where dozens of desperate, hungry and addicted people lived in a makeshift village of tents.

As this account goes on to explain, "for stealing less than $6 in items" the two homeless men that fell into this trap, neither of whom had any prior arrests in Orleans Parish, were charged with burglary, "a felony that can carry up to 12 years in prison . . . a month later the men remain in Orleans Parish Prison awaiting court dates and the possibility they will spend the better part of the next decade in state prison . . . ."[2]

These two scenarios offer peculiar mirror-image reversals of each other, the first an apparently illegal act and the second perpetuated by the representatives of law and order. Both are shadowed and distorted by an ideology that privileges private property. Although these scenes—of residents barred from their homes and police officers conjuring "crime"—might initially seem to gesture toward a topsy-turvy world engendered by the chaos of the hurricane, arguably they are indicative of logic in train before the storm and accelerated in its aftermath. These post-Katrina "criminals" recall the "looters" of the immediate aftermath, those with the presence of mind to enter private property to retrieve food, water, and diapers as a matter of survival. As social justice lawyer and public housing advocate Bill Quigley has powerfully argued, those "left behind" during Katrina, the sick, the disabled, the elderly, children, and the poor, are precisely those constituencies left behind by the "recovery." This fact is no more accidental than the actions of police officers deliberately baiting homeless people. It is the result of policies that have for decades targeted the urban, racialized poor. While, as the previous chapter discussed, all sections of society suffered as a result of the market-driven rebuilding process, the vulnerable suffered the most.[3] This chapter charts the accelerated processes of privatization after Katrina, processes that disproportionately affect low-income communities dependent on public services and spaces. Most significantly, it explores the various ways that these constituencies have attempted to fight back and assert their "right to the city." For Henri Lefebvre, who coined this phrase, given that capitalism requires urbanization to absorb surplus product, the city in turn would be the site of the revolution.[4] In this vein, the "people's reconstruction" envisaged by many on the left after Katrina invoked a transformed city if not the socialist endpoint.[5]

Cedric Johnson's analysis bridges the gap between Lefebvre's Paris of 1968 and our contemporary moment:

> American cities have been especially vulnerable to the volatility of neoliberal world making since they were both critical nodes of capitalist growth and federal investment during the Fordist-Keynesian era and as a consequence, have been severely impacted by welfare state rollback and austerity.[6]

The work of David Theo Goldberg demonstrates the ways in which this process has been markedly racialized. He asserts that "the ghettoized segregation widely associated with the height of American racism was a thoroughly urbanized post-Reconstruction development the full effects of which were realized in cities in the 1920s and 1930s." While legalized segregation often led to the racialization of particular neighborhoods, the "informal apartness" that followed formal desegregation, and which was "the effect of privatized preference schemes rather than explicitly institutionalized legalities" has "today more often than not" led to entire municipalities and cities defined by racial apartheid. Ironically then, "at the very time there was growing desegregation—or at least explicit effort—in the public sphere, one could say there was publicly subsidized resegregation in the private." As African Americans were rapidly migrating to urban areas and inhabiting cities in greater numbers than whites by the 1960s, racial redlining and suburbanization meant that inner-city areas were increasingly African American. By 1990, fourteen U.S. cities, including New Orleans, were majority black; in a further eleven cities African Americans represented close to 50 percent of the population.[7]

Goldberg shows that as cities were increasingly identified with the African-American population after the Second World War, the federal government following the Civil Rights movement of the 1960s was increasingly being drawn in the public mind as a "black institution."[8] The idea that cities were places where black people dependent on federal welfare reside goes part way to explaining Quigley's comments on the post-Katrina paralysis with regard to rebuilding New Orleans: "it is easier to convince the country to support war—support for cities is much, much tougher."[9]

This racialized and racist anti-urbanism was clear in the reaction to Katrina evacuees from the city of New Orleans on the part of the surrounding suburban parishes: St. Bernard Parish, with a 93 percent white population, passed an ordinance restricting homeowners from renting property to anyone but a "blood relative." Jefferson Parish, another majority-white suburb whose police had pointed guns at evacuees seeking to cross a bridge from Orleans Parish into Gretna, passed a resolution opposing all low-income, tax-credit multifamily housing, with the sponsoring legislator condemning poor people as "leeches on society." In St. Tammany Parish, the chief law enforcement legislator complained about the presence of "thugs and trash from New Orleans." "People with dreadlocks or 'chee wee' hairstyles" could "expect to be getting a visit from a sheriff's deputy."[10]

And yet the project of "taking back" both cities and government welfare from urban black populations was well underway by the end of the twentieth century. As chapter 1 explored in relation to the so-called war on drugs, the penal arm of the state was increasingly eclipsing issues of social welfare as a way of dealing with unemployed and impoverished communities by the 1980s. This chapter shows the way that, as Loïc Wacquant's work has argued, conceptualizations of the state as vehicle for punishment, on the one hand, and social reform, on the other, are in fact moving closer together in a scenario where the state is increasingly outsourcing its work in both areas to private enterprise and nonprofit agencies.[11] Arguably prior to Katrina these processes in New Orleans lagged behind other urban areas like New York City which had long been subject to widespread privatization and gentrification. In Katrina's aftermath, New Orleans became a zone of free market experimentation.

Despite an incomprehensibly slow reaction to the devastation wrought by Hurricane Katrina on the Gulf Coast, the Bush administration acted swiftly with regard to labor rights: within days of the storm the government suspended the Davis-Bacon Act which would have guaranteed fair pay to construction workers. This meant that a flurry of no-bid contracts were awarded to corporations able to employ undocumented Hispanic workers whose labor was ruthlessly exploited in the construction process, while local, unionized and largely African-American workers were bypassed in the reconstruction. Meanwhile, and before many residents were even allowed back into the city, eviction notices were served on renters all over New Orleans, while a number of properties were bulldozed before residents were able to return to retrieve their possessions. Public housing and Charity Hospital remained shuttered, much of the former soon to be slated for demolition while the latter was never to be reopened. Public transportation was slow to return and downsized after the storm. Public schools returned at a snail's pace, over-shadowed both by the mass firing of 7,500 of the mostly African-American teachers and other public school workers employed by the Orleans Parish School Board, and the emerging charter school movement. Indeed, mass lay-offs in public sector workers after Katrina targeted predominantly African Americans across the socioeconomic sector, with the firing of 4,500 public school teachers often viewed as a specific attack on the black middle class.

The apparent message—that the reconstituted New Orleans would be a wealthier, whiter city, one that was stated quite explicitly by a number of officials[12]—was reinforced when the so-called "green dot" map was issued by the Bring New Orleans Back Commission, suggesting that many flood-prone areas where working families lived be converted to green spaces. This included the majority-black, storm-devastated Lower Ninth Ward that received so much media coverage in Katrina's aftermath. This particular battle will be explored further in the next chapter, and is slightly different from other examples cited here because the dispute over the neighborhood's viability involves high numbers of homeowners. For those without the protection of private property, options in the post-Katrina and rapidly privatizing city were especially stark, defined by what John Arena has described as an agenda of "Negro removal"[13] and what Clyde Woods describes as the "trap economics" of "racial enclosures."[14] The rebuilding process appeared to be a direct attack on local black communities and cultures.

According to Naomi Klein, writing in 2006, "New Orleans' public sphere was not being rebuilt, it was being erased."[15] Klein's influential contention that the post-Katrina city resembled Baghdad's Green Zone was based on early assessments of the rebuilding city. The suspension of labor laws and tax restrictions and the privileging of large corporations over local business interests made post-storm New Orleans, for Klein, a key site of "disaster capitalism," one that paid direct tribute to the "Chicago School" of economics that frame Klein's understanding of neoliberalism. Klein's *The Shock Doctrine* argues that free market libertarians move in soon after disaster strikes in order to render "ground zero" an experiment in neoliberal restructuring. For a number of commentators on post-Katrina economic restructuring in New Orleans, Klein's "shock doctrine" is inadequate for understanding a process that goes far beyond "Chicago School" villains. Johnson suggests that, "inasmuch as she focuses primarily on the corporate skullduggery and White House patronage streams of the Bush era, Klein's arguments neglect the more pervasive and equally consequential phenomenon of *do-good capitalism* where altruism, good will, and even social antagonisms are harnessed to the profit motive."[16] John Arena follows this critique in his work on the role of nonprofits in the destruction of public housing in New Orleans, discussed in more detail below. For Arena, Klein's focus on "shock" neglects the role of consent in neoliberalizing policies, channelled, according to Arena, by nonprofits who provide "progressive cover" for rolling back the social safety net. This point is important for this chapter because it is suggestive of serious constraints on the possibility of resistance.

Klein's thesis emphasizes that "shock" is used as an excuse, a catalyst and an "opportunity" for the introduction of market solutions rather than as a causal factor. Undoubtedly this was the case in post-Katrina New Orleans. But paradoxically her own lexicon of "shock" *as* "doctrine" mirrors the ahistoricity of those Klein critiques. Her analysis does not fully acknowledge that shock tactics are only a fraction of a much larger picture, and that the "doctrine" she describes bleeds far beyond the immediate and apparently isolated contexts opened up by "shock." In this way Klein's thesis does not wholly escape the ideological frame of trauma, in spite of her powerful critique of the conceit of the "blank slate." Klein fails to track the progression of neoliberal policies as forms of "slow violence"[17] that had been in train for decades before the storm; while investing far too heavily in an intentionality—which veers close to conspiracy theory in *The Shock Doctrine*—that overlooks the extent to which free market ideology has permeated institutions and systems.

My conceptualization of "Katrina time" here is indicative of this slow-burning disaster illuminated but by no means caused by or limited to the contexts of the hurricane. While I want to resist the reduction of "Katrina" to a human-induced storm only—as will be explored in the next chapter—here I follow Quigley and others who name "Katrina" as a harbinger of neoliberal reform, and who identify "Katrinas" in urban centers across the United States. As Sheila Crowley, president of the National Low Income Housing Coalition put it at a hearing in Washington, DC, in 2007, "Katrina is about wrenching hundreds of thousands of people from homes to which most will never return. Katrina is about the sudden and complete loss of all that homes mean—safety, respect, privacy, comfort, and security."[18] Correspondingly, "Katrina time" is about the wresting of the future from those very same people; it signifies a temporal collapse that makes of the narrative of "progress" an instance of "cruel optimism."[19]

In contrast, the demand for the "right of return" that frames this chapter resists the post-crisis claim to a much abused narrative of "progress," by gesturing back to a deep historical consciousness that roots particular people to a particular place. The hurricane was undeniably deeply traumatic for all who experienced it, but narrow focus on the language of "shock" masks a much longer running battle for the "right to the city." The first two sections here explore the post-Katrina destruction of public institutions designed for some of society's most vulnerable people: those on federal housing assistance, and children. The demolition of public housing and the dissolution of the public school system are explored in tandem with the limited possibilities for resistance. The third section explores these developments through the frame of the "right to the city," a right that has been most symbolically curtailed by the veritable privatization of the city streets themselves. In all cases "reform" is framed as calculable progress, whereas resistance is couched in the more storied and unquantifiable rhetoric of return.

Right to Housing

In a 2005 publication on gentrification as the "new urban colonialism," New Orleans is not much more than a footnote in the story of globalized gentrification trends. This specific collection, *Gentrification in a Global Context*, wants to push beyond the gentrification debate's focus on "global cities," that has been in play ever since Ruth Glass gave the term currency in 1964 in relation to London.[20] As the contributors point out, "footloose capital and a footloose middle class" have been transforming communities well beyond Mike Davis's Los Angeles or Neil Smith's New York.[21] Policies to not only "open up" the housing market—i.e., the greenling of previously redlined districts—but also to clamp down on homeless people with "zero tolerance" policies and police harassment have proliferated across the globe as a means to reconsolidate the interests of a predominantly white property-owning global elite. In spite of New Orleans' relative absence from this particular volume, low-level gentrification patterns had transformed the French Quarter and Fauborg Marigny by the 1990s, and had begun, as discussed in chapter two, to creep into the Tremé. Developers in collaboration with city and federal authorities had already made inroads into the city's public housing stocks, which were to take a massive body blow after Katrina. By the end of 2005, the stage was set for New Orleans to become a key site of gentrification in the United States. And by the end of the first decade of the twenty-first century, New Orleans exemplified the fact that the project of "taking back the city" had moved well beyond global urban centers, and into cities, like New Orleans, that are either located in, or have much in common with, the global South.

Writing in 1995 Neil Smith argued that in the United States, the colonialist practices of gentrification are inflected with a nationally specific "frontier thesis." Smith writes,

> For [Frederick Jackson] Turner, the expansion of the frontier and the rolling back of wilderness and savagery were an attempt to make livable space out of an unruly and uncooperative nature. This involved not simply a process of spatial expansion and the progressive taming of the physical world. The development of the frontier certainly accomplished these things, but for Turner it was also the central experience which defined the uniqueness of the American national character. With each expansion of the outer edge by robust pioneers, not only were new lands added to the American estate but new blood was added to the veins of the American democratic ideal.[22]

Smith suggests that postwar suburbanization and neighborhood redlining led to the conceptualization of an "urban wilderness." The city "was, and for many still is, the habitat of disease and disorder, crime and corruption, drugs and danger." And, as suggested above, the raced body: in the U.S. context the "urban" has become almost synonymous with "blackness." And yet, as early as the 1960s, Smith identifies the emergence of a new, sanitizing discourse that might save the inner city: the "urban frontier." Smith writes, "in the language of gentrification, the appeal to frontier imagery has been exact: urban pioneers, urban homesteaders and urban cowboys became the new folk heroes of the urban frontier."[23] This, Smith argues, was a successor discourse to "urban renewal" that, by the 1980s, was imagining the pioneering middle classes as the saviour of the crumbling and ghettoized inner city.

In the New Orleans context the "frontier thesis" of gentrification is especially tempting because the perceived cultural clash that gentrification engenders is particularly pronounced. Nonetheless, as Smith contends, "the frontier language camouflages a raw economic reality."[24] Where early discussions of gentrification often implied that trends were driven by consumer choice, for Smith—from a Marxist perspective—gentrification was first and foremost a "movement of capital, not people." An appreciation of the "rent gap"—the gap between the actual value of "devalued" land given its uses, and its potential value, given its central location—is what, according to Smith, drives capital investment in a previously redlined neighborhood. This analysis doesn't undermine the importance of the cultural clashes engendered by gentrification, but it treats culture as symptomatic rather than causal. Gentrifiers themselves thus emerge not as the drivers but as the followers of capital. According to commentators like Smith, by the beginning of the twenty-first-century gentrification was part of neoliberal urban policy unfolding in the United States and in urban centers around the world. The story of the demise of public housing in New Orleans, severely exacerbated by Katrina, is singularly illustrative of this picture.

There is perhaps no more potent a symbol of the dystopic potential of U.S. cities in the national imaginary than the soaring and apparently soulless public housing projects. As John Arena writes in his study of the destruction of public housing in New Orleans, "in the public imaginary, high-rise projects signified black welfare dependency, crime, and much of what was perceived as wrong about urban America."[25] In fact, in New Orleans, the projects consisted of low-rise buildings in line with the city's distinct architectural traits—and many argued that they should be protected for their architectural merits alone.[26] Nonetheless, as elsewhere, New Orleans' projects became notorious for being centers of delinquency, welfare dependency, crime, violence, and drug abuse. As Arena explains, the erection of public housing came out of the progressive movements that arose on the back of the Great Depression in the 1930s. But soon public housing became linked with a state subsidized "racially discriminatory suburbanization model":

> With passage of the 1949 and 1954 housing bills, public housing was progressively linked to rehousing inner-city poor communities displaced as part of federally financed inner-city urban renewal projects and highway construction.[27]

By the 1990s, these sites of "racial ghettoization" had themselves—in a tragically ironic and circular fashion—come to be seen as "Keynesian artifacts," impediments to profit-making that not only blocked site development but which depressed property values in entire neighborhoods. The destruction of public housing has thus been central to gentrification as neoliberal urban policy. As Arena outlines, "between the mid-1990s and 2010 the federal government and local housing authorities demolished over 400 public housing projects, eliminating approximately 200,000 public housing apartments out of an original stock of 2.4 million."[28] While the administrations of Ronald Reagan and Bush senior had established the economic and ideological scaffolding for the removal of public housing, it was the Clinton administration that really moved on the issue, under the cover of a reimagined "war on [concentrated] poverty." Clinton's euphemistically named HOPE VI project awards federally financed grants for the purposes of public housing demolition and the subsequent construction of "mixed income communities." Thus HOPE VI was one of the many federal programs that subsidized the privatization of public assets, by turning substantial numbers of former public housing units over to the market. In a proliferation of ironies, government officials, bolstered by a chorus of sociologists providing supposedly objective commentary, have decried the deplorable state of public housing projects that led to concentrated poverty and generational cycles of unemployment and crime. Vice President Al Gore stated that these projects were "monuments of hopelessness."[29] Meanwhile, Clinton promised in his 1996 State of the Union address that "the era of big government is over." While this speech made clear that this involved dramatically scaling back the welfare state, the reduction of government did not preclude enormous federal investment into the expansion of prisons and the penal arm of the state more generally.[30] As the Housing Authority of New Orleans proceeded with plans to privatize the projects, it invested more and more in policing, betraying its own arguments that the end of public housing would mean less crime and less need for policing.

Thus, rather than maintaining the dilapidated projects—something which public housing residents have tended to be vocal in demanding—authorities with their eyes on demolition have adopted a policy of "benign neglect," failing to repair apartments or fill empty units, despite growing waiting lists. HOPE VI has thus usually occasioned evictions for the poor, especially since a 1995 executive decree ended the requirement that the demolition of affordable housing units be subject to one-for-one replacement. As Engels presciently pointed out in 1872, "in reality, the bourgeoisie has only one method of solving the housing question after its fashion—that is to say, of solving it in such a way that the solution perpetually renews the question anew."[31] While Engels was thinking of Haussman and Second Empire Paris, David Harvey points out that this process would "recur again and again in capitalist urban history"—with Robert Moses taking a "meat axe to the Bronx," public housing construction and highway construction driving out the heart of Tremé, and then the ultimate destruction of public housing across the United States beginning in the late-twentieth century. As Engels suggested, the poor "are merely *shifted elsewhere!*"[32]

Such was the case with the St. Thomas housing project, which Arena casts as a kind of prelude to the post-Katrina demolitions of the so-called "big four"—St. Bernard, Laffitte, B. W. Cooper, and C. J. Peete. As one of the most organized of New Orleans' public housing projects, Arena argues that the process of privatizing St. Thomas, which was eventually made reality by a HOPE VI grant, demonstrates the truth behind the oft-voiced rhetoric of "de-densification" that surrounds public housing discourse. Arena suggests that what initially alarmed officials about the project's supposed "density" was the potential for organizing and political activity. He explains that the administration of Lyndon B. Johnson paid particular attention to the kinds of collective action enabled by public housing in its attempts "to contain the black revolts sweeping U.S. urban centers in the mid- to late 1960s."[33] This view was supported by the Black Panther presence in the Desire public housing project in the Ninth Ward, where the group set up tutoring and food programs for children, and which occasioned the well-known stand-off with the NOPD in 1971. Certainly the views expressed in Luisa Dantas's film, *Land of Opportunity* (2010), discussed in the previous chapter, suggest that contrary to stereotypes about public housing, and the undisputed fact that many of the projects had lapsed into states of serious disrepair and some were plagued by crime and violence, projects like St. Bernard also hosted crucial social networks conducive to mutual support and collective consciousness. Thus what was eventually framed as the benevolent task of purging cities of the projects becomes another way of repressing not "blight" or crime or poverty, but dissent. Arena concludes that "the demolition of public housing communities at St. Thomas in New Orleans and across the country has destroyed not only badly needed affordable housing but political power, community identity, and neighborhood support systems, as well."[34]

For Arena, what eventually quashed the opposition on the part of resident-activists to the proposed privatization of St. Thomas was the introduction of the "non-profit complex."[35] Residents were offered the opportunity of gaining a seat at the table by forming their own nonprofit that would steer St. Thomas in the direction of the private sphere and, in return, offer residents some measure of "self-determination." Thus, according to Arena, individual residents were seduced into attractive roles with financial and social rewards, lost their ability to challenge power and thus sold out their fellow residents, most of whom ultimately faced eviction—from the new mixed income development that was not renamed "The New St. Thomas," as residents had proposed, but rather unilaterally renamed "River Garden" by developers.

Arena's assertion that in the wake of Katrina, public housing residents were similarly disempowered via the creation of various nonprofit entities— which then splintered resistance—is convincing. Clearly the post-Katrina opposition to demolition, at one point a strong and unified movement, fractured along lines that suggested a difference of opinion in terms of the best means to challenge the status quo. Arena's own account, offered as a participant-observer, charts this process of splintering by flagging up differing attitudes to race, class, and resistance. For Arena, anything short of direct action signifies a concession to power, whereby opposition is channelled into consent. Nonetheless, in a social context with a "law and order" agenda that was arguably shaped by the criminalization of civil disobedience—the civil rights tactics of Martin Luther King and others who challenged racist and unjust laws in the name of social justice—possibilities for direct action are seriously constrained. Arena wishes to push against the prevailing ethos of TINA—the idea that "there is no alternative," a phrase employed frequently by the former British Prime Minister Margaret Thatcher to suggest there was no alternative to market liberalism—but refuses to recognize that the confrontational tactics he advocates did not yield results for public housing residents, however important they are in the armoury of nonviolent resistance to oppressive power. It is hardly surprising that residents, physically barred from their homes by authorities who seized on Katrina as an opportunity to push through long-planned goals to rid the city of public housing, were tempted by the possibility of a seat at the negotiating table—even if that did represent a concession to the forces of privatization.

Like Arena, who has long been involved with the organization C3/Hands off Iberville, the social justice lawyer Bill Quigley has been involved in housing issues in New Orleans for decades. Unlike Arena, Quigley's involvement in the post-Katrina movement to save public housing involved advocating a range of tactics to resist demolition plans. Significantly, Quigley credits the human rights framework, and specifically the principle of the "right of return" at the heart of the United Nation's Guiding Principles on Internal Displacement, with providing post-Katrina housing activists a vocabulary in which they could articulate their demands. "No principle," Quigley writes, "has proven more helpful to Gulf Coast advocates than the international 'right of return.' The right to return has no parallel in U.S. law, which makes it even more important in advocacy and analysis."[36] The right of return outlines an obligation on the part of national governments to enable those displaced in post-conflict and post-disaster situations to return home. In this scenario Katrina evacuees are considered not "refugees" but "internally displaced persons." Where for Arena, the human rights rhetoric that began circulating among housing activists soon after the storm became a distraction from the movement, and the involvement of the United Nations "an end in itself, a fetish, a diversion,"[37] for Quigley, these engagements provided activists with crucial energy and support, even if they did not achieve the ultimate goal of saving public housing.

As Quigley explained to me in an interview in November 2013, the right of return filled a void because it provided a way of advocating for the most marginalized of Katrina evacuees: renters on public assistance. While the outrageous treatment of homeowners in post-Katrina New Orleans, including low-income, African-American homeowners in places like the Lower Ninth Ward, gleaned support across the political spectrum—and from some very unlikely right-wing quarters like Fox News—those unable to appeal to property rights had no sanctioned narrative by which they could chart a path back to their homes. Quigley explained that even relatively privileged renters, like law students at Loyola University, often returned to discover that their former homes were now rented to different people, their possessions duly discarded. Those on public assistance are, Quigley maintains, at the bottom of the pile, exposed to this prevailing view: "you're just lucky to have a place, that the government gives you a place. It's not a question of justice, it's a question of charity. And charity can be cut off at any time, you have no entitlement to charity." In contrast, the rhetoric of the "right to return," that quickly evolved from this human rights framework in post-Katrina New Orleans, emphasizes entitlement—as indeed does the language of rights in general.

Initially, public housing residents shut out from their homes in New Orleans were offered resettlement elsewhere, as if location had no meaning for those without financial means. Quigley summarises, "because housing is housing and you can exchange it just like that." The residents Quigley worked with wanted to assert something different:

> We were saying that's not the way we see it and that's not the way people experience it. There's a lot more to housing than the materials under which you're sheltered, there's this connection of relationships particularly among people who are low-income and racially segregated. It is friends and families and communities and churches and doctors and choirs and parties and that sort of stuff that keeps people together. And it's not just this box that I live in.[38]

Quigley's writings are vocal about the idea that social justice lawyering should not be about leading movements but should rather lend itself to movements, while ensuring that legal action is considered as just one option among many tactics, including direct action. He explains that the impetus for legal action that he and other lawyers took on behalf of public housing residents after Katrina came from the residents themselves. They all knew it was a long-shot, but saw the legal case as a vehicle to organize around. When their day in court arrived, with many residents having travelled from relocated housing in Houston and Memphis and elsewhere, residents asked Quigley to argue their case on the basis of the right of return. As Quigley made the case,

> the room just became absolutely silent. I was able to identify and talk about this thing, the right of return. Through no fault of their own these people had been displaced. And these folks can't be displaced just on the basis that the government decides they don't want to do their housing. I explained how essential to human dignity the right to return was. It was like the whole room was breathing together while we were doing it.[39]

Though unsurprisingly, the judge turned down the case on the basis that there was no precedent, it gave Quigley a chance to articulate what he believes everybody in that courtroom knew to be true: "what's in people's hearts, and their consciousness: that this is wrong, even if the law doesn't know how to respond." It also gave Quigley the chance to articulate a narrative that arguably quite literally picks up the baton of the human rights framework that black nationalists and socialists like Malcolm X were arguing for in the latter stages of the '60s freedom movement. Ultimately, developers got their way and the council voted unanimously for demolition. The view of city council president Oliver Thomas, who himself later went to prison for corruption, won out: "There's just been a lot of pampering, and at some point you have to say, 'No, no, no, no, no! . . . We don't need soap opera watchers right now."[40] The federal government in the form of Housing Secretary Alphonso Jackson put it more benevolently: "we should not put them back into the drug-infested, killing-infested environment that they came out of, and anybody who says that really don't care much about these people."[41] At least 5,100 units, most of which survived the storm remarkably well—indeed "the bricks" had long been seen as viable shelters from hurricanes—were destroyed after Katrina, as homelessness soared. The demolitions were part of a narrative of "progress" that did not include the city's public housing residents in its vision of the future. It's highly likely that public housing residents are disproportionately represented in the estimated 100,000 African-American residents who have not been able to return home to New Orleans. As Quigley put it:

> We are 100,000 people less than we were. That's a lot of people. They're not talked about, they're not grieved, they're not missing

in the public discourse. It's like, well we're a smaller town, we're a whiter town, we're a richer town, we're the charter school capital of the world. We've privatized as much as we can privatize, but we're still looking to do more. They trumpet this as an opportunity town. And more than one thing can be true at the same time. There are opportunities here. We are happy to have the new people that are here. But this city is still configured in such a way that 100,000 couldn't make it back.[42]

Right to Education

If prior to Katrina New Orleans lagged behind other U.S. cities when it came to gentrification patterns, after Katrina it positively led the way on education reform. In the case of housing, the international right of return was jettisoned as a principle in favor of Mayor Ray Nagin's neoliberal version of the right to return—an individualistic rendition that simply encouraged those with the means to do so. The response to the Bring New Orleans Back Commission that the mayor established, and which will be discussed in the next chapter, was so virulently hostile that it gave way to successive waves of planning, principles, and aspirations, which ultimately let the market decide post-Katrina redevelopment patterns. Where the government seized its chance to exit from public housing provision in New Orleans after the storm, it similarly made a poignant retreat from education, opening the way to market penetration. The movement to save public housing essentially lost its raison d'être—i.e., quite literally the structures themselves, to defend. But the debate about the privatization of public schools in the post-Katrina city continues to rage, despite the fact that those resisting the reforms confront a transformed landscape: in May 2014 the last directly run school in New Orleans' Recovery School District was turned over to a charter, making it the first school district in the United States to have no traditional public schools. Commentators from across the political spectrum are arguing that New Orleans has entered untested waters in an experiment in urban education. Where state-sanctioned demolitions removed perfectly viable housing stock from a city that lost tens of thousands of structures to the hurricane, and which was suffering from an acute shortage of affordable housing, the privatization of public schools denied traumatized children the stability of neighborhood schools at a time when they were most needed. In ways even more fundamental than with public housing, the removal of neighborhood schools fractured possibilities for political mobilization in myriad ways.

The immediate aftermath of Katrina saw widespread denunciations of the state of public institutions in New Orleans—institutions that were held responsible for the impoverishment of a large proportion of the city's residents. Where public housing loomed large in this conversation, arguably public schools took a larger hit. Education has long been considered *the* vehicle of social mobility, and this role has been accentuated with the neoliberal retreat of state welfare and a more holistic response to the problem of persistent poverty. Just as calls for improvements were trumped by the desire to sweep the decks clean with public housing, public education was similarly subject to large-scale and traumatic overhaul. It was widely declared that incremental reform had failed. As with the destruction of public housing, the scaffolding for the privatization of schooling was already in place by the time of the storm. The Recovery School District, tasked with taking over failing schools from the notorious Orleans Parish School Board, was established in 2003. Soon after the storm Louisiana Governor Kathleen Blanco raised the threshold for what counted as a failing school, while simultaneously significantly relaxing the regulations by which charter schools could be established. Consequently, the RSD took over the vast majority of New Orleans' schools, many of which were rapidly turned over to charters. According to Adrienne Dixson, this legislation, which appeared to target the much maligned Orleans Parish School Board, precipitated "the conditions that led to the firing of the entire teaching force in OPSB" as well as the effective dismantling of the teachers' union.[43] The mass firing of 7,500 of its teaching and support staff, mostly African American, has since been declared illegal in district courts, but in the meantime it brought New Orleans to the forefront of market-driven educational reforms that have gained cross-party support since the 1990s.

Diane Ravitch explains that calls in the 1960s for the decentralization of schools initially came from parents and teachers seeking more local control, and were only later hijacked by the language of "choice" and the norms and values of the market. This appropriation occurred in part because of the chronological coincidence of the 1960s critique of state bureaucracy and the 1970s deregulation of the market. This latter development paradoxically cannibalized the leftist critique of the state for a right-wing market agenda, in a way that has fractured progressive politics. The charter school movement is the product of these contradictions. Ravitch, once an avid believer in the school choice movement, now an ardent critic, had an insider perspective on the emergence of education reform in the 1990s, and explains that the new thinking—now ensconced in both parties—saw the public school system as obsolete, because it is controlled by the government and burdened by bureaucracy . . . Democrats saw an opportunity to reinvent government; Republicans, a chance to diminish the power of the teachers' unions, which, in their view, protect jobs and pensions while blocking effective management and innovation.[44]

Charter schools, which receive relatively little "interference" from government, have become the vehicles for "school choice." Officially, this choice is encapsulated in a parents' right to withdraw a child from a school at any moment, supposedly making these schools more "accountable" to parents who can contemplate a marketplace of schools rather than putting up with failing neighborhood schools. In reality, school choice constitutes widespread selection practices on the part of the schools themselves. In a system made up entirely of charter schools, this means that no family can take it for granted that their child will attend their local school.

Writing on the cusp of the educational reforms emerging in the 1990s, Donald E. Devore and Joseph Logsdon, in their groundbreaking work, *Crescent City Schools* (1991), suggest that "in New Orleans, as in so many large American cities, the public schools are facing a major crisis. As most privileged citizens of the nation have abandoned our central cities, they have left urban schools underfunded and filled with the society's poorest children. The Orleans Parish Schools now face an awesome challenge."[45] Paradoxically, prominent school reformers have seen themselves as the saviours of the system that Devore and Logsdon champion, even as they have transformed it beyond recognition. One such self-proclaimed saviour is the former president of Tulane University, Scott Cowen. Cowen clearly has some qualms about the direction of schools in New Orleans, and the institute that he's founded has published a number of reports not uncritical of New Orleans' charter schools. Cowen nonetheless has become a prominent champion of the new arrangements. In his account of his emergence as a "leader" in post-Katrina New Orleans—a leader, one might note, with no democratic mandate—he acknowledges the mixed results of the education reforms, but he takes what he identifies as a "pragmatic approach": "action meant hard things: challenging tradition, breaking rules, disrupting the status quo, causing pain."[46] It was important, he restates throughout *The Inevitable City* (2014), which is also a kind of "leadership manual," to seize the opportunity. Seizing a neighborhood school for Tulane University was one of these "hard calls," possibly made easier, he freely admits, by the fact that he is "somehow separated from the [local, New Orleans] culture."[47]

Another leadership quality that Cowen touts is the ability to "compartmentalize": he describes the way in which chartering Lusher as a selective school for Tulane affiliates, to ensure the return of this elite private university, required repressing emotion that might stray into the territory of a much larger, more pressing tragedy. Scruple would have to be left at the door as well: "were we bumping neighborhood African-American kids to make room for the privileged white kids of Tulane faculty? . . . Was Lusher somehow discriminatory? Was Tulane saying one thing but doing another?"[48] Leadership requires tough choices, we are told. Initially the two-tiered system that Cowen rightly alludes to appeared to be between the new successful and largely selective charter schools, with Lusher at the top of the food chain, and schools still languishing under the control of the Recovery School District. With all but a handful of schools in the city of New Orleans now chartered, it is clear that those tiers remain within the new decentralized "system." Top-performing schools continue to ruthlessly select, weeding out not only those with low test scores, but also, and notoriously, many students with special needs. Meanwhile those with open enrolments tend to take on the most challenging cases and are often close to 100 percent African American. More and more of these schools are of the "no excuses" variety. "No excuses" is an extreme expression of the charter school movement more generally, which adheres to the idea that poverty is no excuse for a failing school, and that teachers have a duty to close the achievement gap between white and black students. While these schools put enormous pressure on their own teachers, essentially saying that they have "no excuse" for not graduating successful college entrants, however challenging their social contexts might be, the "no excuses" mantra is also routinely turned back on the students themselves, who often find themselves subject to "zero tolerance" environments.

Arguably it is the highly regimented teaching methods employed by these schools that leads to disciplinary measures that many observers feel are not just excessive but oppressive and cruel. Children as young as five are asked to walk on lines in corridors, sit through "silent lunches," and are often denied recess and thus any chance to play or socialize. Some schools employ methods of shaming for transgressions as minor as lateness and missed homework, transgressions that are often well beyond the control of individual children. As Sarah Carr's fascinating account of several New Orleans charter schools in the post-Katrina period, including two well-known "no excuses" institutions, demonstrates, these disciplinary regimes assert control over both the mind and body.[49] Schools like Sci Academy and particularly the KIPP (Knowledge is Power Program) school that Carr observes expect children to "track" their teachers with their eyes at all times and, as is the case with KIPP, adopt a host of ritualized communication signs to ensure that nothing holds up the crucial business of "preparing students for college." The sense of urgency that circulates around this task is fuelled by data-driven standards of success that in turn creates a stressful pedagogic environment with an inevitable emphasis on "teaching to the test." Just as sinking businesses go bankrupt, schools that don't reach their targets are routinely closed down, reinforcing the fact that "choice" for parents often means fielding a constantly shifting landscape, where some students are herded from failing school to failing school. As well as the obvious interruptions and setbacks to educational progression that this entails, many students have to endure the insult of transitional phases where the impending closure of their schools see simultaneous invasion of a new school that might take over the old school's libraries and gyms, depriving them of crucial resources, but might not necessarily wish to educate its current set of students. Sold as "consumer" choice, the resulting chaos is in fact a top-down process that appears to favor business over and above the students they are meant to be educating.

Indeed, as Carr explains, many suspect that these schools are not really preparing children for college at all. The intense focus on reading and math—on which children are constantly tested—eschews the broad-based education favored by the middle classes, and the regimented teaching methods in many of the "no excuses" charters discourage creative or critical thinking. Obedience and submission are, as Carr explains, more suited to low-skilled, minimum-wage jobs in punitive employment contexts; as opposed to the university setting, which requires independence and assertion, as well as good grades. As many have pointed out, the middle-class board members who run these schools in all likelihood wouldn't dream of sending their children to schools like this—and in practice they do not. As even Cowen admits, his wife, Margie, who acts as the conscience of his text, was upset by visiting a "no excuses" KIPP primary school. Cowen reflects:

> I am not as observant, or maybe not as sensitive, as Margie, but I know what she means: The environment was extremely strict, bordering on harsh. It reminded me of boot camp. "But think about the backgrounds they're coming from. They may need the structure to concentrate."[50]

Carr partially supports this view, by asserting that studies suggest that many low-income families, in contrast to middle-class counterparts, are often supportive of these strict disciplinary regimes. There are myriad reasons for this, including the fact that lower-income families have fewer options: "faced with a choice between a school they perceive as safe and focused on college and one they perceive as unsafe and disorganized, they usually, and understandably, select the former."[51] And yet clearly, as Carr also points out, there is a not so concealed acceptance here—on the part of schools themselves—that children from different backgrounds require different schooling. In the New Orleans context, as in many other inner-city environments, the ghost of segregated schools, and then the trauma of integration supported by the bussing of students across residentially segregated areas, hovers. Only now, the spectre of "bussing" students out of their neighborhoods arises in paradoxical tandem with the reassertion of a rationale for racially segregated learning. As Carr reports, foundations that fund "KIPP-like charter schools so view their mission as educating poor, minority children that they do not provide philanthropic support for schools with significant white or middle-class populations."

> The result, whether intentional or not, is that their money disproportionately supports some of the nation's most segregated schools—and charter school founders may have a financial incentive to keep them that way.[52]

Just as these new vessels for segregated learning do not even provide the salve of educating children in the comfort of their own neighborhoods, neither do they offer culturally sensitive approaches to the demographic they're teaching. These schools tend to imagine their students just like some dared to imagine New Orleans after Katrina: as "blank slates." In line with the marketplace ethos, children's brains have, in some schools at least, been quite literally reimagined as places where "data" can be banked. As one teacher that Carr observed told his class, "feelings are just data your brain sends you about how it thinks you should be feeling. The choice you make to give up or keep going is what makes you who you are."[53] And as another educator told his students, "this is not a place where your past matters at all."[54] It should be noted that this latter statement arises in the context of an open-enrolment school that wishes to send the positive message that previous misdemeanors will not be held against students, and that the school is an opportunity for them to return to a "clean slate." Nonetheless, this notion permeates the philosophies of these schools, which imagine the histories that their students bring with them as baggage to be discarded, deficits to be cleared. The school will in turn "raise up" these underprivileged children, who are mostly taught by people not from their own neighborhoods or city, but rather by "fresh-faced" recruits from predominantly Ivy League universities, many of whom have had little more than five weeks of teacher-training.

Teach for America is a national organization that has been at the forefront of the market-based transformation of U.S. inner-city schools. It takes what it views as the best graduates through a rapid training period and then plants them in what are supposedly some of the most "troubled" schools in the nation. In New Orleans, TFA recruits, and others from similar organizations, have in large part replaced the teachers that operated under the Orleans Parish School Board prior to Katrina. Where these teachers were mostly African American, experienced educators with teaching certification, TFA recruits are largely white, recently graduated, and have no teaching qualifications. One of the many ironies that attends the planting of TFA recruits in New Orleans' schools—in order, so the argument goes, to make poor black children "college ready"—is that they have inadvertently supplanted previous generations of African Americans who did make it to college and who have achieved some measure of social mobility. It is little wonder that some are calling this veritable ethnic and class-based "transfer" of New Orleans' teaching force cultural imperialism. It is an approach championed by people like Scott Cowen, who imagine the ills of urban America transformed by a crusading middle class—as manifested in his service-learning program for Tulane undergraduates.[55] Yet the reentry of this crusading middle class into the inner city does not signify the return of a much-needed tax base, but rather displaces poor black residents and school children and imagines their "rescue" via charitable rather than redistributive measures.

The investment on the part of TFA graduates is, of course, far deeper than the superficial belief that contact with the middle class is going to somehow counteract brutal social inequalities. TFA recruits enter classrooms burdened by the notion that they are quite literally all that stands between their students and what is posited as their path to salvation: a college education. They are thus pursued by the same logic that led to the mass firing of the city's pre-Katrina teaching staff: teachers alone are responsible for failing schools. This is where these young, underpaid, over-worked, and largely non-unionized recruits—some argue that TFA is a union-busting organization[56]—themselves fall victim to the theory of the "blank slate." According to this view, education takes place in a bubble that has no relationship to issues surrounding poverty: housing, health, employment, racism. As New Orleans parent advocate Ashana Bigard explained to me in an interview in October 2014, while she initially felt real hostility toward TFA and its young recruits, a training session she offered for TFA staff on post-traumatic stress syndrome led to an unexpected outcome: "everybody broke down, crying, saying that they have second-hand trauma, how they are so ill-prepared, they've been lied to, they don't have the support, they've been set up." Bigard concluded that "there's a second wave of victims here. They're being abused."[57]

Nonetheless Bigard, and the growing number of people who are speaking out against education reform in New Orleans and elsewhere, are primarily concerned for the "first wave" of victims: the students who stand at the center of the petri dish of the new experiment. In New Orleans, many of these students, who are being told by these schools to bracket their feelings, their hunger, their history, and their cultural identities, are still visibly suffering as a result of the physical and psychological disruptions of Katrina. According to Bigard, the post-Katrina reforms suggest that "poor black traumatized children apparently have different brains, alien brains, that we cannot educate as we can white, middle class kids." These children are entering schools that are criminalizing behavior that you might expect from trauma victims, like a lack of ability to concentrate, poor time-keeping, tiredness. In addition, many of these schools employ elaborate systems of "demerits" that label students for normal, appropriate, and desirable behavior, like consoling other students who may be upset. Bigard recounts one incident where an eight-year-old boy was suspended from his school for regularly greeting one of the cafeteria staff he knew from his neighborhood. The last straw was when he moved out of line to embrace her, having learned of a family bereavement, in spite of the fact that he had repeatedly been told that it was inappropriate for him to engage with this woman. In Bigard's view, these schools are both criminalizing children and depriving them of the means for appropriate socialization:

> When you have pre-school and kindergarteners with quiet lunch and no recess, they're not getting social development time. Anti-social behaviour is criminal behaviour. So they're not going to learn appropriate social behaviour. Everything in this world is networking. We're going to have a whole generation

of kids that do not know how to communicate with people. It breaks down the social fabric. This is something that we will not be able to easily repair, that these kids didn't get the social development fundamentals. People say to me, what about the parents. And I say, *what* about the parents. They're putting their kids on buses sometimes at 5.30am. They are working two jobs, seven days a week.[58]

Bigard's stories speak to another related trend in the recent development of U.S. schools, charter and traditional public schools alike, and this is the penetration of schools not just by corporate logic but by the police. As Bigard recounts, after Katrina, many public schools were opened under the "protection" of hordes of police, the National Guard, private security firms, and perhaps one, single, counsellor to address a traumatized school population. The heightened police presence in schools is in part fuelled by the war on drugs, as it is by the Columbine shootings and the persistent threat of gun violence in schools. A rationale that was initially at least in part informed by the desire to protect children has apparently turned on them. Bigard's example of one six-year-old taken before a judge for possession and distribution of drugs, for taking Rolaids—common antacids—into school to share with his friends, on the mistaken belief that they were candy, is part of this picture. It took Bigard and her coworkers five months to get this child back into school; with no traditionally accountable school board, no one would take responsibility for the decision that had led to a six-year-old boy being sent to an "alternative school"—a breed of school viewed by many as warehousing for those deemed unteachable.

Bigard explains that while working with an organization representing the families of incarcerated children, she was asked to identify at what point most of these kids were entering the criminal justice system. She explains that on examining these figures for New Orleans in 2008, her jaw dropped as she realized that most children were going directly from schools. Against the conventional wisdom that says that keeping poor kids in school and off the streets is the best way of avoiding jail, in fact, as Bigard puts it, "your kid who is cutting school is a hell of a lot safer than if he's in school every day." Where the commonplace of, for example, two eight-year-olds getting into a fist fight in the classroom would have formerly received an in-house response, now teachers routinely call the police and involve a criminal judge. "The same eight-year-old is going to be handcuffed, put in a police van, gain a record of some kind, and could be expelled."[59] Charter schools anxious about test scores are incentivized to adopt this approach: frequent expulsions is a common way of eliminating "difficult" cases that might drag down a school's numbers.

According to Kenneth Saltman and David Gabbard, this is part of a wholesale militarization of U.S. schools that has gone hand-in-hand with market-based solutions.[60] And according to Bigard, with the New Orleans reforms in mind, the results are a "denigration of democracy." As Devore and Logsdon argue in *Crescent City Schools*, early public school reformers like Horace Mann were animated by the belief that schooling was central to the creation of the national citizenry: "free public schools lay at the foundation of the democratic order and decency in the United States."[61] That Mann ultimately turned his attention to the cause of abolition is testament to the idea that at least intimations of racial equality informed this early vision of public schools. That the early experiment in public schooling in New Orleans and across the South involved a series of racial exclusions and discrimination is also testament to the fact that education has long been linked in the public mind to the issue of political agency. The right to education has been a key battleground in the black liberation struggle, from challenging the laws that prohibited slaves from learning to read, to the emergence of black students and educators in the Reconstruction period, through the period of "benign neglect" of black schools and teachers—who for decades were denied equal pay—during the Jim Crow years, and then the tumultuous years of integration and bussing. The post-Katrina emergence of an all-charter district in New Orleans is arguably another chapter in this racialized trajectory.

If, as Catherine Michna writes, "neighborhood schools serve as rallying points around which communities can organize broader struggles for equity in the city and the nation's public sphere,"[62] then, as with the removal of public housing, the removal of neighborhood schools has restricted the means for political activity and dissent among the city's working-class African-American population. Moreover, the sinister picture of "no excuses" charter schools painted by Bigard, Carr, Kristen Buras[63] and a host of other commentators is suggestive of a system that is not trying to produce enquiring, politically engaged citizens. As Bigard explains, these schools ask children "to leave your humanity at the door. This is not about education, this is about conditioning for low-wage jobs." Or indeed, prison. These schools are teaching the values not of collective action but rather submission to authority. They are thus part of the same logic that has denied public housing residents a place in the post-Katrina city. Under the guise of rescuing them from unsafe living quarters, these residents have been deprived of housing that also afforded community solidarity and support, just as underprivileged school children have been wrested from the potentially more nurturing environments provided by neighborhood schools. Quite apart from centralizing these underprivileged school children in the narrative of progress that characterizes the "new" New Orleans, school reform has condemned them to the futureless landscape I have been calling "Katrina time."

Right to the City

Days after Katrina, Naomi Klein called for a "people's reconstruction" that would recognize the rights of all New Orleanians to return to a safe, fully functioning city, that would include affordable housing, viable schools, public transportation, accessible healthcare, and jobs with a living wage. She suggested that "evacuees must be at the center of all decision-making," and that the authorities must be accountable to those most victimized by the storm.[64] This vision recalls that of Henri Lefebvre in his 1968 treatise, "Right to the City." Paraphrasing Lefebvre, David Harvey explains that this entails "a right to change and reinvent the city more after our hearts' desires. It is, moreover, a collective rather than an individual right, since reinventing the city inevitably depends upon the exercise of a collective power over the processes of urbanization."[65] Unfortunately, despite many efforts, the "right to return" to a New Orleans that might better reflect the "heart's desires" of the majority of New Orleanians failed to materialize.

Alluding to recovery dollars at that moment pouring into national and international relief agencies, Klein wrote that "New Orleans' evacuees should draw strength from the knowledge that they are no longer poor people; they are rich people who have been temporarily locked out of their bank accounts." They remained locked out. As Jordan Flaherty and other local activists and grassroots organizers announced in an open letter to funders:

> Instead of prioritizing efforts led by people who are from the communities most affected, we have seen millions of dollars that was [sic] advertised as dedicated towards Gulf Coast residents either remain unspent, or shuttled to well-placed outsiders with at best a cursory knowledge of the realities faced by people here. Instead of reflecting local needs and priorities, many projects funded reflect outside perception of what our priorities should be.[66]

As Flaherty recounts, "the message from major funders was that New Orleanians could not handle the money appropriately."[67] Local organizations were disenfranchised via claims of a "corrupt" culture in the same way that developing countries—like Haiti after the 2010 earthquake, as discussed in chapter 1—are routinely denied self-determination by a paternalistic and arguably parasitic foundation world. Flaherty's book, *Floodlines: Community and Resistance from Katrina to the Jena Six* (2010), is testimony to the fact that after Katrina, a host of progressive, left-identified organizations with roots in the city were mobilized to bring about a just recovery. And yet his account also speaks to internal weaknesses: Flaherty speaks of schisms that fractured organizations like Common Ground Collective and the People's Hurricane Relief Fund along the lines of race, gender, and class. Even in those grassroots organizations with some legitimate local roots, the presence of outsiders, often volunteers, some with short attention spans, similarly led to friction among these groups. These fractures clearly relate to issues around control, power, and representation, exacerbated by the fact that many of them were competing with each other over a tiny pool of resources.

What remains silent in Flaherty's account of post-Katrina "resistance" movements is the question of what, exactly, these groups were resisting. As with Spike Lee's post-Katrina documentaries discussed in the previous chapter, many of these groups, most of which had a 501c(3) tax exempt, nonprofit status, have a deeply ambivalent attitude toward the state. Immediately after Katrina, popular anger against the Bush administration and apparent federal incompetence was widespread. While this anger largely stemmed from the fact of state disinvestment in public infrastructure and services, the reaction often paradoxically advanced this state of affairs by dismissing the government as a possible vehicle of social good. As will be discussed further in the next chapter, organizations like the Common Ground Collective did not seek to make demands on the state but instead established a roster of largely volunteer-staffed services, including a highly successful health clinic. According to Cedric Johnson, these diverse groups can be understood as examples of "anarcho-liberalism." Johnson writes:

> Anarcho-liberalism's roots can be traced back to the New Left politics of the sixties, but its more immediate sources can be found in the anti-capitalist politics that first crystallized against corporate globalization during the Clinton years, and surged again during the Occupy demonstrations. The defeat of "actually existing socialism" had a powerful effect on left politics during the nineties, producing a strand of anticapitalism leery of the path to socialism that was attempted throughout much of the twentieth century—the seizure of state power and initiation of

nationalization and large-scale planning to abolish private property
and redistribute social wealth.[68]

Ironically, those activists whose aims stop considerably short of the creation of a communist society via the abolition of private property, but who
still imagine a positive, redistributive role for the state, appear in the new
context to be embracing "reform" rather than "revolutionary" solutions that
look beyond the state. Many community organizations and nonprofits that
emerged in response to Katrina are defiant in asserting their independence
from government. Instead of imagining socialist solutions to the problems of
inequality in New Orleans highlighted and exacerbated by Katrina, Johnson
suggests that these groups seized on the idea of "horizontal" organizing that
paradoxically, and as discussed with regard to Rebecca Solnit's work in the
introductory chapter, mirror neoliberal arrangements.[69] "Parallel" services
that essentially perform work previously expected of the state both ostensibly
remove the rationale for state involvement while forwarding the neoliberal
mantra of "self-help."

In the New Orleans context, where these organizations see themselves
as working for a majority-black constituency—if they are not majority-black
themselves, and many are not—issues around black politics, and in particular the history of civil rights, further complicates this picture. A number
of the post-Katrina grassroots organizations, including Common Ground,
were founded by former members of the Black Panther Party. As Flaherty
explicitly states, former Panther member Malik Rahim's leadership of Common Ground in its early years lent a sense of legitimacy and authenticity to
the organization. And yet Common Ground is Black Pantherism stripped
of its radical redistributive and black nationalist politics. A collective ethos
remains, but its limits are highlighted by the fact that the organization
relies on a volunteer labor force. Despite its slogan "solidarity, not charity,"
the political rationale for this is not clear, and its ultimately unsustainable
model means that solidarity, like charity, might dry up. Indeed, while the
organization's ethos is a variant on the self-help theme, the services performed by largely white volunteers from out of state on behalf of a largely
black, native population, don't even afford the latter the satisfaction of
self-empowerment. This point is particularly important for New Orleans'
poor black communities, who have often historically responded to the reality
of government abandonment by pooling resources and investing in forms
of self-help that are also mutual aid.

While left-identified, Johnson argues that "anarcho-liberal" groups
display "an aversion to politics" inasmuch as agenda-setting requires some

measure of leadership and centralization.[70] Unsurprisingly, those activists who have opposed specific examples of privatization have tended to move in the opposite direction. Particularly in the debate about education reform, those who critique the charter movement tend to be in favor of centralization and unionization, i.e., they imagine a state that, with public pressure and accountability, might be made to work on behalf of the people. Ashana Bigard envisions her activism around education in the context of the black Civil Rights movement, which notably attempted to enlist the federal government as an ally in the struggle for racial equality. She suggests that one of the "biggest barriers" to organization around education is "public perception . . . somewhere along the way the non-violent resistance movement of the 1960s got told in a different way. As if Martin Luther King and everyone was being polite as well as non-violent. That's not what the hell happened but it's what they put in the books." Echoing Arena, Bigard notes a contemporary aversion to confrontation:

> If I raise my voice or I'm passionate about it, I'm crazy about it, no one will listen to me. I'm an "angry black woman." They tell me to be calm, to be polite. But the destruction of my community, city, and all the lives of the children in this city that I am from, I am damn passionate about. And yes I'm angry, I'm hurt, I'm distraught . . . They are killing us.[71]

For Bigard and others confronting privatization, lobbying for a public sphere that might be overseen by the state does not preclude a politics deeply invested in the local. As Johnson claims, "public policy—healthcare, schools, public safety and so forth are also expressions of community values,"[72] and arguably this is particularly the case in New Orleans. For Bigard, the apparent attack on New Orleans' neighborhood schools is part of a larger, racist attack on the city's distinctive black culture that has both relied upon and celebrated the public sphere in notable ways. She points to the way the recovery has not only locked many local African-American workers out of myriad jobs that would formerly have been public sector work, crippling its precarious black middle class. She sees a "new New Orleans" that has quite literally criminalized activities that have always been part of the culture here—activities that often involve collectives or non-private spaces.

New Orleans now has one of the strictest curfews for under-16s in the country. Unsurprisingly, the enforcement of this curfew has raised concerns about racial profiling, given that it overwhelmingly affects black youths. In the new mixed-income developments, as well as conducting stringent background checks on would-be residents, including credit and criminal record checks—few developments will house those with prior convictions—they also often prohibit people sitting on their porches past a certain time, despite the fact that in New Orleans and indeed across the South, this has historically been a prime gathering place. Most controversially, after Katrina there has been a perceived crackdown on music and noise in New Orleans. The city's noise ordinance, long on the books but unenforced, has come under the microscope as the city is tightening up its laissez faire reputation through more rigorous regulation. Where many venues hosted live music under the radar of the law, they now require permits. Most notably, in 2007, in response to a shooting at a second line parade the year before, the city raised the permit fees for a second line parade by 500 percent. While the new punitive fees were successfully challenged by ACLU on the grounds of free speech, the apparent criminalization of New Orleans' iconic second line parades, routinely appropriated and commodified by the tourist industry, represented for many an incursion into a community ritual that celebrated the "right to the city" like no other. A practice that began in the nineteenth century, second line parades evolved from the jazz funeral. They are run by social aid and pleasure clubs who dance, with a band, onto the city streets on one nominated Sunday per year. Together the club and the band constitute the first line, while those that dance behind them are the second line. Joel Dinerstein describes these "little cultural miracles" as "rolling block" parties.[73] Anthropologist Helen Regis has argued—both in her scholarly work and in the testimony she gave as part of ACLU's case against the city—that second line parades are community rituals in working-class African-American neighborhoods that expressly reclaim streets that have been branded unsafe due to crime.[74]

Scholar and musician Brice Miller concurs with this view, claiming that the second line, along with the city's brass bands and Mardi Gras Indian cultures, are indigenous cultures "that grew up in black neighborhoods of New Orleans, as ways of countering racism and class vulnerability."[75] For decades the city's tourist industry has hijacked these symbols of New Orleans' black culture for the purposes of profit; now regulation poses a threat of a different kind, as well as what many perceive as an uprooting of deeply rooted traditions that have been devalued since the storm. For Miller the solutions must be "bottom-up," but he too questions the legitimacy of many groups that have sprung up post-Katrina under the "grassroots" banner. In the absence of a "people's reconstruction" that would have enabled collective, democratic power over public decision-making, the horizontal structures that have filled the void left by the state, while frequently contesting the deleterious effects of late capitalism, often ultimately mirror existing inequalities. In the "new" New Orleans black residents across the socioeconomic spectrum have been disenfranchised.

As discussed in chapter 2, arguably since Katrina there has been a deeper disconnect between the conceptualization of "New Orleans culture" and its residents. Thomas Jessen Adams and Matt Sakakeeny, in a 2014 conference and in a forthcoming publication, argue that since Katrina "culture bearers" have been privileged in the recovery, with a host of nonprofits established with the aim of returning the city's fabled "cultural community," particularly its musicians. Musicians' Hurricane Relief Fund, New Orleans Musicians' Assistance Foundation, and Habitat for Humanity's Musicians' Village were part of a context that imagined the rescue of New Orleans as saving "America's Soul," in a way that overlooked the basic needs of the entire city in favor of a romantic view of New Orleans that serves its tourist industry.[76] As Bill Quigley comments, "it was the outsider's definition of what made us special. So they would send a hundred musical instruments, which was wonderful, but they wouldn't try to save people's houses."[77] And yet despite the rhetoric, and a handful of dollars earmarked to help specifically musicians, many of the city's musicians have returned to a context seemingly hostile to the grassroots music traditions that have made New Orleans famous. Not only have many street bands been subject to increased levels of police harassment, but music education—that in New Orleans has tended to focus on jazz—has been notably scaled back in the post-Katrina city. As Miller notes, New Orleans "culture is being celebrated and attacked by the exact same people."[78]

Miller, who worked on a jazz program in public schools prior to the storm, is himself one of the 7,500 public school workers who were "unceremoniously" fired after Katrina. While some music education has crept back into the city's schools since the storm, the "no excuses" schools, which tend to educate some of the city's poorest students, also tend to narrowly focus on math and English, which are constantly tested, over and above a broader curriculum including art, music and physical education, which are not. For Miller, this subverts the process whereby music education in New Orleans's schools has traditionally provided a path to social mobility, enabling teachers to "replace the gun in the kids hand with a trumpet."[79] "The question is," says Abram Himelstein, who co-directs the Neighborhood Story Project with Rachel Breunlin, "whether we're going to stop testing poor kids long enough to find out who they are."[80]

Himelstein and Breunlin run a writing program that evolved from a desire to empower those exploited by a media industry that not only profits from its own misrepresentations of violence in black neighborhoods; its unethical reporting can also sometimes exacerbate that violence, making the subjects of its stories less safe. The NSP counters mainstream media narrative with "our stories told by us." The organization pays people to produce books about their social worlds, not only providing a vehicle whereby they can "write back" to power, but also renumerating those not usually afforded the luxury of developing their intellectual capital. As Himelstein told me in an interview, "rich people's education is already about personal agency largely because they're at the top of the colonial pyramid." The NSP, which started out in schools and which still partly operates in them, works with people it perceives to be at the bottom of this pyramid, to counteract this inequality. By starting with the questions "who are you?" and "who are your people?" the program adopts a pedagogy that challenges the "blank slate" approach of "no excuses" charter schools, which operate on the reverse assumption that a student's identity, social context, and history is better left outside the classroom.[81]

The NSP has its origins in Students at the Center, another nonprofit that works in New Orleans' schools. Students at the Center draws on the work of the late Brazilian educator Paulo Freire whose *Pedagogy of the Oppressed* (1970) argues that narrative is both the basis for oppression and liberation. As Kristen Buras explains, SAC adopts Freire's idea that "education must begin with the solution of the teacher-student contradiction, by reconciling the poles of the contradiction so that both are simultaneously teachers *and* students."[82] In distinct contrast to the "no excuses" adoption of a strict code of discipline and authority, SAC and NSP emphasize equality, largely through a practice known as the "story circle." As Michna explains, this practice began with John O'Neal and the Free Southern Theater, which was based in New Orleans in the 1960s. This form of communal storytelling thus began its life as part of the cultural arm of the Civil Rights movement, and those who continue to practice it, like Kalamu ya Salaam and Jim Randels and their coworkers at SAC, and the NSP, self-consciously identify themselves in this lineage.[83]

And yet story circles have proliferated across many progressive groups working in the post-Katrina city, just as the slogan "right to the city" has been claimed by a host of groups across the political spectrum. It's not always clear what these groups have in common with the Civil Rights movement, much less Lefebvre and 1968. What is clear is that the Civil Rights movement and the claim to the "right to the city" both imagine democratic power over an invigorated public sphere. In the context of a charter school movement that in some guises sees *itself* as a continuation of the Civil Rights movement, and of the 1960s call for local control, the emphases on the *public sphere* and *democracy* needs to be made particularly clear. For many critics, charter schools subvert and undermine both.

According to David Harvey, asserting the "right to the city" has yet to lead to a coherent social movement. Instead we have seen the fracturing of the left over issues of identity, funding, and perhaps most significantly, the role of the state. Harvey suggests that one way to unify struggle is "to focus sharply on those moments of creative destruction where the economy of wealth-accumulation piggy-backs violently on the economy of dispossession, and there proclaim on behalf of the dispossessed their right to the city."[84] The post-Katrina period saw two stark examples of "accumulation by dispossession" in New Orleans, in the destruction of public housing and the dismantling of public education. The attack on public healthcare in the form of the closure of Charity Hospital provides another case study. Unfortunately, despite resistance to these developments, there was no unified response to these brutal examples of neoliberal restructuring. But if the disinvestment revealed and exacerbated by Katrina are part of a gradual but determined backlash to the successes of a fundamentally incomplete Civil Rights movement, a "repossession" of both the city and the government on behalf of a ruling class, then it is perhaps the ideals of that movement that most fully speak to the "right of return" that so poignantly expressed the longing on the part of New Orleanians to return to the place they called home. If "Katrina time" traces an arc of neoliberal urban policy that has deprived particularly poor black communities the resources through which to meaningfully invest in the future, then the Civil Rights movement—which, in its latter call for social and economic rights invoked human rights and thus powerfully articulated the "right to the city"—remains a central touchstone for resistance in the project of returning to that foreclosed future.

Conclusion: Public Time

In the collection *Pedagogy, Policy, and the Privatized City* (2010), Jim Randels and Kalamu ya Salaam write:

> Before and After. New Orleans has a new time line. A new zero point. However, a natural event is by no means the sole cause for our new era. To understand post-Katrina, you have to understand pre-Katrina. Many folks in post-Katrina New Orleans, particularly in terms of public education, don't follow

this simple pre- and post-postulate. They are salivating to start from scratch, to establish a new day and a new order, with nothing but disdain for the prezero.[85]

Writing in response not to Katrina but 9/11, Barnor Hesse and S. Sayyid claim that the western reaction to the "ground zero" apparently realized in lower Manhattan was not just a "war on terror" but a "war on politics." They write:

> Through the lens of Western governments, the idea of politics has become discredited as a democratic form of idealisation. In the UK and the US it is being dissipated by lifestyle escapisms, subverted as an expression of sociality, and mortgaged to the commodity fantasies of the corporate take-over of the state. In cynical reason, there is no politics, no contemplation of social change, and no ethical alternative to the Western world order.[86]

Ironically, the "emergency time" symbolized by post-9/11 New York and apparently echoed in post-Katrina New Orleans becomes the opportunity to implement a "post-political" agenda ascendant—and seemingly irresistible— well before the apparition of these particular crises. According to Lauren Berlant, the widespread precarity that arises as a result of neoliberalism and the situation of "crisis ordinariness" that it engenders, gives way to a time not of politics but rather survival. Berlant notes in contemporary art in general, and one example of post-Katrina documentary in particular, a "turning away from politics and the political, a becoming-private that ranges from a desperate self-hoarding . . . to embodiments of the neoliberal subject aspiration that equates entrepreneurial activity with sovereign, democratic personhood."[87]

According to many educators, this is precisely the model of agency taught in U.S. schools, where citizenship has been reduced to an act of consumption. As Henry Giroux writes in the preface to *Education as Enforcement* (2003), "any struggle to make schools more democratic and socially relevant still have [sic] to link the battle for citizenship to an ongoing fight against turning schools into testing centers and teachers into technicians . . . schools are increasingly defined less as a public good than as sites for financial investment and entrepreneurial training, that is, as a private good."[88] Giroux claims that "educators need to challenge the idea that politics is dead." He then goes on to make a distinction between "emergency time," or the time wherein "the imaginable future" becomes what Kenneth

Saltman terms "a repetition of a bleak present,"[89] and "public time." Following democratic theorist Cornelius Castoriadis, Giroux argues that public time signifies "the emergence of a dimension where the collectivity can inspect its own past as the result of its own actions, and where an indeterminate future opens up as a domain for its activities."[90] Giroux's call for a critical pedagogy in U.S. schools hinges on this notion of temporality that counters the depoliticizing effects of "emergency time" and thus might be the condition of possibility for a new kind of politics.

I would like to appropriate the notion of "public time" for the New Orleans context, where arguably a variant of public time is always already a part of the culture here, and where "emergency time" has been experienced as a particularly violent invasion. In *Coming Out the Door for the Ninth Ward* (2006), a book written by members of Nine Times Social and Pleasure Club and produced by the Neighborhood Story Project, one interviewee emphasizes that where Katrina was a terrible loss, it was the destruction of the Desire public housing project, several years prior to the storm, that constituted for her the "total loss."[91] As Helen Regis and Rachel Breunlin argue in the article that they researched while working with Nine Times on this book, the post-Katrina dispersal of New Orleans' working poor recalled "multiple diasporas" that preceded it and which the former Desire community struggle against in order to maintain their connections.[92] This community had experienced "emergency time," or what I have in this book been calling "Katrina time," well before the advent of Hurricane Katrina. And they suffered this violent and futureless temporality in the name of "progress."

Himelstein identifies *Coming Out the Door for the Ninth Ward* as the NSP's "Katrina book" and it was one of the organization's bestsellers. Like many of NSP's books, the narrative is a work of collaborative ethnography that involves extensive interviews with community members. The result is therefore not an individual achievement but rather a work that is viewed by about twenty-five collaborators as "their book."[93] The subject is the world created by the Desire housing project located in the Ninth Ward. The narrative traces the founding of Nine Times there in the late 1990s, the project's destruction by HOPE VI in the early 2000s, and the afterlife of Desire's destruction in the experience of Katrina, as well as Desire's symbolic resurrection in Nine Times' parades through the former site.

What emerges is a "collectivity" inspecting "its own past as the result of its own actions." Desire is a world built by its residents, one that undoubtedly descended into difficulty in the late 1980s and '90s due to the effects of racialized poverty, drugs, and crime, but which is overwhelmingly recalled by Nine Times as a place of community and love. They evoke a community that has not suffered the privatization of the family and the social atomization that this entails. The book is full of defamiliarizing accounts that describe, for example, a shooting that led to a hospital ward being overwhelmed by concerned visitors from the project: the aftermath of tragedy that is seldom reported by the mainstream news media. As Regis and Breunlin argue, social aid and pleasure clubs trace a "subaltern map" across the New Orleans landscape that is being rendered increasingly unstable in the post-Katrina landscape.[94] *Coming Out the Door for the Ninth Ward* is a prime example of narrative-based resistance that exposes and challenges the violence of neoliberal urban policy. It does this primarily by evoking an interruptive temporality that defies the devastatingly short-term market logic of Katrina time; in their preface to the book, anticipating their first post-Katrina parade, the authors write:

> We've come a long way, but the struggle isn't over. We have our sights set on November 19, 2006, when Nine Times will come out again on the 3400 block of Louisa Street. From there we'll go up Louisa Street through Press Park, over that bridge to visit our people on the other side, to Franklin Avenue on our way back home to Desire Street, down Desire to that Florida Project back over the tracks and—get ready—it's time to go through that mighty Desire once more. Keep this in your prayers and it will happen.[95]

In awakening the ghost of Desire in collective memory, and invoking a claim to the geography of New Orleans that has no relationship to property rights, Nine Times inaugurates a "public time" that is also arguably a "New Orleans time." This temporality involves an orientation toward the past as pathway for a different kind of future, a crucial oppositional tendency given that social forgetting is central to neoliberal world making. The rest of this book will explore modes of survival through the lens of "New Orleans time," which I have been arguing here offers a variation both on the elusive progress of "American time" and the dead-end of "Katrina time." As Berlant writes, "the urgency is to reinvent, from the scene of survival, new idioms of the political, and of belonging itself, which requires debating what the baselines of survival should be in the near future, which is, now, the future we are making."[96] As a seminal figure of past resistance who was too far ahead of his times to be fully *with* the times, the New Orleans civil rights campaigner, Homer Plessy, who claimed public space on behalf of all the city's residents, is perhaps a good model of the past *as* future, as a symbol of the kind of city New Orleanians might want to return to. Rather than viewing Plessy as a symbol of failed resistance, he might be remembered as a political activist, working within a human rights tradition, who audaciously imagined a racist colonial government as possible ally against racist local politics; thus envisioning the transformation of the state by a subversive, anti-racist, Creole urban counter-public.

Part III

New Orleans Time

5
_____

New Orleans and Water
Remapping Ecologies of the Gulf South

In an early sequence of Spike Lee's *When the Levees Broke: A Requiem in Four Acts* (2006), a number of residents from New Orleans' Lower Ninth Ward describe both hearing and feeling an explosion coming from the levee bordering the Industrial Canal.[1] This would likely have been around 7.45 a.m., Monday morning, August 29, 2005, when New Orleans had just narrowly escaped a direct hit by Hurricane Katrina. Reinvigorated by the unusually warm waters of the Gulf of Mexico, Katrina was then downgraded from a category 5 to a category 3 storm before making landfall in Jefferson Parish, Louisiana. New Orleans had not, as many had dared to hope, "dodged the bullet." Catastrophic levee failures led to the inundation of 80 percent of the city. The most devastated area was the Lower Ninth Ward, where the cross-currents of race and class, money and power, land and water, have, as it were, exploded in New Orleans' post-Katrina landscape.

Some speculated that the explosion they heard might have come from the electrical supply, while others wondered if it hadn't come from a collision caused by a neglected barge smashing into and breaching the levee at the Industrial Canal. Others imagined a more deliberate act. As Spike Lee observes of this particular sequence in his director's commentary, "these folks will swear on a stack of bibles that they heard an explosion . . . many African Americans, and I include myself in this group, don't put anything past the United States government when it comes to black people." Lee would likely have had many historical episodes in mind when making this statement, but underlying them all, if we leap-frog the brief moment in the twentieth century when the federal government was paradoxically enlisted as an ally of black rights, is a founding national crime: slavery. Lee's interviewees, this sequence of footage suggests, recall more recent disasters, in which black suffering had undoubtedly been enormously exacerbated if not caused by government authorities. As former New Orleans Mayor Marc Morial observes in the film, it became almost an "article of faith" that the levees in the Lower Ninth Ward were dynamited following Hurricane Betsy in 1965—which led to catastrophic flooding in the Ninth Ward, an experience that seemed to uncannily repeat almost exactly forty years later. The rumor that circulated after Katrina was in turn fuelled by events during the 1927 Mississippi River flood, when city elites had undoubtedly stage-managed the dynamiting of the levee that protected St. Bernard Parish, in order to save New Orleans for business.[2]

The near mirror-image scenario that the 1927 flood offers Katrina, as well as the interlude between these two catastrophes, tells us much about the relationship between what is perceived as "natural disaster" and human agency. In 1927, though already facing a downward trajectory, New Orleans was still by far the wealthiest city in the South, and its elite representatives were able to persuade state authorities and the federal government to sacrifice the rural parishes to protect the city. By 2005, New Orleans was not the scene of wealth and power but rather of disinvestment and poverty.[3] While it is highly unlikely that the breaches of the levees in the Lower Ninth Ward were the result of dynamiting, their failure was still the result of criminal negligence on the part of the federal government. The levees did not overtop; they collapsed. The 1927 flood led to huge federal investment in the levee system across the entire Mississippi Valley, for the first time shifting responsibility from local to federal authorities. As John Barry explains in *Rising Tide: The Great Mississippi Flood of 1927 and How it Changed America* (1997), the flood represented a watershed "when the nation first demanded that the federal government assume a new kind of responsibility for its citizens."[4] Though public sentiment was well ahead of the government of the time, the 1927 flood was followed closely by the Great Crash, Depression, and the New Deal—a sequence of events that initiated a massive expansion of the state. This, in turn, enabled the federal government to respond decisively to the 1950s and 1960s Civil Rights movement. And yet, by 2005, the political forces that brought the welfare state into being had disintegrated. As Clinton declared in 1996, "the era of big government is over."[5]

Following Katrina, understandable anger at government failings crystallized around the U.S. Army Corps of Engineers responsible for maintaining the levees. Many insisted, and still insist, on describing the post-Katrina flooding of New Orleans a "federal flood." The advocacy organization, levees. org, even awards " 'Seals of Approval' to reporters who properly characterize the flooding in metro New Orleans as due to levee failure rather than blaming the flooding solely on a storm, a practice," their website explains, "which denies human responsibility."[6] While, as discussed in previous chapters, the post-Katrina anger at government inaction and disinvestment often bred the desire for alternative arrangements—opening up spaces for nonprofits and private enterprise to fill the apparent void—when it came to the levees, it was clear that no agency other than the federal government could even aspire to live up to the task. One popular slogan that arose in this period, and which has also become the name of another advocacy website, was "levees not war"[7]—thus calling a hollowed-out security state back to the task of citizen welfare and protection.

But one of the ironies of this slogan is the fact that, as explored below, levees themselves wage war on water, in ways that are often counterproductive and unsafe. While the crumbling New Orleans levee system was undeniably part of a crumbling infrastructure irresponsibly neglected by the state, and which led to possibly hundreds of fatalities, the system itself is part of a larger vision of human control over the environment that is itself fallacious and dangerous. In Louisiana the levee system emerged from a very particular colonial perspective that originated with the French—an empire that tended, as Craig Colten points out, to claim hydrologic territories. And yet, as Colten also points out, waterways were considered by French, Spanish and British imperial powers as "public domains." "Unlike terrestrial property," Colten explains, "water was fluid and moved, and thus did not have the same exclusive ownership qualities as land."[8] Thus while efforts to colonize and privatize bodies of water have been long-standing and are ongoing, New Orleans' watery geography testifies to the various ways in which water subverts understandings of both private property and sovereignty. The relationship that binds South Louisiana to water—that which is public and non-sovereign—cannot simply be engineered away.

In the previous chapter I argued that after Katrina New Orleans was afflicted by a racialized anti-urbanism. But this is only part of the picture. Here I complicate this suggestion with the idea that paradoxically, this anti-urbanism has been exacerbated in the New Orleans context by the attendant idea that the Crescent City's project of urbanization is fundamentally unstable, incomplete. This in turn has combined with the residual sense, discussed in chapter 1, that New Orleans is somehow "foreign" within the national imaginary. As Stephanie Houston Grey argues, "residing as it does at the mouth of the Mississippi River, the city of New Orleans has been historically characterized as a site of expulsion, waste, and excess."[9] For Grey, the alluvial plains of the lower Mississippi are imagined as sites of pollution in an allegory that combines understandings of geography and ethnicity. In this racist narrative of disposable populations, New Orleans' watery excess corresponds with its perceived legacy of racial mixing, in a narrative in which black and white, land and water, are disciplined via mechanisms of social and environmental control. And yet these fluid boundaries will not be fully disciplined. Just as the city's transgressive cultural and racial legacy lives on, despite their cooptation by the tourist industry, the region's abundant water is not contained by the vast system of levees and canals designed to exploit natural resources while keeping "nature" in check.

The primary victims of this watery excess, this fundamentally incomplete project of urbanization, are undeniably the region's low-income and predominantly black populations. African Americans were of course disproportionately hit by the levee breaches in New Orleans, just as the health of black neighborhoods has suffered as a result of Louisiana's toxic petrochemical corridor that lines the Mississippi River between New Orleans and Baton Rouge. What was once a strip of slave plantations has been left to the descendants of black sharecroppers who inhabit land now dubbed "cancer alley." Out toward the Gulf, the land is literally being swallowed up by the oil industry, displacing native wetland communities, driven back from the Louisiana mainland in successive waves by white supremacy.[10] And yet while it is these vulnerable and disenfranchised populations who bear the burden of exposing environmental hazard, degradation, state negligence, and corporate violence, the cultures of these communities also point in the direction of a different relationship with the region's "natural endowment." This relationship encapsulates recognition of human limits when it comes to controlling the environment. And this difference, I argue in this chapter, engenders an alternative attitude toward time. It gestures toward a temporality that interrupts what Wai Chee Dimock usefully terms "the short chronology of a young nation."[11] This is a temporality that registers environmental agency, and that I have been calling in this book "New Orleans time." This final section of the book will pull out the various possibilities suggested by this term.

This chapter explores the relationship between land, water, power, and culture, through the vastly differing temporal lenses offered by post-Katrina New Orleans on the one hand and Louisiana's rapidly eroding coast on the other. The first section explores the unravelling attempt to tame the water bodies that constitute New Orleans' fluid foundations, concluding with a discussion of Rebecca Solnit's and Rebecca Snedeker's "New Orleans Atlas,"

Unfathomable City (2013). The second section explores the ways in which this "struggle for New Orleans" has been projected in the post-Katrina period onto the "struggle for the Lower Ninth Ward." Why has this neighborhood within the area that Richard Campanella describes as the city's "poor third" become the focus of such fierce debate and contention since Katrina?[12] What relationship persists between the Lower Ninth and the rest of New Orleans? How do the supposedly unstable ecologies of the Lower Ninth Ward relate to the web of community organizing that has sprung up in this now iconic New Orleans neighborhood? The final section extends beyond the geography of the New Orleans metro area to consider the imaginative territory opened up by Benh Zeitlin's *Beasts of the Southern Wild* (2012).[13] It views New Orleans from the perspective of the Bathtub community, in order to contemplate the relationship between indigenous communities, the urban environment, and the state, when it comes to confronting the reality of rising sea levels. What shape will the map of coastal Louisiana take in one-hundred-years' time? And, as Lower Ninth Ward residents asked in Katrina's aftermath, who let the water in?

Conquering Water: The Struggle for New Orleans

Craig Colten claims in *An Unnatural Metropolis: Wresting New Orleans from Nature* (2005), that "keeping the city dry, or separating the human-made environment from its natural endowment, has been the perpetual battle for New Orleans."[14] While "the big river" that defines New Orleans' famous crescent kept its indigenous name, the Europeans who colonized Louisiana did not intend to accommodate the Mississippi as had the first inhabitants. These semi-nomadic peoples frequently moved around the Mississippi basin following inundations. The Europeans "intended to stay put," and so began the long process of straitjacketing the river so that it, too, would stay within its banks.[15] The result would be a feat of engineering that would artificially prevent "this immense writhing snake of a river"[16] from shifting its flow in its effort to find the shortest route to the sea.

The decision to locate New Orleans, the capital of the Louisiana colony, on the original site of the French Quarter, is still a matter of historical speculation. Geographer Peirce Lewis describes New Orleans as the "inevitable city" on the "impossible" site,[17] implying that commercial advantages afforded by the Mississippi River and its proximate but apparently safe distance from the coast trumped geographic and environmental considerations. Lawrence Powell claims that Jean-Baptiste Le Moyne, Sieur de Bienville, was acting in pure self-interest when he founded New Orleans—he had considerable land holdings in the area that would dramatically increase in value with site development.[18] Richard Campanella characterizes the founding of the Crescent City as "Bienville's dilemma," and imagines that personal gain came into play alongside issues of "accessibility, defendability, riverine position, arability, and natural resources, plus a lack of better alternatives." Campanella also distinguishes between the city's "site"—its physical footing—and its "situation," meaning "its regional context and how it connects with the world."[19] New Orleans' site was hazardous, its situation superb. And the investment—financial, commercial, strategic—a risk worth taking, but a gamble nonetheless.

While New Orleans' waterborne threats now emanate primarily from its complex system of navigation and drainage canals, as well as the rapidly eroding coast, initially, the greatest challenge was the Mississippi River. This was also New Orleans' boon. Powell captures the paradox, when he explains the way in which the city, in its "lush decades" in the nineteenth century, absorbed the vast wealth created in what "proved to be the richest valley on Earth;"[20] he writes, "it was as though the city were the drain plug in an immense bathtub. And as the basin released its bounty, so the city's coffers swelled."[21] And yet this also anticipated New Orleans' future bowl shape—or rather, network of hydrological sub-basins—into which enormous amounts of rain and flood water could and would be dumped. In the nineteenth century large parts of New Orleans had yet to sink below sea level, but successive floods in its fledgling years inspired the French to begin erecting artificial levees on the site of the natural levees created by the sediment of the river itself. In time it would become apparent that the man-made levees deprive the soil of the water and sediment that builds the land—and which indeed built the entire deltaic plain via the rhythms of the Mississippi's natural flood cycle—and keeps it from collapsing in on itself and sinking. In the meantime, the unintended consequences of levee construction was out of sight, and this process of asserting control over the river was reaching its zenith toward the end of the nineteenth century—with Louisiana now marked as American territory.

According to John Barry, to aspire to contain the Mississippi "requires hubris," and turned out to be "the perfect task for the nineteenth century":

> This was the century of iron and steel, certainty and progress, and the belief that physical laws as solid and rigid as iron and steel governed nature . . . man had only to discover these laws to truly rule the world.[22]

As Barry's book shows, in fact, the triumph of the "levees only" approach to river control by the early-twentieth century was as much about personal power and ambition as it was about science. Scenes from the 1927 flood showing black workers forced at gunpoint to sandbag the levees, sometimes using their own bodies as fortification, graphically illustrate the interpenetration of one system of control with another.[23] The imperatives of flood control and social control were then repeatedly reinforced in the months following the catastrophe, during which black workers were coerced into refugee camps along the natural levee, for fear that the Mississippi Delta would be drained of its supply of cheap labor. Often suffering appalling conditions and abuse, these workers were only allowed to leave if they were summoned back to the plantation by their white "masters."[24]

While the catastrophe of the 1927 floods taught fundamental lessons about the need to concede to water—via the creation of outlets and spillways—in order to stop the levees building up pressure and themselves becoming time bombs, reliance on levees continued. Indeed, as suggested above, they became vast, federally managed structures that attempted to dwarf the river. And yet it was also clear by this point that the importance of the river in commercial terms was declining. As Campanella explains, "the lion's share of New Orleans' spectacular wealth and meteoric rise between the Louisiana Purchase and the Civil War can be traced to river-related activity." And yet "the city's supreme confidence in its geographical advantage" blinded it to the competition coming from other waterways as early as 1825, with the completion of the Erie Canal. With the coming of the railroad, the flow of trade shifted decisively northward. While New Orleans' business elites focused on "exploiting today's boom" rather than "preparing for tomorrow's bust," a series of navigation canals were excavated with the idea of boosting the city's competitiveness.[25]

The Inner Harbor Navigation Canal, commonly referred to as the Industrial Canal, opened in 1923, finally achieving the goal of connecting the river with Lake Pontchartrain to the rear of the city. The construction of the Intracoastal Waterway in the 1940s, which intersects with the Industrial Canal, provided another route from New Orleans to the Gulf. Finally, the Mississippi River Gulf Outlet (MR-GO), a brainchild of the Second World War, was completed in 1968. As Campanella explains, after Katrina many would ask: "why score and scour thin, delicate soils and invite dangerous water bodies into the heart of a bowl-shaped metropolis?"[26] These seaways funnelled enormous storm surges up into the urban core in 2005, breaching the levees that protected the Lower Ninth Ward, St. Bernard Parish, and New Orleans East. MR-GO, itself an economic failure, also "destroyed

8,000 acres of wetlands during its inception," and "subsequently caused severe coastal erosion and salt-water intrusion."[27] Coastal erosion has in turn drastically reduced New Orleans' natural hurricane protection in the form of barrier islands.

From Lake Pontchartrain, on August 29, 2005, water flowed into the 17th Street and London Avenue drainage canals, breaching the levees and flooding the central city. Municipal drainage, alongside levees, is another major reason for New Orleans' subsidence, with many areas of the city falling below sea level in the early part of the twentieth century. New Orleans' backswamps, which represented a route into freedom for the region's escaped slaves but which conjured disease and degeneration for European settlers fearful of tropical climates, were cleared with the arrival of new pumping technology at the end of the nineteenth century. This enabled the city to expand rapidly toward the lake. As Campanella explains, these drainage canals that funnel excess water into Lake Pontchartrain themselves necessitate a whole new system of levees and floodwalls that have lured people into harm's way.

The city's suburban expansion on reclaimed land coincided with another boom that was to similarly reshape and devastate the landscape, this time via resource extraction. The Louisiana oil industry, which imploded in the 1980s but which is still very much in evidence today, has scored and scoured vast stretches of the state's undeveloped wetlands that lie between New Orleans and the Gulf of Mexico. The fastest depleting landmass on earth, water reclaims marshy land at the rate of more than one football field every hour. Thus New Orleans faces coastal erosion and soil subsidence even before you factor in rising sea levels and the increased frequency and severity of hurricanes that we can anticipate with climate change. The physical footprint of New Orleans today is the result first of a colonial vision that deployed levees to contain the river, followed by an American vision that expanded the levees, oversaw the expansion of the metro area via suburbanization, and became utterly dependent on oil.

Arguably oil extraction and suburbanization are the twinned ingredients of what I have been calling in this book "American time": the temporality of the so-called American Century, which encapsulated a vision of rising living standards for all. The fallacy of this myth, as explored in previous sections of the book, is now very clear to see. With the veritable abandonment of the social safety net and the deepening of inequalities, not just in terms of economic and social outcomes but also, and perhaps most fundamentally, in terms of the degree to which we are exposed to environmental risk, the continued perpetuation of this consumerist vision requires turning a blind eye to the future. This is the point at which a national dream long fuelled by a claim to the future gives way to what I have here been calling "Katrina time," the time of neoliberalism in which short-term gains are bought at the expense of long-term security.

In New Orleans' case, the levees themselves are a symbol of the false sense of security that has driven the development of the now sprawling metro area. As Richard Campanella argues in relation to the era prior to the 1927 flood, short-sighted approaches to river management meant that the region's repressed waters were "waiting to create a mega-catastrophe every 50 years rather than minor overtoppings every couple of years."[28] With some qualification, the same can be said today of a policy approach that puts far too much emphasis on engineered solutions to environmental threat. This approach means that once in a generation, Katrina-like catastrophes are experienced as unanticipated trauma, from which people only wish to be delivered into normalcy. Trauma as a category is very easily appropriated by ahistorical and short-termist authorities eager to conceal their ongoing role in courting disaster. Where the French colonists gambled on a site for New Orleans that many argue hardly constituted "land," the stakes of the current risks are now much higher, as the landmass sinks and shrinks in front of our eyes.

According to Lauren Berlant, " 'trauma' has become the primary genre of the last eighty years for describing the historical present as the scene of an exception that has just shattered some ongoing, uneventful ordinary life that was supposed to just keep going on and with respect to which people felt solid and confident." But "the extraordinary always turns out to be an amplification of something in the works, a labile boundary at best, not a slammed-door departure."[29] It is the very slammed-door departure represented by the levees themselves that so magnifies the effects of flooding and creates the slammed-door effect of trauma. In the previous chapter I argued that Naomi Klein's equation of neoliberalism with the shock tactics of disaster capitalism obscured the much larger historical canvas of "Katrina time." Here I suggest that the characterization of the post-Katrina flooding of New Orleans as an unanticipated rupture limits our understanding of the recovery to the restoration of the pre-traumatic moment. To reiterate, this is not to claim that Katrina was not an enormous source of trauma for the myriad individuals who suffered as a result of the hurricane and the disaster of the aftermath. But it is to claim that trauma as a paradigm often conceals the slow, nonspectacular and human-engineered violence walled out by levees and a discursive context wedded to a false sense of security punctuated by violent and sometimes catastrophic interruptions.

Wai Chee Dimock suggests that interest shown by New Orleans'
Times-Picayune in the Dutch flood control system after Katrina offers an
"alternative timeline" to the "short chronology of a young nation." In the
Dutch response Dimock notes "a trajectory of action at once local and
national, an instance of democratic politics that would have been helpful
if it had indeed 'flooded' the United States, if its crosscurrents had indeed
permeated these shores."[30] These images of water permeating the landscape
are now central to Dutch flood control policies, which long ago learned
the lesson of over-reliance on levees and floodwalls. The Dutch Dialogues
project, initiated by New Orleans architect David Waggonner, continues
John McQuaid's Pulitzer Prize-winning work for the *Times-Picayune* by
launching a long-term project to oversee the exchange of ideas between
these two delta regions. While the Dutch have adopted the principle of
"safety first"—not overly apparent in the New Orleans context—they have
also embraced the idea of "living with water." In this vision water is considered not just a threat but also an asset that cannot, in any case, be
safely banished from water-logged landscapes. New Orleans' large expans-
es of concrete and asphalt testify to the attempt to do just this; and yet
the water speaks otherwise. New Orleans' roads are dotted with potholes,
the sidewalks buckled by tree roots and often impassable, betraying the
persistent existence of water that won't be tamed. As Waggonner puts it,
"we're living on the isle of denial, and we're living in denial, because we
don't accept this condition of wateriness."[31]

Waggonner's Urban Water Plan is a visionary document that proposes
that arteries of water run through the Crescent City in a way that might soak
up excess rainfall and reduce the pressure on the city's overworked pumps.
Apart from the many practical benefits to a city in which large areas now lie
below sea level, Waggonner's plan involves important aesthetic and psychological dimensions: in a city in which the fear of drowning understandably
looms large, the "living with water" approach aims to restore the idea that
water can be an amenity. Most importantly, perhaps, it keeps water in sight,
thus counteracting the tendency of this urban culture to repress the precarious fact of its own existence. As Waggonner explained to me in an interview
in October 2014, this collaboration with Dutch planners is indeed about
stretching the timeline of a young nation to encompass other chronologies:
"we in the US seem to think that everything needs to be invented everyday.
There's no wisdom to that, everything's old. Our egocentrism isn't so good
either . . . What I do affects somebody else. I don't just have to let raw
market forces determine everything. There could be balance."[32]

In an essay titled "The Cement Lily Pad," Rebecca Snedeker, inspired by Waggonner's ideas, asks us to:

> Imagine New Orleans as an emerald green lily pad, a healthy circulatory system with the vitality and structure that comes with hydration. A floating city, with skin that breathes, within a delta coast. Let us saturate ourselves with wonder, let us embrace and fathom the water in the city. Or prepare to visit this place with a snorkel.[33]

This essay is part of a collection of maps and essays curated by Snedeker and Rebecca Solnit. These maps attempt to capture a host of circulatory systems and trace their intersections within New Orleans' complex urban landscape. Many of the maps place one vector in relation to another, often creating unexpected juxtapositions. What is striking is that water runs through and often defines most of these ecologies. Founding and draining the city, coastal erosion and its effect on Native peoples, the racial and economic spatialization of the city which is in turn profoundly shaped by topography; the issue of human burial, an enormous challenge in a location and climate that often collude to turn graveyards into swimming pools; the transatlantic slave trade and its cultures of resistance; when oil displaces water, as it did during the BP oil spill or following those other, unnoticed accidents that occur in the Gulf every day; the strategies of containment inherent to both levees and mass incarceration; the cultural significance of proximity to mud; seafood and sex. These watery maps with fluid boundaries excavate a city that has already in part opened the metaphorical floodgates to water, which inevitably shapes much of the city's DNA, in spite of the fact that for much of the city's history, the Mississippi River—New Orleans' raison d'être—has largely been obscured from view.

From multiple perspectives these maps explore the specificities of a culture that has evolved from a city residing "at the bottom of a big river." In his commentary on a map about the journeys made by human remains, Nathaniel Rich suggests that the city, known in the nineteenth century as the "Wet Grave," is peculiarly determined by this "other city" of the dead; one that breaks through the film of what is usually a culture's unconscious to manifest in distinct ways in New Orleans. As discussed in this book's introduction, it is clear to any tourist visiting the city that this is a place engaged in the sale of death. From its famed above-ground cemeteries to its zombie tours, the city's ghoulish imagination is fuelled by something that runs deeper than merely commercial interests, and can be traced back to inordinately moist soil that refuses to bury the dead. As Rich writes, "New Orleans may be subsiding, but its corpses continue to rise."[34]

Arguably, then, while water itself may be repressed in some respects in the Crescent City, knowledge of its implications is not absent from the archive: as discussed in chapter 2, the founder of New Orleans' Ashé Cultural Arts Center, Carol Bebelle, told me in an interview in December 2013 that this is a city in which people walk around with the memory of boats floating over their heads.[35] New Orleans is haunted by its historical status as a key site in the transatlantic slave trade as well as the domestic trade in human beings that followed. The city's deeply precarious location, the levels of environmental risk and social despair that its histories have incubated, lead many commentators to question the sanity of choosing the Crescent City as a place to live. Billy Sothern's map of the city's "revelations" contemplates New Orleans' many cultural compensations, and evokes a culture that meets despair "with a constant call to the immediacy of the present."[36] This call manifests most obviously in the city's myriad parading traditions which routinely bring large parts of the city to a standstill. As discussed in chapter 2, Mardi Gras is only the most prominent example in a cultural context that provides a powerful riposte to the national Protestant work ethic. The New Orleans tradition that most clearly disrupts conventional notions of temporality, and calls us to the present moment in all its pleasure and pain, is the jazz funeral. The jazz funeral is part of a raft of parading and performance traditions in New Orleans that recognize and celebrate finitude in ways that not only contradict a national culture fixated on the future, but which also attest to the city's irrepressible foundations in a fluid that both represents life and holds out the possibility of drowning. These are urban cultures that are often described as having "bubbled up" from the streets, those buckled sidewalks that gesture to a city visibly laboring under—and dancing to the tune of—myriad social and environmental stresses.

In their introduction to the "New Orleans Atlas," Solnit and Snedeker point out, as do so many introductions to volumes on the Crescent City, that while New Orleans may be "drenched in the past," it is geologically one of the youngest places in the United States, "a region of soft alluvial soil that turns to mud, melts away, and erodes into the surrounding waters." Their introduction places the city under the sign of annihilation: it is "imperiled, [sic] and may disappear altogether"; though its place in the cultural memory of the United States, they suggest, is assured.[37] Yet their cartographic interventions tell a different story. The city may be one of "amorphous boundaries," but their maps represent the human endeavor to carve out pictures, to draw straight lines that do not really exist. For this reason the ecologies they map resist the courting of the death drive so central to New Orleans culture, the tendency to focus on the material present at the expense of imagining the future. A love of life that often harbors a disturbing fatalism. As one contributor asks, "how can you turn being muddy into a positive?"[38]—without, we might add, losing the critical negativity that so defines this place in collective memory. Does future planning necessarily entail forgetting, especially in a place where the future seems so uncertain? Conversely, does "living with water" mean giving in to it?

While knowledge of environmental precarity and a temporal arc that transcends our own existence helpfully counteracts the delusion that human beings can bend "nature" to their will, planning for future survival requires the imperious art of map-making. New Orleans today would not exist if it were not for the colonial vision of the French settlers who began the long and perilous task of subduing the Mississippi River. After Katrina, some called a halt to this kind of planning, arguing that it was time to give the city—or at least parts of the city—back to the sea.

Conceding to Water: The Struggle for the Lower Ninth Ward

In March 2012 Nathaniel Rich wrote a piece for the *New York Times* suggesting that six years after Katrina, "it was clear that nature had triumphed" in the Lower Ninth Ward. Titled "Jungleland: The Lower Ninth Ward in New Orleans Gives New Meaning to 'Urban Growth,' " Rich's piece claimed that prior to an attempt by city authorities to "clean-up" and reclaim the neighborhood in 2012, the Lower Ninth "no longer resembled an urban, or even suburban environment. Where once there stood orderly rows of single-family homes with driveways and front yards, there was jungle." Describing the fact that much of the Lower Ninth is still characterized by abandoned lots a whole six years on (at the time of writing) from Katrina, his article depicts a landscape of snakes, stray dogs, racoons, and unchecked invasive weeds strangling the native fauna. "The neighborhood has become a dumping ground," Rich writes, "for many kinds of unwanted things."[39]

Unsurprisingly, Rich's article sparked anger from many quarters. Questions about the Lower Ninth Ward's viability have clung to the neighborhood ever since Katrina, and this piece undoubtedly breathes new life into those questions. Rich's Lower Ninth Ward is largely unpeopled, mirroring the kind of voyeuristic gaze opened up by the bus tours that his article describes, and which tend to focus on monuments of devastation and blight as opposed to the more prosaic realities of a slow recovery. Worse still, the fact that the predominantly African-American population that has made this place home are hardly mentioned here means that a host of potentially racialized metaphors enter this article via the back door, where they might have been explored and exposed. It is hard to read about "unwanted things" in Katrina's aftermath without being reminded of the apparently disposable bodies that floated in the city streets days after the storm, or the large-scale displacement of many of the city's poor black population (many of whom would have been residents of the Lower Ninth Ward). It is hard to read about "jungleland" in this corner of South Louisiana without being reminded of the highly racialized interpretation of this semi-tropical landscape formed by European explorers when they first "discovered" it. As will be explored below, since the 1800s the Lower Ninth, the city's swampy, lowermost corner that initially attracted a low-income immigrant and black population, has long been considered "distant and uncivilized."[40]

The story that many bloggers offered as counter-narrative to Rich's piece was the deeply politicized human odyssey behind both the abandoned lots and indeed those which are now inhabited (roughly one-third of pre-Katrina residencies).[41] This story started almost as soon as Katrina hit, when a host of commentators suggested that the city should not be rebuilt. Beyond those who liked to point out, often in religious guise, that one meaning of "Katrina" is "to cleanse," these arguments largely focused on the fact that much of the metro area lies below sea level. On September 1, 2005, Republican House Speaker Dennis Hastert observed in an interview that "it looks like a lot of that place could be bulldozed."[42] Seeking to contain the outcry caused by his comments, Hastert nuanced his statement by suggesting that the government needed to think very carefully about where federal rebuilding dollars would go. This kind of thinking occurred on a city level in the form of Mayor Ray Nagin's "Bring New Orleans Back" Commission, which reported in January 2006. Following recommendations by the Urban Land Institute, the Commission put a question mark over the future of several devastated and relatively low-lying neighborhoods in Orleans Parish. Crudely interpreted by a graphic in the *Times-Picayune*, these question marks translated into the now infamous "green dots" that hovered over Village de L'Est, Lakeview, Hollygrove, Broadmoor, and the Lower Ninth Ward. The confused message that went out was that these low-lying neighborhoods could be converted into "green spaces" that might also act as floodplains. Rich's article goes as far as to suggest that "much of the Lower Ninth has fallen into the very condition that New Orleanians after the storm were desperate to avoid: it has become green space."

This statement eclipses the efforts of myriad neighborhood organizations that sprang up while residents were still in exile to defend the Lower Ninth Ward, in addition to the numerous nonprofits that have stayed to aid rebuilding efforts in the long term. In fact, following the controversy of BNOB, Mayor Nagin abandoned the commission's recommendations for footprint shrinkage. While no actionable plan for the rebuilding of New Orleans emerged, the Unified New Orleans Plan, which included the entire metro area and which involved widespread neighborhood consultation, embraced the principle of the "right to return." Moreover, Nagin sought to reassure his black constituents that New Orleans was going to be a "chocolate city" once more. Despite expressing reservations in private about the safety of rebuilding in the Lower Ninth Ward, he repeatedly insisted publicly in the ensuing months that this neighborhood in particular would be rebuilt.[43]

And yet, as noted in the previous chapter, the invitation to rebuild in any flooded neighborhood was a neoliberal one: it came with no real assistance, and thus ensured that resettlement was a market-driven process. Affluent neighborhoods like Lakeview, also devastated by Katrina and identified as a future flood risk by the Urban Land Institute, were in a much better position to regroup. Village de L'Est, with its sizeable Vietnamese enclave, though dealing with floodlines in many cases just as high as in the Lower Ninth and with a similarly low-income constituency, was able to call on the organizational capacities often at work in immigrant communities. Just a few months after Katrina, Village de L'Est had the highest return rate in the city. While, as the world would come to know over the next months and years, the Lower Ninth is itself a close-knit community proud of its deep roots, a number of factors meant that the neighborhood's return would be protracted and, at the time of writing, fundamentally incomplete. Residents in the Lower Ninth Ward remained scattered for much longer. This was because the neighborhood was sealed off for longer than any area in the city, and when it did finally open for "look and leave" visits, basic services were slow to return; a moratorium on building further stalled rebuilding efforts. As Dan Baum notes, many were refused entry into the Lower Ninth Ward in those first few months after Katrina, and "the residents were furious."

> Their frustration nourished a whole new crop of conspiracy theories: the city wanted to turn the Lower Nine into an industrial park; developers wanted the Lower Nine, with its riverfront and view of downtown, for condominiums; somebody's cousin's cousin saw Donald Trump drive through in a limousine.[44]

Many believed that the Lower Ninth had been singled out because of its majority black and working-class makeup, and these beliefs were not without foundation. As Tom Wooten reports in his book that charts the plight of the so-called "green dot" communities, in September 2005 "speculation was rife that New Orleans would come back only as a 'boutique city,' with a much smaller footprint and a whiter, wealthier population."[45] Property developer Joseph Canizaro, chair of the BNOB commission, argued that Katrina had offered up a "clean sheet" on which to plot a "new" New Orleans. For many, the Lower Ninth Ward, as the worst hit area in the city, represented the "ground zero" of this particular disaster.[46] In the same way that the demolition of public housing (discussed in chapter 4) was identified as key to "deconcentrating" poverty in the city, many commentators—who characterized the Lower Ninth as a poor and crime-ridden area already blighted by significant numbers of abandoned houses—suggested that this now iconic neighborhood would not be reconstituted as it was.

As Richard Campanella explains, located in what was until 1852 designated as the "Third Municipality" and which was also nicknamed the "dirty third" and the "poor third," the Ninth Ward's downriver geography, lying on the outer boundary of the city limits, meant that it has long been "first on the list for urban nuisances, last in line for amenities."[47] The area has been home to a slaughterhouse, a sewage treatment plant, warehouses, and industrial plants. Anathema to those located upriver on the wider natural levee next to a river unpolluted by refuse, these "nuisances" have provided jobs while depressing property values. In 1918, city officials managed to overlook the 25,599 people living in the Ninth Ward, claiming that it was an ideal location for the Industrial Canal because it was uninhabited.[48] Anticipating the coming of Interstate 10 that drove out the heart of the Tremé, in 1923, the completed Industrial Canal carved out the lower section of the Ninth Ward, in effect isolating it from the rest of the city. With the construction of the Intracoastal Waterway in the 1940s, "the 11,556 residents of the Lower Ninth Ward, long severed from the other 97.7 percent of the city's population by the Industrial Canal, were now surrounded on three sides by water bodies, even as their underlying soils subsided."[49] The Mississippi River Gulf Outlet in the 1960s further endangered the hydrological sub-basin occupied by the Lower Ninth Ward and St. Bernard Parish. The combination proved deadly in 1965 with the storm surges that came with Hurricane Betsy.

Thus the Lower Ninth Ward concentrates many of the city's environmental hazards into one small area, while similarly acting as a microcosm of the city's changing demographics. In the 1960s the Lower Ninth became the center of New Orleans' vicious school desegregation debate, which stimulated white flight all over Orleans parish and particularly from the Lower Ninth, a movement that was then exacerbated by Betsy. In an intensification of trends across the city, the neighborhood experienced rapid population decline from 1960 and went from being a racially mixed area—with, as Campanella explains, a predominantly white "front of town" and a predominantly black "back of town"—to being 95 percent African American by 2000.[50] During this forty-year period, crime rates rose, leading one commentator to describe the area as the "murder capital of the murder capital."[51] It is little wonder that when Katrina thrust the Lower Ninth into the limelight from its pre-storm obscurity, the neighborhood became the "poster child" of New Orleans' environmental and social woes. Its peripheral location on the city's outer boundary mirrors New Orleans' own position on the margins of the national imaginary, just as the long-term municipal neglect of the Lower Ninth reflects disinvestment in New Orleans as a whole on the part of state and federal bodies. The close ties in the neighborhood forged as a result of the Lower Ninth's physical isolation also captures and magnifies New Orleans' reputation as a place where roots run deep.

Thus, after Katrina the neighborhood became a symbol of the city's embattled future. As Richard Campanella explained to me in an interview in October 2014,

> It's the biggest example, it's the worst example, it was the hardest hit, it had the highest velocity flooding, it had the deepest flooding, it double flooded with Rita, it has history it has geography it has culture, it has the racial dynamic, there's the white flight—it has it all. And that's why people have been drawn to it, it's a helluva story.

Another facet of the Lower Ninth's microcosmic role is that in fact, and contrary to the assumption of many outsiders to New Orleans looking in, the neighborhood is neither the poorest in the city nor is it the lowest lying. The survival instincts spurred by a post-Katrina media narrative that has encouraged both of these assumptions, as well as painful experiences like BNOB, have set out to disprove these two myths about the Lower Ninth Ward. As Wooten points out, if the Lower Ninth was going to prove to apparently sceptical city authorities that the neighborhood was "viable," if it was going to save itself from being quite literally written off the map, then adopting a narrative of "sustainability" might just be the "magic bullet."[52]

Wooten's book shows that all of the "green dot" communities were severely alienated by the initial planning process that failed to include them, and adopted robust counter-narratives that emphasized their "self-reliance." As urban critic Roberta Gratz explains, "the top-down attempt to shrink the city galvanized an enraged citizenry into a level of civic involvement that did not exist before the storms." Writing in 2010, Gratz describes a New Orleans overtaken by a "can-do spirit" that has defied predictions that the city would not fully return.[53] This spirit was particularly apparent in the Lower Ninth Ward, where a host of community organizations and nonprofits sprung up to fill the void left by a government that would only half-heartedly give the go-ahead for rebuilding in this neighborhood. And yet arguably, what Gratz characterizes as insurgent "grassroots" activities have only reinforced the government's laissez faire position. As suggested in previous chapters, the image of citizens pulling themselves up by their own bootstraps, fiercely independent from government, is entirely in keeping with the neoliberal state.

It is hard to read the literature produced by nonprofits working in the Lower Ninth Ward without being told that the area has historically boasted higher home ownership rates than elsewhere in the city or the nation.[54] This is usually a bald assertion that seems to gesture to home ownership as an unquestioned good that naturally entails certain rights.[55] Prior to Katrina about 60 percent of Lower Ninth Ward residents owned their homes. This is unquestionably important given the enormous constraints historically placed on the ability of black people to acquire assets and economic security. The Lower Ninth Ward, though maligned in the media, *is* a symbol of black social mobility, just as the teaching profession has traditionally provided a key route into the middle classes for African Americans. The Lower Ninth Ward was threatened after Katrina just as thousands of black teachers were fired by the Orleans Parish School Board. As Silas Lee told Dan Baum, "the area represents African-Americans' cultural and historical significance, and their financial stability. They're not going to let anybody take that away."[56] And yet, appealing to the unquestioned rights of property owners precludes solidarity with the many renters who found themselves with nothing after Katrina. It appeals to a narrative that equates respectability with wealth. Albeit a precarious wealth: statistics confirm that African-American homeowners were disproportionately bypassed by Road Home money. This context makes it all the more plain both why black homeowners would want to insist on their property rights and the way in which a system in thrall to private property and wealth enshrines inequality. As discussed in chapter 3, many black homeowners could not access standard mortgages and so financed their homes via unconventional means, with the result that they did not then have the paperwork deemed necessary by Road Home to prove title to their properties.[57]

In addition to insisting on the twinned values of self-reliance and homeownership, community organizations and nonprofits working in the Lower Ninth have also often sought to counteract the idea that the area is environmentally unstable. New Orleans' post-Katrina reputation for building back green is largely thanks to efforts in this particular community. From resident organizations like Holy Cross Neighborhood Association and its offshoot, the Lower Ninth Ward Center for Sustainable Engagement and Development, to nonprofits organized largely by transplants like Common Ground, to the larger scale and celebrity-inspired organizations like Make it Right and Global Green, sustainability has become a buzz word as well as an admirable aspiration in the rebuilding of the Lower Ninth Ward. The emphasis is not just on resilience to flooding but also on the more lofty goal of carbon footprint reduction as well as the practical reality of cheaper bills.

The most visible and commented upon development in this area is Brad Pitt's work through the Make it Right Foundation. The foundation aims to combine cutting-edge design with the latest technology in green building, and it concentrates its efforts in the very worst hit location in the worst hit neighborhood: right on the site of the largest levee breach of the Industrial Canal in the Lower Ninth Ward. Describing his location of choice, Pitt told the historian Douglas Brinkley in an interview that "it was obliterationville . . . it was a blank, blank, blank canvas."[58] While Pitt's assessment of the physical site used language that insensitively mirrored that of the political forces he was ostensibly opposing, his aim to rebuild this most devastated site, and thus prove that anywhere in New Orleans could be rebuilt, has made him a local hero to some. There have been murmurings that the consultation process his foundation instigated was not responsive enough to the community, and although the project claimed to be concerned to preserve the vernacular architecture, some feel that the new houses stand out in curious and unsightly ways. Nathaniel Rich's reference to the project as resembling "a Special Economic Zone" takes in both this latter criticism and the widespread sense that the financial costs of this kind of rebuilding are so high that they defeat the whole point of Pitt's project: beyond the hundred or so that Make it Right has pledged, it is unclear that this model could be rolled out on the mass scale required to repopulate the entire area.

But arguably a much larger question in relation to the "Pitt homes" is one that concerns the very nature of the gesture itself. Campanella suggests that "if you build an architecturally sustainable building and you put it in a geographically unsustainable place, then you've not really accomplished much, have you."[59] Campanella was one of the experts who made recommendations to the "Bring New Orleans Back" Commission and who advocated for the consideration of footprint shrinkage through the deployment of a GIS-based methodology to measure and map four potentially conflicting principles: the desires of residents to return to their respective neighborhoods; the level of damage of those neighborhoods; the neighborhoods' historical and architectural character; and their future environmental and geographical risk. Such a methodology, he suggested, would shine light on those flooded areas which most, and least, warranted the effort of rebuilding. The methodology was not adopted, and eventually all neighborhoods were allowed to rebuild, regardless of demand or risk. What Campanella calls the "Great Footprint Debate" is, he asserts, history. At least for now. Among other reasons, the absence of government funds needed for mass buyouts to relocate residents to higher ground ruled this option out.

The commission created by Governor Kathleen Blanco, the Louisiana Recovery Authority, ultimately decided that homeowners would be awarded the pre-Katrina value of their properties. Quite apart from discriminating against homeowners from areas with lower property values, this ruled out the prospect of enticing people out of floodplains. In the context of the Lower Ninth this might, for example, have involved concentrating returning homes, shops, and amenities in the Holy Cross area, which sits closer to the river and thus on the natural levee. As Baum concludes, "instead of encouraging people to move to higher ground, Blanco's commission ended up doing the opposite: encouraging people, especially those in the lowest-lying and poorest neighborhoods, to stay put and fix up their houses."[60] While, as Campanella concedes, what has been—perhaps ominously, perhaps realistically—renamed the "risk reduction system" has been significantly strengthened in the Lower Ninth Ward, the neighborhood is now even more geographically isolated than it was before the storm. He questions the wisdom of those who encouraged the idea that "coming back to a lonely and destroyed neighborhood was an act of urban resilience."[61]

The absence of an ideological or financial commitment to planning—which necessarily needed to be a democratic process quite unlike that initiated by BNOB—means that redevelopment in the Lower Ninth is uneven and haphazard. Vast sections of undeveloped land do lend some credence to Nathaniel Rich's contention that after Katrina, at least some parts of it have been returned to nature. As the ecologist Michael Blum explains, where two years after Katrina much of the Lower Ninth Ward resembled an agricultural field, now these areas are "more like a secondary forest." Blum, whose ideas, alongside Campanella's, are featured in Rich's article, explains that the area has become the center of a scientific study precisely because it features a particularly rich "novel ecosystem"—which is an interface between a natural and anthropogenic environment. Arguably, given the relatively tiny areas of the earth's surface that remain "untouched," all ecosystems are novel to a certain extent; but New Orleans in general and the Lower Ninth in particular offer up a singular case study.[62]

Unlike other instances of urban depopulation, which often lead to incidences of urban areas being ceded to various stages of wilderness—Detroit is a good example—post-Katrina New Orleans has seen the rapid "reassembling of the landscape." Mass evacuation followed by slow but steady return to an area "adjacent to some of the most significant natural areas of the Gulf Coast" means that the Lower Ninth has much to teach us about urban risk. Thus Blum and a team of collaborators are engaged in mapping the relationships between social and "natural" systems, with diversity as the key vector. As Blum explains it, ecological diversity increases as you descend into New Orleans' topographical bowl, while social diversity declines.[63] While Blum and his team carefully avoid making value-laden statements, the questions raised by this study are clearly fascinating: how does community and environmental resilience map on to social and ecological diversity? The idea that poverty must be "deconcentrated" and that "mixed-income communities" are desirable—the supposed rationale behind the demolition of public housing—suggests an assumption that with diversity comes strength (it should be noted that this is not the thrust of Blum's study, which pursues a greater understanding of diversity rather than privileging it). And yet, as the previous chapter explored, tight-knit communities can achieve high levels of organization that in turn constitute forms of social "resilience." Similarly, while biodiversity is often assumed to be a good thing, new combinations of species potentially pose new threats, as Rich's article illustrates.

Blum explained to me in an interview in September 2014 that a "novel ecosystem" is the scientific corollary of "a Frankenstein community," which is the way he describes it in Rich's article. Possibly statements like this inadvertently contributed to the sense of offense with which this article was widely greeted by residents—read impressionistically (a tendency that runs counter to Blum's precise, scientific deployment of this term) the statement contributes to the idea that the Lower Ninth is somehow unnatural (or excessively "natural"). And yet this literary allegory—which, in Blum's formulation, refers to biological data, not people—is highly instructive for considering the relationship between natural and human history. It is a common mistake to confuse Dr. Frankenstein with the monster that he creates, and indeed this confusion is in some ways part of the story. To what extent can we take an ethical distance from that which we create? What responsibility do we ultimately have for the creation of a system that might turn out to exceed our ability to control it? Mary Shelley was asking these questions from the vantage point of a rapidly industrializing Britain, at a moment when human beings were fundamentally altering their relationship with the natural world. Arguably the apparition of the modern city constituted the most monstrous and dynamic human-authored machine of all.

Some residents of the Lower Ninth Ward have responded to the charge that their community is unsustainable with a move that reimagines the fine line between human beings and "nature" in the urban environment. The neighborhood has long been cut off from Bayou Bienvenue, which, prior to the 1960s, formed a stretch of wetlands which reached out to Lake Borgne and the Gulf of Mexico. Older residents can remember the day when this wetland area adjacent to the Lower Ninth's "back of town" was a place of recreation where people could hunt and fish. Crucially, it also formed a natural barrier against storm surges. The excavation of the Mississippi River Gulf Outlet in the 1960s brought saltwater to this freshwater environment, killing off trees and eroding land. With the closure of "MR-GO," Lower Ninth residents are seeking to breathe new life into this drowned cypress forest. An observation deck—installed within sight of a wary Army Corps of Engineers, without their explicit blessing—now enables residents to peer over the floodwall to what used to form a kind of natural levee system.[64]

This invitation to view the Lower Ninth Ward's border with now destroyed wetlands—and indeed to restore those wetlands—represents a desire to partially wind the clock back on the city's long project of banishing its swampy foundations. It is also a reminder of the fact that residents of the Lower Ninth Ward have long viewed their semi-rural neighborhood as the "country," which makes the post-Katrina crowning of this area as a symbol of urban blight all the more ironic. In this way again, the Lower Ninth crystallizes New Orleans' complex relationship with its surrounding waters, at the same time that many alienated residents are looking to St. Bernard, rather than Orleans Parish, as the center to which they might gravitate. In this sense, returnees, many of whom see themselves as "pioneers," are indeed staking out new, reimagined territory.

Between Land and Water: Louisiana's Retreating Frontier

When Benh Zeitlin's *Beasts of the Southern Wild* appeared in 2012, some observers suggested that the film allegorizes the Katrina experience of the Lower Ninth Ward.[65] There are some parallels. Yet the defining physical feature of its fictive community, the Bathtub, is that it exists on the "wrong side of the levee."[66] Like the inhabitants of Isle de Jean Charles, Terrebone Parish, Louisiana, the principal geographical inspiration for Zeitlin's film, the Bathtub residents reside in a watery world that they fully embrace. Their problem is not the absence of (functioning) levees, but rather the fact that adjacent urban communities live behind them. As Hushpuppy, our remarkable child-narrator, tells us at the start of the film:

> Daddy says up above the levee, on the dry side, they afraid of the water like a bunch of babies. They built the wall that cuts us off. They think we all going to drown down here. But we ain't going nowhere.

This statement of resilience belies a stark fact: as salt water invades marshes, this receding patch of land is starved of the freshwater from the Mississippi River that carries the sediment to build more land. As experts who proposed artificially engineering the river's natural flooding of coastal wetlands have long since discovered, the network of dams and locks that extend up the Mississippi's vast continental network means that the river itself now only carries a fraction of the sediment that it once carried at the dawn of the industrial era. Coastal restoration projects that involve sediment mining and land building are now underway, but currently they are nowhere near to keeping pace with coastal erosion. And most projects are time-limited. As Campanella explains, "any long-term solution to the sediment budget problem cannot have a project end-date."[67] Zeitlin's protagonists inhabit the dilemma bequeathed by a society addicted to short-term gratification and thus ill-equipped to deal with the unintended consequences of urbanization. Tragically, their community is haunted by the proximity of an end-date, which arrives in the film as a Katrina-like catastrophe.

In a mirror image of the New Orleans experience of Katrina, residents of the Bathtub who decide not to evacuate see their home swallowed up by water as a direct result of a *functioning* levee—in this case working to keep others dry. This fact both highlights the unequal protection provided by flood control systems while anticipating the most controversial scene of the film: the dynamiting of the levee on the part of the remaining Bathtub residents. This act can be seen as that of a desperately poor rural community, residing at the bottom of capitalism's pyramid, seeking survival at the expense of a modern, urban world that they define themselves against. As Hushpuppy tells us in the exuberant opening sequence of the film, "up in the dry world . . . they only got holidays once a year. They got fish stuck in plastic wrappers. They got their babies stuck in carriages. And chicken on sticks and all that kind of stuff." In contrast the film shows images of an edgy kind of freedom: dancing, costuming, drinking alcohol, fireworks. The reckless abandon that characterizes these scenes similarly drives Hushpuppy's father and his friends to destroy the levee—that has become a symbol of the straitjacketed, engineered, and highly administered world that apparently lies behind it.

As a number of critics have rightly pointed out, the wild freedom of the Bathtub community carries a strong libertarian strain. Though this is a community ostensibly living on the margins of capitalist society, arguably what one critic describes as this film's "explosion of Americana"[68] marks the Bathtub as classic frontier country. In this context the community's violent act of civil disobedience is about more than just survival: it is symbolically anti-state. This is reinforced when, following the destruction of the levee, government officials issue a mandatory evacuation of the community, placing Hushpuppy and her extended Bathtub family in a hurricane shelter where social and healthcare workers are portrayed in sinister, Foucauldian lights. As Hushpuppy comments, "it didn't look like a prison it looked more like a fish tank with no water. They say that we're here for our own good." In this way "the government"—imagined monolithically—condescendingly pathologizes its subjects, depriving them of their watery freedom, and subverting the Bathtub's strong sense of self-reliance. Even Hushpuppy's physical appearance is disturbingly disciplined in these scenes. When she and her father, Wink, escape the grim clutches of government, the viewer is rooting for them. This sequence led one critic to describe the film as a "Republican fantasy."[69]

Cedric Johnson goes so far as to write his review of *Beasts* under the subheading, "This is What Neoliberalization Looks Like!"[70] For Johnson, Zeitlin's film encapsulates the anarcho-liberal politics that he sees elsewhere defining the response of nonprofits to Hurricane Katrina. As discussed in the previous chapter, and mentioned above in relation to the Lower Ninth Ward, the popular anger at government inaction in the aftermath of the hurricane led in many cases to a fierce rejection of the state in general, that instead emphasized volunteer labor and the activities of nonprofit agencies. Arguably these activities reinforce the government inaction they ostensibly oppose, by stepping into the breach, while providing progressive cover for the neoliberal retreat of the welfare state. Where many nonprofits working in these roles only inadvertently support the ideology of a system that they outwardly seem to resist,[71] for Johnson, this move is deliberate in the context of the "cynical politics" of *Beasts of the Southern Wild*. Johnson writes that "benevolent elements of the state, such as the national guard, flood control systems, and the disaster shelter which serve as critical life lines in real disasters, are all depicted in *Beasts of the Southern Wild* as impersonal and corrupt." Moreover:

> The most apparently heroic act in the film, when Wink and his friends stuff an alligator gar fish with dynamite and bomb the levee to relieve flooding in the Bathtub is in fact, an anti-social and selfish act. . . . Here, Wink and his conspirators sabotage the public good and the safety of thousands of citizens for the benefit of their small village.[72]

The dynamiting of the floodwall is indeed a selfish act: far from being "the most apparently heroic act in the film," it is rather the most troubling one. Johnson's often very convincing analysis seemingly relies on the idea that the film (disingenuously) depicts the Bathtub community as the utopian antithesis of all that modernity is not. He suggests that "after viewing this film," despite *Beasts*'s powerful subtext on climate change, "some might walk away with the sense that the solution to our current crisis is to return to pre-industrial, quaint ways of living. We can turn back the clock, reject modern technologies like the Bathtub denizens, and live off the land (or sea) in small, autonomous communities."[73] And yet, despite its loving portrayal of the Bathtub, *Beasts of the Southern Wild*'s power lies not in an unqualified celebration of its way of life but precisely the reverse. In fact, the film seems to suggest that this community have much in common with the urban world onto which it projects its demons.

In an early scene, Wink points to an oil refinery behind the levee and tells Hushpuppy, "ain't that ugly over there. We've got the prettiest place on earth." Yet, as Patricia Yaeger points out in a strikingly insightful blog, the food that Hushpuppy brings back from her apparently fantastical journey for her dying father is carried in Styrofoam, which is itself made from oil. Moreover,

> images of acetylene torches, gas stoves, and gas engines remind us that although the film's characters are battered by the forces of global warming and their carbon footprint is small, creating

a carbon-free democracy is not their concern. The citizens of the Bathtub practice a dirty ecology, making do with what they can salvage from other waste-making classes.[74]

Just as the urban world pathologizes the scavenged world of the Bathtub, which Johnson claims evokes a "slum aesthetic,"[75] so the Bathtub denies its affinities with industrial modernity—while living on its scrap heap. In this sense, the mythical, prehistoric aurochs that haunt this film—that we see being slowly released from the melting polar ice caps—present as much of a challenge to the Bathtub as they do to the world behind the levees. Indeed, existing as they do on the frontline of climate change, the Bathtub community are among their first victims.

Hushpuppy is herself replete with survivalist mantras inculcated by her dying father. In repeatedly declaring herself "the man" she defies not only her gender and her age but her fragility as a human being: in the closing scenes of the film, when she comes face to face with the aurochs, she feels herself at one with their power. But in the scene that follows Hushpuppy must confront her father's finitude. In fact, as Yaeger points out, "the vulnerability at the heart of *Beasts* is staggering":

> Hushpuppy steers through her world in underpants, wearing white plastic boots covered in mud, her parents lost, the camera lens that follows her scratched or marred. She jousts perilously with sparklers; she lights a gas range and burns down her house; neglected and feisty, she is more wild than free, and her thoughtful face summons archetypes of abandonment.

A number of scholars, most notably bell hooks, have suggested that the depiction of a semi-naked six-year-old black girl constitutes "a crude pornography of violence" that reinforces racist stereotypes of black women. hooks suggests that the film's valorization of "nature" naturalizes relations of domination and Hushpuppy's condition of abandonment: this is the life she can expect.[76] And yet hook's review, like Johnson's, relies on the idea that she is the only critic to note that Hushpuppy does not inhabit a "vibrant" utopia but rather a brutal and often violent world. Picking up on Hushpuppy's insistence on strength and masculinity, hooks fails to see that the protagonists' evident vulnerability and craving for maternal care might complicate the message of the film itself. Indeed, while hooks charges the film with displaying "the mindset of white supremacy" that imagines "black children no matter their age" as "miniature adults," she overlooks the fact that a childlike perspective is precisely what Hushpuppy offers the viewer. Her fantasy of strength and resilience is the hubris of youth, an attitude that the film constantly offsets with images of striking precarity. In this sense, and contra the views of commentators like hooks and Johnson, *Beasts of the Southern Wild* offers no solutions or agendas. Rather, it tragically diagnoses our modern condition, wherein fantasies of perpetual survival are both necessary to continue and the root of our own self-destruction. In this sense we are all doomed to one day inhabit floodplains, whichever side of the levees—now essential in Louisiana, even with their deadly side-effects—we reside. Quite apart from being the pickaninny of racist imagination, Hushpuppy is the "philosopher-child" who expresses society's deepest, but ultimately unrealizable, wishes. As she poignantly states, "I want to be cohesive."

This is most fully encapsulated in Hushpuppy's adoption of the future anterior when she imagines "the scientists of the future" who will know that "once there was a hushpuppy and she lived with her daddy in the bathtub." Her innocent and unfaltering sense of her own self-importance is a stark commentary on the delusions of the adult world, while the film's prehistoric imagery is strongly suggestive of a temporality that exceeds Hushpuppy's anthropogenic imagination—and indeed the Anthropocene itself. This layering of perspective, in which Hushpuppy is both simultaneously an object of identification and the vessel of a childlike gaze, contrasts sharply with another, earlier and now very famous rendering of the relationship between Louisiana's natural landscape and the built, manufactured world. Robert Flaherty's *Louisiana Story* (1948), commissioned by the Standard Oil Company, is a docudrama that tells the story of the burgeoning Louisiana oil industry through the eyes of a Cajun child.[77] While the boy's parents are wary of the new oil rig established close to their home, their son is fascinated by the machinery and drawn to the friendly and benevolent workers on the site. Following a blowout, the company quickly and efficiently cleans up and moves on, with no lasting damage to the environment—or so a fictitious newspaper story tells us. While Flaherty's wetlands are visually stunning and seem to harbor an enchanting way of life, the derrick, initially a noisy, dirty interruption to the apparently pristine wilderness, by the end is allowed seamless passage through the water as it exits the site. The boy sadly wishes it farewell, sensing the opportunity it represents.

Clearly a work of propaganda, *Louisiana Story* is also prophetic. *Oil and Water*, directed and produced by Alan Robert Davis and David Winkler-Schmit, premiered at the 2014 New Orleans Film Festival.[78] Made in the shadow of the BP-oil spill and indeed Hurricane Katrina, it captures the paradoxical relationship that persists between Cajun coastal communities, fishing, and the oil industry. The filmmakers explain that while the media coverage of the oil spill focused on the ways in which the oil industry threatens Cajun culture by polluting fishing waters and cannibalizing land, it failed to report that many Cajun families remain supportive of the industry's presence in coastal Louisiana. It is essential to their livelihoods. The aim of this film is to dramatize the plight of a family directly suffering as a consequence of the environmental costs of a "modern lifestyle," one that they are simultaneously dependent on.[79] *Oil and Water* is painfully aware of the dilemma at the heart of its narrative, where *Louisiana Story* is untainted by a contradiction not yet fully apparent, and in any case obscured by the optimistic moment in which it was made.

Nonetheless, Flaherty's seductive portrait of the ultimately harmonious relationship between nature, man, and machine now has sinister overtones given what we know about the role played by the oil industry in "scoring and scouring" the Louisiana wetlands, opening them to saltwater intrusion and, ultimately, reclamation by the sea. The major role played by fossil fuel extraction and consumption in global warming and rising sea levels globalizes and dramatically magnifies the devastating local effects of the oil industry. No such vision of innocence stands unopposed in *Beasts of the Southern Wild*. Its protagonists sport a complexity that defies the claim that they are either courageous pioneers or the primitive "scroungers" constructed by the racist imagination in Katrina's wake. The film's magical realist forays demand interpretive strategies that take nothing for granted. Rather than the seamless narrative we are offered in *Louisiana Story*, which skilfully borrows from the genre of the documentary to weave its spellbinding and dangerous fiction, *Beasts* is self-consciously impure, as much generically as it is thematically. Just as its apparent critique of capitalism is in fact a tale of complicity, its apparent theme of the anti-urban returns us imaginatively to the scene behind the levees—and to New Orleans itself, which, culturally, has much in common with the Bathtub. As Hushpuppy and her girlfriends embark on their apparently magical realist journey into the waters of the Gulf, they encounter a floating bar and brothel named Elysian Fields. This sad and sleazy symbol of New Orleans culture and geography is, like the world that Hushpuppy inhabits, facing oblivion.

Conclusion: Slow Time?

"Come to a place that's on the front line of the 'end times' in our country . . . come to our great state of Louisiana, to New Orleans, and witness

one of the largest environmental catastrophes ever, the loss of the coast."
Nick Slie, artistic director of experimental theatre ensemble Mondo Bizarro,
issued this apocalyptic challenge to theatre-goers in an interview in 2010.[80]
In October 2013, Slie and collaborators at another New Orleans-based
company, ArtSpot Productions, fleshed out this challenge by opening *Cry
You One*, a site-specific, immersive performance piece which transforms the
Louisiana landscape into the scene of a funeral.[81]

   Cry You One's geographical starting point is Los Isleños Cultural and
Heritage Society Museum in St. Bernard Parish. The museum preserves the
history of the Isleños people who started arriving in South Louisiana from
the Canary Islands in the eighteenth century. Audience members are greeted
by guides who promise to take them on a journey to the "edge of Louisiana."
Before boarding the bus that transports the audience and performer-guides
alike into what is described as "the nature," the boundary between per-
formers and spectators is already blurred. "Are you dreaming?" emerges as
a refrain throughout the performance. By the time you are dancing a last
waltz for Louisiana, having been asked by "Mr C" (capitalism?), who claims
to have seduced everybody, what you might save from the debris of the
landscape, this sense of the surreal is fully realized. This last dance, followed
by a display of destroyed artifacts of late capitalist society—radios, televi-
sions, computers—and then the invitation to put mud on our faces, was
clearly about saying goodbye to a world devastated by human intervention.

   The next "act" involved boarding a boat that took us to the other
side of a canal and delivered us to the man-made levee that borders St.
Bernard and separates it from Lake Borgne and the outlying waters of the
Gulf of Mexico. The drowned cypress forest that was dramatically presented
to us, spread out as far as the eye could see, was a disturbing lesson in
how incredibly beautiful images of destruction can appear to the human
eye. This set the scene for a funereal procession for a mile or so along the
levee, followed by a horse and carriage that provided transport for weary
mourners. As is the tradition in South Louisiana, this walk was punctuated by performances, song, installations. Bread and fruit were thrown out
to audience members, and there was even a shower of what looked like
champagne on offer to those willing to catch it in their mouths. The lively
Cajun-inspired fiddle gave way to the beat of a drum that transformed the
occasion into a kind of jazz funeral. If this was a goodbye, a last supper,
it was also a celebration.[82]

   Like Hushpuppy in *Beasts of the Southern Wild*, who sees "everything
that made me flying around in invisible pieces" and senses that if any
part of this mesh is broken, all might be lost, *Cry You One* initiates audience members into a temporary community to come together and realize

their own interconnectedness, with each other and with the land. It is a dramatization of various forms of solidarity, of fun, and the challenging and apocalyptic message that all this might be lost. Interestingly, though clearly rooted in the place-specific story of Louisiana's land loss, *Cry You One*, since I participated in one of the first performances in St. Bernard in October 2013, has gone on an extended tour across the United States. In inviting Americans beyond Louisiana to engage in this frightening act of witnessing, *Cry You One* not only brings to national attention the fact that large parts of U.S. territory are falling into the sea. By asking Americans to dance with death, it dramatizes their own complicity in a drama of modern consumerism that is sacrificing the future.

While the erosion of Louisiana's coast is visible to the naked eye, and can thus be experienced in real time, the catastrophic effects for the vast majority of Americans—who don't actually inhabit these wetlands, including New Orleanians—is postponed, delayed. As Rob Nixon argues in *Slow Violence and the Environmentalism of the Poor* (2011), "in an age that venerates instant spectacle," disasters that are "slow and long lasting" garner little attention.[83] No matter how many times the word "rapid" is inserted into sentences about Louisiana's land loss, the urgency of this catastrophe is subject to a disturbing amnesia. I locate this amnesia at the interstices of two of the temporalities treated in this book, "American time," or a time of forward-moving pressure fixated on a particular type of progress, and "Katrina time," or the time of a neoliberal, "turbo-charged" capitalism that has paradoxically dropped its vision of the future in favor of a race for instant gratification in the present. In her book, *This Changes Everything: Capital vs. the Climate* (2014), Naomi Klein argues that "market fundamentalism has, from the very first moments, systematically sabotaged our collective response to climate change, a threat that came knocking just as this ideology was reaching its zenith."[84] She suggests that, beyond all the studies that have explored the psychology behind the apparent desire to stick our heads in the sand over climate change, we need to appreciate the extent to which our current brand of capitalism depends on this attitude.

My tentative suggestion in this book is that New Orleans offers an interruptive temporality that might challenge the dominant modes of cannibalizing time and thus eclipsing the future. Like *Beasts of the Southern Wild*, this alternative temporality offers no solutions or agendas but rather diagnoses a problem and challenges us to stare it in the face—or at least dance with it. Culturally and environmentally, New Orleans dramatizes risk and precarity, and thus presents the rest of the nation with the suggestion of finitude. Its environmental and transnational legacies taunt the national imaginary not because it lies outside of that sphere but rather because it remains within, unravelling its coherence and challenging its boundaries. It is the first major U.S. metropolitan area to face the imminent threat of being reclaimed by water. The rapprochement of New Orleans with the Gulf is a fitting symbol for an age stalked by images of self-destruction.

The survival instincts kicked into gear by Katrina understandably often sought to pave over the cracks and repress—yet again—New Orleans' watery foundations; rather than to fully face up to what "living with water" might mean. Given the poisonous atmosphere that framed proposals for footprint shrinkage, in a landscape historically marked by myriad forms of environmental racism,[85] it is hardly surprising that a neighborhood like the Lower Ninth Ward was unwilling to be sacrificed. While arguments for relocating to higher ground are in many ways persuasive, it is clear that processes of this kind would—and will—take place at the expense of the poor and the disenfranchised.

And yet community resilience, without action at the governmental and indeed global levels, cannot change the fact that the city lies in a region that faces its own end within a generation or two. This brings with it a temporality that is not exactly slow, but which demands a certain kind of attention that reaches beyond that of the spectacular and the instantaneous. In October 2014, Richard Campanella speculated that those who suggested that New Orleans be abandoned after Katrina "might have been one hundred years ahead of their time. Which is to say, they were premature. But they were also prescient. And if current trends continue, and all indications are that they're going to worsen, then predicting the twenty-second century here is tough."[86] New Orleans has not accepted water as has the Bathtub. Nonetheless, as will be explored further in the concluding chapter, it fundamentally troubles what Dimock describes as the "nation's timeline"—thus putting into play new modes of survival, and platforms for reimagining the political.

6

New Orleans and the Nation

Legacies from the Future

Moira Crone's character Malcolm de Lazarus is a "not yet," a human being taught to disregard his past and rely on a "Trust" that will secure a constantly postponed and deeply uncertain future. He is positioned as an aspirant to the ascendant class of "Heirs," who have been endowed with immortality, determined to experience their privilege at the expense of the "Nats" ("Naturals"), the "diers" who make up the larger, disposable population left to squabble over dwindling resources. The spectacle of these earthly and finite existences provides entertainment for Heirs in this rigidly hierarchical and divided society. Centered on the sinking "New Orleans Islands," Crone's speculative fiction has transfigured the United States into the "United Authority," an entity that exercises a weak sovereignty over this "De-Accessioned Territory" that creates a point of stark contrast with the disinfected "Walled Urbs," the preferred residences of the dominant class. Conceived prior to Katrina but published a number of years after, *The Not Yet* (2012) stages a clash between what Zygmunt Bauman usefully describes as a weightless "liquid modernity" and a fading New Orleans physically and culturally marked by the ravages of time.[1]

For Bauman, "liquid modernity" has transcended the long-term investments of "heavy capitalism" in favor of fleeting engagements that have liberated capital from its antagonistic dance with labor. While Bauman acknowledges that capitalism was always interested in "melting the solids," "heavy modernity" envisaged new solids: "progress meant growing size and spatial expansion,"[2] symbolized by the "iron cage" of the factory in which capital and labor, unequal as they may have been, were caught in "mutual engagement." Weightless modernity "let one partner out of the cage . . . in 'liquid' modernity, it is the most elusive, those free to move without notice, who rule."[3] In the world of *The Not Yet*, it is the quite literally weightless and wealthy Heirs who rule, in contrast to the solid Nats who remain rooted to their mortality and their poverty. No longer maintained by a welfare state seeking to guarantee capital's "reserve army" of labor, these supposedly redundant bodies live in a world in which, in Bauman's words, "safe ports for trust are few and far between, and most of the time trust floats unanchored vainly seeking storm-protected havens."[4] And yet the liquid precarity of the "New Orleans Islands," the scene of a fully realized "neoliberal deluge,"[5] nonetheless harbors an alternative temporality to the "Katrina time" that I suggest, later in this chapter, is the status quo of Crone's novel.

This final chapter explores the ways in which New Orleans resists narratives of a rootless, liquid modernity—a reality that the floodwaters of Katrina undoubtedly carried with them. In so doing this conclusion seeks to examine what is at stake in the idea that the Crescent City in some respects pushes against the grain of national trends. This idea has animated each of the previous chapters: chapter 1 explored eighteenth- and nineteenth-century New Orleans as both subject and object of an American empire, and the way in which this doubled position has often cast it as an exotic, possibly foreign, colonial outpost within the larger nation. Chapter 2 traced the fundamentally incomplete process of "Americanizing" New Orleans in the twentieth century, and the way the ascendant tourist industry eventually settled on a narrative of decline that could be quaintly commodified for a national culture in step to the tune of "progress." It assessed the extent to which New Orleans' untimeliness vis-à-vis the United States transcends tourism's script. Chapters 3 and 4 suggested that Katrina brought this apparently peripheral city center-stage in the nation's tale of economic restructuring, which has both cannibalized the past and eclipsed the political imagination of the future. They explore the suggestion that displacement followed by privatization were experienced as particularly vicious assaults by New Orleans' working-class African-American residents, for whom "home" has been historically imagined as rooted, precious, and in many respects public as well. Chapter 5 charted New Orleans' intimacy with water, examining the precarious bases on which the city has claimed itself as "land." It argued that while New Orleans has historically repressed its watery foundations, its cultural archive nonetheless bears witness to the city's proximity to finitude and death. This discussion of death returns us to one of the principal concerns of the introductory chapter and it features in this concluding chapter too.

The introduction noted the risk and rewards at play in the association between New Orleans and the death drive, exploring the extent to which the cultural visibility of death in the city sets it apart from a nation that, at least at its zenith in the twentieth century, saw itself as the quintessential embodiment of the future. Arguably the destruction wrought by Katrina symbolically remade New Orleans into the blank canvass of the national imagination. Not only has this engendered a violent "flight from history" that has threatened the viability of communities in the city that reach back generations. It has also landed New Orleans squarely in the midst *not* of an optimistic, future-oriented "American Century," but rather in a neoliberal milieu that has annihilated this vision of the future—a collapsed temporality this book has named "Katrina time." The dilemma posed in this opening chapter is encapsulated by Lee Edelman's challenge to what he calls "reproductive futurism" in his polemic, *No Future* (2004). For Edelman all politics calls on and appropriates the "image of the future child," which is itself a fantasy designed to divert us from present injustices. In contrast Edelman poses the figure of the "queer" as an agent of the death drive that disrupts all political imaginings that are always already conditioned by this cynical and disingenuous appropriation of the future.[6] Edelman's warning against political opportunism is apt in the context of a post-Katrina New Orleans that has, in the ten years since Katrina, been ruthlessly reimagined as a shiny new laboratory for neoliberalism, at the expense of its poorer, largely African-American residents and their cultural history. And yet the introduction also suggested, as Nina Powers puts it, that while Edelman's thesis is "incredibly compelling" it is, "at the same time, historically dispiriting."[7] It essentially capitulates to the neoliberal mantra that "there is no alternative," while narcissistically and individualistically revelling in the corollary that has been the disastrous outcome for vulnerable residents in New Orleans and across the United States: "no future." This final chapter picks up the question of the city's critical negativity with respect to the larger nation, in order to envisage ways of imagining the future and being political that are not held hostage to an infinitely deferred endpoint: Edelman's future child or, as has been a consistent theme of this book, the mythology of progress apparently bankrupt at the end of an American Century.

The first section of this chapter explores the idea of "dead cities," as a way of charting a larger U.S. decline narrative around the themes of urban decay and the ever-increasing gap between the rich and the poor. It focuses on Chris Hedges's and Joe Sacco's collaborative work of graphic journalism, *Days of Destruction, Days of Revolt* (2012), which singles out a handful of "national sacrifice zones" in order to narrate a larger predicament: the death of the American dream.[8] I argue that while the Katrina crisis works well as a metaphor for the larger national crisis Hedges and Sacco depict, the fallout from post-storm New Orleans is also partly a consequence of the kind of representation at work in *Days of Destruction, Days of Revolt*. The second section explores David Simon's and Eric Overmyer's television series, *Treme* (2010–2013), in order to examine a mode of representation that apparently eschews the "dead cities" thesis in order to celebrate what is, in contrast, portrayed as a vital New Orleans culture.[9] And yet, despite its often sympathetic portrait of post-Katrina New Orleans and some of its political struggles, *Treme* does not, I argue, avoid the pitfalls of certain kinds of documentary projects. Neither does its variant of "New Orleans exceptionalism" ultimately escape the larger, clichéd stereotype of a New Orleans culture in love with stasis and death—one that has paved the way for the city's violent post-storm transformation. The final section returns to Moira Crone's projection of New Orleans' and the nation's future in *The Not Yet*. I suggest that in science fiction, Crone has imagined a critical temporality that is distinctly New Orleanian without sacrificing intimations of the future. This extraordinary and deeply strange post-Katrina novel thus leaves us with the suggestion that New Orleans' defiance of national trends need not simultaneously be an act of self-annihilation.

Dead Cities

In *Days of Destruction, Days of Revolt*, Chris Hedges's narrative on Camden includes one commentator who describes the city's predicament as "a slow-moving Katrina": "Camden is the poorest, richest city in America . . . It is like a third world country. You have the rulers and the rich. They control everything while the people die and perish."[10] Certainly New Orleans' status as one of the most unequal cities in America bears out the implied analogy. According to data analysed by Bloomberg in August 2014, nine years after Hurricane Katrina, New Orleans ranked the second most unequal city in America, on a par with Zambia. The only U.S. city that topped New Orleans' inequality measure was Atlanta which, as the *Times-Picayune* noted, has a "median household income" that "was $46,466, more than $12,000 higher than that of New Orleans."[11] That inequality has risen significantly since the storm suggests that New Orleans, like Camden, has been subjected to a protracted Katrina, one that has deepened the divisions so vividly on display in the late summer of 2005.[12]

As Hedges's and Sacco's reportage demonstrates, post-Katrina New Orleans underscores a crisis that is national in scope. *Days of Destruction, Days of Revolt* singles out what it identifies as four "national sacrifice zones." The desolate Reservation at Pine Ridge, Dakota, the destroyed landscape of Camden, New Jersey, the bombed out mountains of Welch, West Virginia, and the scenes of contemporary slavery in Immokalee, Florida, are the focal points for two observers who customarily attend to foreign conflict zones. These are the ravaged landscapes of what this angry book characterizes as America's war between the rich and the poor, which has crucially involved the corporate hijacking of government—and thus democracy itself. Camden, Hedges's and Sacco's signature example of urban decline, is stalked by many of the problems that trouble New Orleans: racialized poverty, homelessness, crime, dysfunctional municipal services. As in New Orleans, poverty is screened from view: "a multilane highway, a savage concrete laceration, slices through the heart of the city. It allows commuters to pass overhead, in and out of Philadelphia, without seeing the human misery below." For Hedges and Sacco, the quintessential symbol of twentieth-century mobility, the car, has perversely buried this place: "Camden," we are told, "is a dead city."[13]

In an essay of the same name, Mike Davis suggests that "dead cities" in the U.S. context suggest that "urban dereliction has become the moral and natural-historical equivalent of war."[14] Davis explains the different waves of neighborhood destruction that have occurred in inner-city areas across America since the Second World War: urban renewal and freeway construction in the 1950s and '60s; ghetto insurrection that particularly targeted commercial centers; and finally, and by far the most significant, the 1970s and '80s saw widespread "disinvestment in the older central cities" which was "led by the banks, endorsed by federal policies, and reinforced by ensuing local fiscal crises and contraction of lifeline municipal services."[15] Davis compares the consequent "urban dead zones" to the bombed-out cityscapes of post-war Europe. He observes:

> No civilization—especially not one so rich and powerful—had ever tolerated such extensive physical destruction of its urban fabric in peacetime.[16]

This tolerance for—indeed the active encouragement of—the decline of key inner-city areas across the United States contrasts starkly with attitudes toward urban destruction at the height of the industrial age. Kevin Rozario's analysis of the rapid reconstruction of Chicago after a cataclysmic fire in

1871 and San Francisco after a major earthquake and fire in 1907 points to a culture with faith in the future. He argues that "the foundations for the restoration of both Chicago and San Francisco were undoubtedly laid by an expansive industrial economy," that was in turn fired by "the art of optimism." Indeed, Rozario suggests that the narratives constructed around these events played a central role "in helping Americans to conceive of disasters as instruments of progress."[17] Rozario locates the origins of this attitude in colonial America and the Puritan tendency to interpret events as evidence of God's design. "Indeed, an argument can be made that this expectation of reformation and growth via adversity would become the sustaining force behind that most powerful of myths: America as the land of infinite possibility and renewal."[18] As Rozario's article suggests, this mythology is an ideal breeding ground for the creative destruction of capitalism,

> a (business) culture in which ruination was a necessary means of renewal and in which the demolition of obsolete products was understood to be necessary for the innovation and streamlining that supposedly stimulated economic growth and promoted urban development. In such a dynamic economic system, the decimation of a major metropolis presented itself as an opportunity for growth and expansion.[19]

And yet in more recent history, the creative destruction of capitalism has rendered whole swathes of cities "obsolete," their ruination the opportunity not for growth and expansion but rather "planned shrinkage." In this post-Katrina New Orleans stands out as an exemplar of this logic, a city that suffered both the "slow violence" of urban decline and "benign neglect" and the rapid destruction wrought by natural disaster—coupled with disaster capitalism—that enormously accelerated these trends. The pace of rebuilding in New Orleans is suggestive of a culture no longer invested in bricks and mortar but rather the liquid capital at work in abstract, speculative finance. As discussed in chapter 3, the private corporations responsible for distributing recovery dollars after Katrina soon realized that real money was to be made not in ploughing this money into rebuilding the city but rather in delaying this process for as long as possible. The "inefficiencies of profit"[20] on display in twenty-first-century New Orleans contrast sharply with the optimistic faith in future progress at work in the aftermath of disasters that unfolded at the height of "heavy capitalism." In Lee Edelman's terms, here the "figure of the future child," which accommodated the deaths of staggering numbers of construction workers in the name of progress and industry,[21] gives way to its alternative, "no future"—a time that, contrary to Edelman, is not infused with an ecstatic *jouissance* but rather stalked by hopelessness and despair.

Rozario invokes Aristotle to explain the late-nineteenth and early-twentieth-century equations of disaster and progress in the United States. He suggests that "a key ingredient of any plot is what Aristotle called the *peripeteia*, the turning point or reversal that moves a story forward . . . Without it, we have stasis. We have no story."[22] This anti-narrative is what this book has been calling "Katrina time," a moment in which the homelessness that resulted from the storms and the wreckage of tens of thousands of properties was compounded by government policy which oversaw the demolition of many more. In this sense Katrina anticipates the national foreclosure crisis that arguably originated in predatory sub-prime mortgage lending which in turn contributed to the conditions that precipitated the global financial crash of 2008. Just as African Americans in post-hurricane New Orleans faced the greatest difficulties in terms of reclaiming their homes due to a labyrinth of discriminatory fiscal contexts, so too did African Americans suffer disproportionately from the evictions that ensued across the nation as a result of the sub-prime mortgage scandal. For Hedges and Sacco, the outcome of the financial crash—which shored up the banks at the expense of ordinary people, many of whom were forced onto the streets—is the terminus of the "American dream," the anti-narrative that renders bankrupt the vision of a nation of property owners that briefly came into contact with reality (though a largely "for whites only" affair) in the postwar years. "Take a look at the American dream," says one observer in Camden, as he points to a tent city: "In today's society no one is exempt from Transitional Park. Everybody is one paycheck away from being here."[23]

In *The Price of Inequality* (2012), Nobel Prize-winning economist Joseph Stiglitz provides statistical evidence for the portrait of U.S. decline that *Days of Destruction, Days of Revolt* paints. This decline is sketched not in the terms of diminishing influence on the world stage, as has surfaced so often in recent Republican rhetoric nostalgic for imperial power. Rather it is articulated in terms of the neoliberal abandonment of the social contract. As Stiglitz explains,

> For thirty years after World War II, America grew together—
> with growth in income in every segment, but with those at the
> bottom growing faster than those at the top . . . but for the

past thirty years, we've become increasingly a nation divided; not only has the top been growing the fastest, but the bottom has actually been declining.[24]

Stiglitz argues that the redistribution of wealth upward has been supported by government policies that have helped create the context in which incentives are "directed not at creating new wealth but at taking it from others." Predatory capitalism has resulted in stagnating or declining incomes for an increasingly "hollowed-out" middle class, and despair at the bottom end of the social pyramid.[25] Minorities have suffered the most:

> Between 2005 and 2009, the typical African American household has lost 53 percent of its wealth—putting its assets at a mere 5 percent of the average white American's, and the average Hispanic household has lost 66 percent of its wealth.[26]

The precarity that has come with the Great Recession has compounded a situation that has seen the disappearance of secure jobs and the decline of wages, meaning that "more of the money is going to the top, more of the people are going toward the bottom."[27] This bottom is defined by poor health indicators and a declining life expectancy for America's poor. Interestingly for a study which has centralized a drowning New Orleans and which has turned its attention to "liquid capitalism," Stiglitz uses the aqueous metaphor for negative equity: the growing numbers of Americans who owe more on their homes than those homes are worth, are, so the terminology goes, "underwater."[28]

In contrast to Stiglitz, Patrick Sharkey's study of economic mobility deploys not a liquid metaphor to think about social paralysis but rather it invokes solidity: his study of the "inherited ghetto" is titled *Stuck in Place* (2013).[29] Like Stiglitz, Sharkey challenges the commonly held idea that the United States offers more social mobility than comparable counterparts in western Europe. In particular, he is interested in the striking fact that there has been so little improvement in the economic fortunes of the vast majority of African Americans in the decades following the Civil Rights movement. Post-Katrina New Orleans is introduced in his text as a key symbol of the persistence of the problem of concentrated racialized poverty in America. While Sharkey clearly wants to distance himself from analyses that blame black communities for their own need, in the way that the post-storm media discourse so clearly did, it is hard to avoid the conclusion that for him there is something almost pathological about the apparent attachment of African Americans to ghetto environments.

Unlike the Moynihan Report of 1965, which famously placed the burden of responsibility for black poverty on "the negro family," however well-intentioned the authors of the report may have been, Sharkey consistently identifies external factors that have shaped racial inequality. He rightly takes the federal government to task for its uneven and often punitive treatment of inner-city neighborhoods. Nonetheless, the novelty that his study apparently offers is the insight that part of the intergenerational disadvantage that parents pass on to their children is "place": "evidence suggests that the inability to advance out of the ghetto appears to be closely related to individuals' attachments to specific places—cities and metropolitan areas—that have fared poorly in the post-industrial economy."[30] According to Sharkey, this means that even if a family does advance out of poverty, they might be sucked back into it at any point due to a proximity to or enmeshment in the "ghetto environment." This poses problems for a study that privileges mobility and only recognizes economic vectors: the "sense of 'belonging'" that a person may feel "in a working class area" cannot be comprehended or contextualized, leading to the apparently irrational and self-defeating outcome that this attachment might trump "the desire to move to a new environment."[31] Sharkey notes that residential mobility isn't necessarily the only way to escape the deleterious effects of the ghetto on economic opportunity—although he implies that this is probably the most effective route out of poverty. But some of his recommendations for the alternative, neighborhood investment, do not look very different: the demolition of public housing is held up as one salutary method of altering a neighborhood's trajectory in the "long-term."[32] And yet, as Engels suggested (and as cited in chapter 4), in this scenario, the poor "are merely *shifted elsewhere!*"[33]

Sharkey's inability to recognize the potentially positive effects of working-class residential concentrations on neighborhood solidarity and potential collective action—trends discussed in more detail in chapter 4—are mirrored in the commentary of *Days of Destruction, Days of Revolt.* "Once Camden died," Hedges writes, "its carcass became a dumping ground." Joe Sacco's accompanying comic strips offer a slightly different perspective, which works to partly counteract the unremittingly bleakness that the commentary dwells on. The sequence on Joe Balzano, Hedges tells us, helps to "recreate the Camden that was lost."[34] Yet the visual representations of a thriving city go much further than this. Balzano's memories unsettle the clear bound-

ary between past and present that the commentary establishes in such a
heavy-handed way. The visual juxtaposition of different temporal moments
draw Camden's industrious past into Balzano's present, demonstrating his
agency as a storyteller as well as a rationale for his continued investment in
Camden. Similarly, Sacco's illustrations of Lolly Davis's difficult story tell a
tale of generosity and solidarity, and "great affection" for Camden in spite
of its decline.[35] Sacco's comics thus refute the idea that abandonment of
the apparently "dead city" is the only logical route to follow.

The concluding section of *Days of Destruction, Days of Revolt*, focuses
on the hope seemingly held out by the Occupy movement. This section
most transparently reveals the class identifications through which the book
is rendered: following a powerful description of neoliberal disinvestment
and the emergence of the security state, the commentary tells us "we will
all be sacrificed":

> The suffering of the other, of the Native American, the African
> American in the inner city, the unemployed coal miner, or the
> Hispanic produce picker is universal. They went first. We are
> next. The indifference we showed to the plight of the underclass,
> in Biblical terms our neighbor, haunts us. We failed them, and
> in doing so we failed ourselves. We were accomplices in our
> own demise.[36]

Thus, despite the first-person accounts glimpsed in Sacco's drawings, this
conclusion leaves no doubt that the subjects of the books are the distanced
"others" of classical social documentary (discussed in chapter 3), appropriated as prophetic commentaries on "our" fate. While the book's vision of
an unravelling American dream increasingly catching up with a beleaguered
middle class, and an elite who have "no ideas, no plans, and no vision for
the future,"[37] is convincing on one level, its language of "them and us" casts
doubt on the political vision it offers via its celebration of Occupy. The
characters presented in the book are represented separately from the movement, notably denied political agency. In this sense Occupy becomes the
political equivalent of gentrification, the salvific middle class coming to the
rescue of the underclass, just as the book's insistence that Camden is "dead"
provides a rationale if not for gentrification, then demolition. Moreover,
the book champions Occupy's refusal to "compromise" with power or even
articulate a clear agenda. This is the horizontal language of "ground zero,"
which has abandoned the idea of the state as much as it has abandoned the
post-industrial city. Here there is no clear vision of a "future child," and it
is the "others" of the text's story who suffer this withheld future the most.

The Exceptional City

This style of urban representation ostensibly finds its antithesis in David Simon's and Eric Overmyer's television series on post-Katrina New Orleans. *Treme* chronicles the post-hurricane stories of a number of fictional characters who largely reside in the famed New Orleans neighborhood of the same name. *Treme* self-consciously provides a rationale for the survival of New Orleans in defiance of those who suggested that it should not be rebuilt. As Simon has said, "this show, if we do it right, is an argument for the city."[38] It is, as many have commented, "an ode" to New Orleans culture, a loving celebration that not only dwells on music, food and, to a lesser extent—though still very much part of the series' visual vocabulary—architecture (the so-called "holy trinity" of the city's tourist industry),[39] but also its often long-suffering residents.

David Simon is of course well-known for producing the critically acclaimed television series, *The Wire* (2002–2008), which is not so distant, aesthetically and thematically, from *Days of Destruction, Days of Revolt*.[40] Indeed, many critics have noted *The Wire*'s affinities with the tradition of literary naturalism, which itself arguably emerged in the United States primarily as a medium of fictionalized social documentary—that focused largely on urban experience. Baltimore stars in *The Wire* as possibly *the* principal protagonist, and the series is based on a wealth of local knowledge and meticulous research over a long period of time.[41] And yet, according to Fredric Jameson, " 'Baltimore' is a non-existent concept" in *The Wire*. Jameson's point is paradoxical. He argues that "in *The Wire* nobody knows that other landscapes, other cities, exist: Baltimore is a complete world in itself; it is not a closed world but merely conveys the conviction that nothing exists outside it."[42] The implication is then that the action might take place anywhere—or at least anywhere in the United States. This enables the series to act as a powerful commentary on national decline, one that shines a light on the crushing and determining influence of oppressive institutions on people's lives. In contrast, as Ronald Geerts points out, "the representation of New Orleans in *Treme* rather claims the opposite: the *altérité*, the *créolité*, makes it difficult to extrapolate and to consider it as a metaphor for the United States as a whole."[43]

As Simon's "open letter" to New Orleanians—published in the *Times-Picayune* on the day of *Treme*'s premiere—demonstrates, faithfulness to the realities on the ground is central, as far as Simon is concerned, to the show's success. He writes:

> That we will be held to certain standards by New Orleanians
> goes with the territory. Beginning tonight, you are the ultimate

arbiters—the only ones we really care about—on the question of whether our storytelling alchemy has managed to make anything precious or worthy from the baser elements of fact.

Simon also insists that "at moments, if we do our jobs correctly," *Treme* "may feel real."[44] The idea that *Treme* is addressed primarily to those on the inside of New Orleans culture and that achieving a sense of "authenticity" is therefore key to the show's goals is the focus of much of the scholarly work on *Treme*.[45] What we might think of as "hinge" characters like DJ Davis McAlary (loosely based on the real-life Davis Rogan) self-reflexively dramatize the precarious position the series itself takes up, as self-appointed translator of New Orleans culture.[46] Davis sees himself as a guardian of the New Orleans music that he loves, but the fact that he himself largely identifies these traditions as hailing from black working-class neighborhoods when he is white and comes from an elite, highly privileged New Orleans family consistently positions him as a potential intruder and a fraud, with all the connotations of cultural "slumming." Indeed, the series is full of white characters who problematically imagine themselves as either custodians or protectors of black culture and people. Like *The Wire*, though involving much shorter time spans, *Treme* drew on a lot of local knowledge and talent, and clearly the series is a collective effort including vast numbers of collaborators—black and white, natives and transplants. Yet Simon's highly self-conscious "open letter" reveals his sense that the series, in spite of all good intentions, will inevitably "trespass against" New Orleanians.

Simon's letter positions himself and his team as ethnographers who, in contrast to what Jameson characterizes as the "irrelevance" of Baltimore in *The Wire*, approach New Orleans as, in Marc Augé's lexicon, an "anthropological place." For Augé this is a place

> occupied by the indigenous inhabitants who live in it, cultivate it, defend it, mark its strong points and keep its frontiers under surveillance, but who also detect in it the traces of chthonian or celestial powers, ancestors or spirits which populate and animate its private geography.[47]

This "foundation narrative" might become all the more important, argues Augé, if it has in fact been disrupted by "urban migrations, the arrival of new populations, the spread of industrial cultures"—as is the case with New Orleans. Augé clearly has in mind non-urban cultures, but I argue that his characterization of "anthropological place" largely fits the representation of New Orleans that we are offered in *Treme*. This representation fixates on what it sees as the city's cultural reverence toward "elders" and "ancestor figures," its sharp delineation between "natives" and "transplants." This representation emerges in season two in stark contrast to New York City, which functions in *Treme* as an exemplar of Augé's "non-place," the empty placeholder that he associates with "supermodernity." While for both Delmond Lambreaux and Janette Desautel, New York symbolizes ambition and indeed the future, in contrast to the backwater that New Orleans is sometimes imagined as, for this very reason it is a place of flux and movement that can never represent "home." In this sense it could be argued that *Treme* subverts Patrick Sharkey's argument, summarized above, that the urban ghetto keeps black people "stuck in place"—in part due to attachments that are incomprehensible to a worldview motivated solely by economics. *Treme* instead embraces not a rootless "liquid modernity" but rather the condition of being "in place."

While for Augé, the ethnologist is an intruder of sorts, who wants to "decipher" a culture that might appear to be perfectly natural and in need of no explanation to the indigenous population, the ethnologist also helpfully provides narratives that reinforce fantasies of origin, particularly in moments of contemporary trauma. Augé writes of the ethnologist:

> He may be tempted, like them [the indigenous inhabitants], to look back from the upheavals of the present towards an illusory past stability. When bulldozers deface the landscape, the young people run off to the city or "allochthons" move in, it is in the most concrete, the most spatial sense that the landmarks—not just of the territory, but of identity itself—are erased.[48]

This language of bulldozers, waves of new populations, and the erasure of cultural identity very precisely reflects many of the scenarios that have been playing out in post-Katrina New Orleans—scenarios that *Treme* includes in its storylines. Creighton Bernette surfaces in the first season as the principal mouthpiece of the view that New Orleans is a culture under threat. His rants on Youtube emphasize the idea that the city has been abandoned by the government and the rest of the country—that it has essentially been left to die. This is all the more outrageous, according to Creighton and, one might argue, *Treme* itself, because New Orleans is exceptional; it may embody unhealthy levels of excess culturally and politically, but:

> Day by day, year by year, New Orleans also conjures moments of artistic clarity and urban transcendence that are the best that Americans as a people can hope for. That is if we who bear

witness to them are not too jaded, too spent, and too stupid, to recognize them for what they are.[49]

This fear that New Orleans might give in to its worst instincts resonates throughout *Treme* and is most fully encapsulated by Creighton himself. Creighton is played by John Goodman, notable for his size and physique. According to Julia Leyda, this fact is not incidental: she argues that Goodman's character's fatness reflects the abjectness of New Orleans itself. "Creighton's character embodies, and provokes expressions of, America's paradoxical love and disdain for New Orleans in all its eccentricities and excesses." Significantly, Leyda suggests that "this character's abjection, most visibly signaled by his fatness, ultimately operates as a check on the political critique that his character represents in *Treme*."[50]

Leyda's article proposes that while *Treme* offers a number of more sympathetic portraits of the city's supposed decadence and hedonism—the character of trombone player Antoine Batiste being a prime example— Creighton symbolizes a pathological rendering of New Orleans. While he emerges in season one as a champion of New Orleans, his inability to control his appetite—for food or alcohol—or his temper (more sympathetically in relation to the political situation, less sympathetically with respect to his wife Toni) shows him to be a character who has lost control. This narrative reaches its denouement with his suicide in the penultimate episode of the season, portrayed as an essentially selfish and solipsistic act. Leyda speculates:

> Why did the writers choose to kill off Creighton's character after one season? Insiders say it was simply because Goodman couldn't commit longer, but why suicide rather than a stroke or other natural cause of death? If he, in his excesses and extreme emotions such as grief and righteous anger, represents the city's vocal political critique of the colossal failures that led to the devastation and loss of life and dignity, how can we interpret his defeat by despair?[51]

Creighton's act of self-destruction coincides with an increasingly fatalistic and romantic view of New Orleans: "it's had a helluva run. Now it's done. Whatever comes next is just a dream of what used to be."[52] Creighton's death by drowning vividly recalls his lecture to his Tulane students earlier in the same episode on Edna Pontellier's equivalent act in *The Awakening*.[53] In this lecture Creighton portrays Edna's suicide as spiritual renewal. In a series that envisaged itself as a vessel of cultural survival, this quasi-romanticized, semi-deluded narrative about self-destruction is highly ambivalent. For Leyda Creighton's character and fate reinforces the logic "that essentially blames New Orleans for its own destruction and pathology, much the way popular discourses about obesity distance and mark fatness as abject."[54]

Interestingly, in a preface to what is essentially a New Orleans cookbook which draws on the *Treme* brand, David Simon mentions that New Orleans is regularly cited as one of the fattest cities in the United States, and confesses that he put on weight while making the show. Recalling Nik Cohn's characterization of New Orleans as an unhealthy locale of decadence and death,[55] discussed in the introductory chapter, Simon explicitly equates the city with excess and finitude:

> The town is lethal in so many ways. Its decadence is legendary; its very physicality; a romantic argument for gluttony and sloth and debauch. From ruined shotguns to crumbling French Creole cottages to vacant business district warehouses, New Orleans actually manages to fall apart more beautifully than any other place on earth.[56]

Simon likens his attitude toward the city to a "moth to flame," possibly providing us with a potent clue as to why *Treme* seems to speak far less acutely to power than does *The Wire*. *Treme* does dwell on most of the major political issues that have stalked the post-Katrina city: police brutality; the destruction of public housing, the demolition of many viable homes without permission from the owners or inhabitants; the downsizing of public transportation, the closure of Charity Hospital, the breakup of the public school system; carpet-bagging opportunists willing to make money on the back of human misery. And yet, despite the series' purported desire to stay as close to the "real" as possible, these developments are peculiarly divorced from the larger movements that did in fact spawn them: the movement to save public housing in New Orleans is reduced to what appears to be the personal crusade of the charismatic Mardi Gras Indian chief, Albert Lambreaux. Toni Bernette, the white civil rights lawyer, becomes the principal lens through which to view police brutality. Davis McAlary takes a passing interest in a host of political issues and satirizes them in various song lyrics. Nelson Hidalgo is the principal representative of disaster capitalism in *Treme*, but his characterization veers increasingly toward the lovable rogue as the series progresses, suggesting just how weak *Treme's* political critique is. The treatment of these issues borders on the blasé, not unlike Simon's passing summary of the state of New Orleans in the cookbook: "the crime is epic and appalling. The schools, problematic at best, catastrophic at worst. Government, when it is not inert, is hilariously, shamelessly corrupt. Nothing works quite as it should. Levees collapse. Pumping stations fail."[57]

It's hard not to agree with Lynnell Thomas's conclusion that, despite some stunning footage of New Orleans, and the fact that it clearly did strike a chord with some residents, *Treme* is a sophisticated tourist narrative—for those seeking to go beyond the spaces to which tourists are usually restricted, onto more "risky" terrain.[58] In some ways this is not so far from *The Wire*. As Kecia Thompson suggests, "just as *The Wire* negotiates meaning between its predominately black docu-fictional world and its (arguably) mostly white audience, naturalist texts have a history of negotiating meaning between social classes, including the delineation of urban realities to middle-class readers."[59] Indeed, naturalism at its inception was in part a form of literary tourism, just as the forms of documentary photography to which literary naturalism has been related offered exoticized images of poverty for viewers decidedly external to the camera's purview. And yet, Fredric Jameson argues that the oppressive sense of inevitability that characterizes much realist (and, we might add, especially naturalist) fiction is interrupted in *The Wire* by a "slight crack or rift" which pierces "the seamless necessity." "In *The Wire*," he explains, "it is the Utopian future that here and there breaks through, before reality and the present again close it down."[60] Jameson refers to the numerous creative interventions in *The Wire* which momentarily appear to run against the apparent tide of events. If we agree with his analysis then we arrive at the paradoxical conclusion that the far more obviously dystopian urban drama finds ways out of the determinism that seems to ultimately direct the trajectory of a show that sometimes veers toward the fanciful.

In contrast to the assiduous attention to a multitude of structures and institutions in *The Wire*, the plot of *Treme* seems to be governed by just one over-arching character: that of New Orleans itself. In line with Simon's cookbook analysis of the city as a place of death, numerous characters portray New Orleans as stifling, suffocating, constraining. All the characters with ambition—Janette, Delmond, Annie Talarico—suspect that their beloved city is holding them back. Even the brass band tradition so celebrated in *Treme* is apparently deprived of the oxygen that jazz has apparently been exposed to in New York City. New Orleans is personified through a number of characters but possibly none more powerfully than Chief Lambreaux. Lovable, violent, stubborn and, ultimately, mortal: Lambreaux dies from cancer in the penultimate episode of the final season of *Treme*, mirroring Creighton's death in the first season on some levels; but achieving, perhaps, the cathartic release that Creighton's suicide denies his family and friends.[61] Delmond, Lambreaux's son, himself becomes a father at this point. While when the series began, Delmond was a disaffected New Orleanian having uprooted to New York, the series ends with a partial homecoming: Delmond and his partner will bring up their son with one foot in both cities, and so will keep "the tradition" alive. And yet there is a sense that the characters, and indeed *Treme* itself, has outgrown some of these traditions.

Antoine, another lovable rogue, appears to renounce his former ways and takes on the role of a responsible teacher and father. Davis McAlary, the apparently perennially immature reveller, also seems to "come of age" by the final episode: he starts performing well at work, wears a suit to Mardi Gras, and wants to become a father himself.[62] In this way *Treme* ends by very explicitly referencing the "future child" of Edelman's rhetoric. It's not at all clear though that this vision of the future is compatible with the vision of New Orleans that the series has so relentlessly invoked. Indeed, the final montage is suggestive of the idea that it is time to move on, to transcend the New Orleans of Creighton's and indeed *Treme*'s nostalgic fantasy. One can't help feeling as the final season concludes that we have arrived in a "new New Orleans" that has accepted the obsolescence of the previous model. In this sense the "future child" performs just the kind of redemptive work that Edelman's thesis warns against: it exorcises the "queerness" of New Orleans that has so preoccupied *Treme*. Like the signs on Augé's highway of super-modernity, which gestures back to "local curiosities,"[63] *Treme* retrospectively appears to provide a window not onto New Orleans' post-Katrina future but rather its past.

The problem with *Treme*, we might conclude, is that it buys whole-heartedly into the myth of New Orleans exceptionalism, which not only celebrates the city's distinctive culture and transgressiveness, but also associates it with regression. In narrative terms the transcendence of this vision is almost obligatory. The fetishization of New Orleans that occurs in *Treme*, that so undermines the political narrative the show seemed poised to dramatize, on some levels bears out Walter Benn Michaels's claim that the obsession with identity and multiculturalism in the last few decades has helped obscure the much more pressing issue of growing inequality. Michaels argues that attention to the "cultures of poverty" becomes a vehicle through which to ignore economic realities. He suggests, for example:

> Once we start insisting that working-class literature has its own value and that, as literary critics, we have done the poor an injustice by failing to appreciate their literature—you commit

yourself not only to ignoring but to erasing the inequality, not by removing the deprivation but by denying that it is deprivation.[64]

Michaels's rather literalist polemic seems to itself deny the idea that an appreciation of cultures that emerge from working-class communities might exist alongside a critique of poverty. But his work is a powerful warning against what all-too-often turns out to be apolitical fixation on cultural difference. For Thomas Jessen Adams, the compartmentalized vision that fixates on New Orleans exceptionalism is symptomatic of a much larger trend in U.S. life: the retreat of the state, the breakup of trade unions and the fragmentation of public life brought about by large-scale privatization. Adams argues that the lack of planning and structure that that have typically defined New Orleans has left it particularly wide open to neoliberalization. Therefore an aspect of New Orleans that has often been rendered exceptional—its notoriously inept, laissez faire municipal government—now, according to Adams, might be seen as "predictive." Suggesting that "New Orleans brings it all together," Adams argues, against prevailing trends that have set the study of New Orleans apart from other cities in the United States, that "New Orleans studies" post-Katrina might perform the same role that studies of Los Angeles did in the 1980s and 90s:

> New Orleans, like Los Angeles two decades ago, offers many of us interested in the American experience an apt locale to study not the exceptionalities of its cultures or peoples but the governing structures and institutions of the United States, its national history, and, perhaps, its future.[65]

Thus Adams rejects the notion of New Orleans as a protected "anthropological space" and instead claims it as representative of the nation. The problem though with the wholesale rejection of New Orleans exceptionalism is that it holds the city as rigidly to the script of national example and thus neoliberalism as the exceptionalist narrative holds it to the role of national curiosity or pariah. Neither variant of the story admits the possibility of Jameson's "Utopian moment," wherein an alternative future breaks into the relentless repetitions of the present. The final section of this concluding chapter suggests that Moira Crone's *The Not Yet* holds these two versions together: in her novel New Orleans both encapsulates the national predicament *and* suggests an alternative path, in a narrative solution that envisages a future without sacrificing New Orleans or indeed its future child.

The Liquid City

Where *Days of Destruction, Days of Revolt*, and *Treme* both affirm variants of the "dead cities" thesis, albeit by very different means, Crone's novel also imagines New Orleans through the prism of death. Hedges's and Sacco's book apparently underscores the inevitability of the neoliberal destruction of cities while Simon's and Overmyer's collaboration depicts an exceptional city determined to self-destruct. In weaving together these two possibilities in her speculative fiction, Crone dramatizes a drowning New Orleans in which liquid capital vies with liquid lives.

It is 2121 and the Constitution, and thus the United States, has been abandoned. Instead, the United Authority that replaces them is a loosely federated collection of "Walled Urbs" and "abandoned places." The Walled Urbs are inhabited by Heirs, those who have been able to purchase their immortality. Beneficiaries of "the Reveal," they have been genetically re-described, the privileged recipients of regular prodermal upgrades and the latest implants. Shielded by artificial shells that protect their re-engineered bodies, and controlled climates that keep them under largely artificial skies, this privileged class has "walled out" the vulnerabilities to which the "Nats" or "*the great Untreated*" are routinely exposed. The Nats constitute, we are told, "*an entire generation*" who "*had no future*" in a world where wealth and health has been redistributed upward.[66] This then is a disturbingly recognizable world of the superrich who can afford to insure themselves against risk, in contrast to a disposable population exposed to increasing precarity and forced to compete for diminishing resources. Notably, New Orleans does not emerge in *The Not Yet* as in any way immune to this dystopian future; indeed, as was the case post-Katrina, it emerges in Crone's novel as a drowning geography that vividly performs glaring inequalities. Though New Orleans is placed by Crone squarely in the national predicament, most of it is nonetheless situated in the De-Accessioned Gulf Territory, on the fringes of the United Authority that now exercises a "protectorate" over it. Only the engineered environment of "Re-New Orleans," unmistakably summoning the "new New Orleans" of the post-Katrina imagination, lies within the United Authority's boundaries.

We are guided through *The Not Yet* by Malcolm, the adopted child of Lazarus, a benevolent Heir who established a foundling house for "toss out" children on what has become the New Orleans Islands. Lazarus, who is over 200 years old, is concerned when it becomes apparent that the numbers of the elite are dwindling, and instead imagines a world in which "treatment" might be rolled out for all. His eccentric project thus envisages social mobility for his adopted children, for whom he establishes various "Trusts" which secure their status as "not yets"—those who eagerly await their "boundary time" and the treatment that will eventually make them over into Heirs. And yet by the end of the novel, Lazarus's social and financial investments have all but collapsed, demonstrating that his charitable model—which in no way questions the status quo—has failed. As Malcolm, who has been "waiting and waiting" for his Trust to come good, tells Lazarus, accusingly, "you told me to put off my very life."[67] In this sense Malcolm and the other foundling children are victims of cruel optimism, the literal embodiments of Edelman's "future child"—the infinitely deferred payout of a present defined by denial and precarity.

Thus in the meantime, while they wait, Lazarus sends his children out to act in the Sim shows, as a way of building up their Trusts. By the end of the novel this highly exploitative industry has morphed from the displays of artifice that defined Malcolm's heyday as a child actor, to "more gritty" affairs that stage, quite literally, the spectacle of dying. These shows satisfy the appetite of the lofty, "ghostly Heirs" who perversely crave physical contact with the earthly existence they have supposedly left behind. The De-Accessioned Gulf Territory, or the DE-AX, as it is known, has become the playground for these "earthly delights." As one character tells Malcolm, "this place just exists for their variety."[68] This fringe territory thus recalls the role of contemporary New Orleans and the service industry that has expanded considerably since Katrina.

In an essay that examines the implications of this expansion, Thomas Jessen Adams cites David Simon's comment to the *New York Times* that "lots of American places used to make things. Detroit used to make cars. Baltimore used to make steel and ships. New Orleans still makes something. It makes moments."[69] As Adams points out, Simon's remark is made uncritically, but in it he alludes to the highly commodified time that is central to the political economy of New Orleans. We might add too the fact that Simon's television series, *Treme*, in similarly manufacturing these "moments," participated in the exploitation of service-industry workers by offering precarious, transitional employment.[70] It is the exploitation of the labor of service-industry workers that animates Adams's piece, which argues that the commoditization of human beings that their work entails should be compared to slavery:

> If slavery meant the buying and selling of human beings as
> commodities, then the service economy, with its similar selling of

individuals rather than tangible, physical commodities, engendered somewhat closely related problems in a liberal, market-based society dependent on the self-ownership of free individuals. If liberal freedom grounded in possessive individualism is based on the assumption that no individual can own another, then the buying and selling of human beings in any form represents a profound cultural problem.[71]

The Not Yet brings this possibility to the fore by depicting service industry workers who are basically indentured servants, paying off a "debt" to their Trusts which in all likelihood will never be realized. Indeed, Crone has mentioned in interviews that slavery was on her mind when writing the novel.[72] The metal collars worn around the necks of the "not yets" certainly suggest the comparison. Though race is not a pronounced theme of *The Not Yet*, there are subtle undercurrents indicative of the idea that Heirs do not have dark skin: while the photographs of Lydia Greenmore as an Heir-in-waiting show her to have "dusky skin" like Malcolm's, "dark, wavy hair" and "dark eyes," her reincarnation as an Heir seems to have turned her eyes golden, narrowed her features, lightened her "overskin"—now the "palest taupe"—and her wig is ashen blonde.[73] On the one hand the distinction between Nats and Heirs in the novel could be read as a re-articulation of racial difference; on the other, Greenmore's visual transformation is suggestive of the idea that we are in a world in which those with the means can buy themselves out of the consequences of racial difference, thus emphasizing class as the determining factor. What is pronounced in the novel is the fact that the Heirs are physically insubstantial, their breathing slow, their voices rasping, their weight not much to speak of. In contrast, Malcolm finds himself "ashamed of my heat, my scent, my saliva"[74]—he and the other "Naturals" are endowed with the physical features essential for manual labor. Only they inhabit a technologically advanced world that has rendered most of them redundant, if not regarded as "human waste" then fit only for service and entertainment.

The Heirs on the other hand, while greedily consuming these "moments," have revolutionized their relationship to time. As numerous characters in the novel observe, while time continues to fascinate Heirs, largely in the form of the "diers" (and indeed dying), they are themselves caught in a suspended time, a "timeless time" in which notions of past and future have lost their meaning.[75] In this sense they are the personification of Bauman's liquid modernity, which for him has overseen the annihilation of time. Ironically the Heirs' colonization of time has made them into consumers of what Bauman describes as "instantaneity," the desire *"to pursue gratification while avoiding the consequences."*[76] Lydia constantly reiterates the idea that Heirs "don't *have* to live in consequences"—a fact captured by having eluded the ultimate consequence of death itself.[77] While the consumption of spectacles of physicality on the part of the Heirs may not be fully satisfying, gratification in the present does appear to be the endpoint of what initially presented itself as a "grand plan." Indeed, as Lydia counsels, the idea that "life should mean something, have a purpose," is a "Nat thing," an impulse that Heirs must overcome.[78] Their "floating" lives thus paradoxically represent the short-term thinking that Bauman argues characterizes liquid capitalism.

In this sense *The Not Yet* depicts a social order that has surrendered the dream of progress. While the immortality aspired to by the Heirs might appear to accentuate a national mythology characterized by attachments to the idea of an unbounded future, in fact the immortality of the Heirs has been bought at the expense of the national future. Not only has the United States been discarded but the new, undemocratic entity in its place, dominated by a single corporation, has channelled all of its resources into creating what seem to be unsustainable islands of privilege while the surrounding landscapes are subject to high levels of social deprivation, unchecked rising sea levels, and the inevitable threat of social unrest. This is a world of shrinking frontiers.

In this sense *The Not Yet* makes a distinctively twenty-first-century contribution to American science fiction. As Gerry Canavan and Eric Carl Link argue in their introduction to *The Cambridge Companion to American Science Fiction* (2015), "the science fictional imagination" has been "fundamental to the arc of history across the so-called American Century." This was a century "born in Edison's laboratories and Ford's factories," and it was these expanding visions of possibility that have fuelled American SF.[79] This is not to suggest that this genre has been defined by unqualified utopian visions; quite the contrary. Aldous Huxley's *Brave New World* (1932) is a deeply ambivalent vision of the future inspired by the British author's prophetic sense, articulated as early as 1918, that the aftermath of the First World War would see "the inevitable acceleration of American world domination."[80] While the novel itself opens in a location named "London," clearly the "World State" is the product of a globe that has been colonized by American culture. The mass production of human beings—albeit with population limits in mind—contrasts starkly with the scenario in Crone's novel, in which decreasing numbers of people are of interest to the scientific community. The messianic figure of Henry Ford who looms so large in *Brave New World* has been supplanted by Albers, a twentieth-century scientist whose discoveries, far from dramatically expanding and diversifying the economy, have overseen the catastrophic reduction of economic activity to the treatment and maintenance of wealthy Heirs.

Thus while Huxley's sense that "the future of America is the future of the world" was not for him imbued with much optimism,[81] Crone's twenty-first-century contribution seems to have moved decisively beyond it. *The Not Yet* depicts a vision in keeping with Rebekah Sheldon's claim that more recent SF centered on the United States projects a world "after America." For Sheldon, the visions of social and environmental collapse that you find in novels like Octavia Butler's *Parable of the Sower* (1994) and Cormac McCarthy's *The Road* (2006) exemplify Fredric Jameson's view that the "future frame" of SF is a "strategy of indirection" that allows us to glimpse the "unmediated, unfiltered experience of the daily life of capitalism."[82] Indeed for Sheldon, what appears to be the future frame of much contemporary American SF is in fact a form of what she characterizes as "seeing it again," of telling "*what has been*." Rather than being "near-future fantasies" they are "more accurately understood as historical fictions" that enable readers to "catch up" with the "institutionalization of crisis-forms" that have taken place over the last four decades of neoliberal economic restructuring.[83] Certainly *The Not Yet*, though featuring a clear intensification of current trends, vividly captures the predicament of today's younger generation for whom the future seems to have been indefinitely postponed.

Thus, for Sheldon and for Crone, the neoliberal abandonment of the social contract breeds a scenario in which the ideals for which "America" has historically stood cease to have meaning. And yet as Wendy Brown's work shows, neoliberal rationality has not just killed off aspirations like social mobility—which stand at the center of U.S. mythology—but has also comprehensively challenged the sovereignty of the nation-state itself. As she explains in "Waning Sovereignty, Walled Democracy" (2010), beyond the much-discussed ways in which the "transnational flows of capital, people, ideas, goods, violence and political and religious fealty" have clearly undermined the nation-state, less attention has been paid to the ways in which "the political rationalities of neoliberalism" have eroded national sovereignty: by recognizing "no sovereign apart from entrepreneurial decision-makers (large and small)," by displacing "legal and political principles (especially liberal commitments to universal inclusion, equality, liberty, and the rule of law) with market criteria" and by demoting "the political sovereign to managerial status."[84] In *The Not Yet* the United Authority does appear to have become a vehicle for managing the corporate interests of WELLFI,

which is driven solely by the logic of the market. In this sense, the novel
bears out Brown's suggestion that while the contemporary trend of installing
walls and fences to guard national boundaries conjures the aura of sovereign power, they are in fact "icons of its erosion."[85] The United Authority
is marked externally and internally by a series of walls both demarcating
the national boundaries and sealing in its privileged gated communities.
Here the architecture of security not only fragments the landscape but also
symbolizes the "ungovernability by law and politics" of the populace. As
Brown writes:

> One irony of late modern walling is that a structure taken to
> mark and enforce an inside/outside distinction—a boundary
> between "us" and "them" and between friend and enemy—appears
> as precisely the opposite when grasped as part of a complex of
> eroding lines between the police and the military, subject and
> *patria*, vigilante and state, law and lawlessness.[86]

These boundaries are comparably fragile in *The Not Yet*, and interestingly
breached repeatedly by the novel's liquid metaphors. While at first glance,
it may appear that the Nats are physically solid and earth-bound, while the
Heirs "float" in liquid time, it is imagery surrounding liquids, as opposed to
solids, that frame the novel's vocabulary of precarity. On his return to the
Islands of New Orleans at the end of the novel, Malcolm thinks back to a
time "when all were on the same, watery, unsteady footing, when everyone
knew things could change in an instant, that all was vulnerable, not some
completely vulnerable and some not vulnerable at all."[87] It is the Nats, in
real terms, who are forced to build lives on increasingly watery foundations,
haunted by memories of storms and floods like those brought by "the Great
Katrina." They have to negotiate their own physical footprints vis-à-vis this
increasingly liquid world, one that is less and less accommodating to bodies
rendered "obsolescent" by this new order. And yet, just as national fences
tend to wall out the cheap labor on which nations rely, the walls that
surround the Heirs separate them from the only bodies that they seem to
find compelling and might anchor them to meaning: mortal ones. In this
sense the Heirs too are subject to liquid precarity, not just to the forms of
liquid that condemn them to the blank present of a timeless time, but also
to the finite world beyond, that they both fear and desire.

The principal site of this fear and longing in *The Not Yet* seems to be
the New Orleans Islands, the De-Accessioned Gulf Territory hanging on to
the edges of a United Authority that has apparently lost its center. Unlike

most of the U.A., the New Orleans Islands remains the scene of human variety, where Nats and Heirs not only mix, but blend into various shades of grey in the form of the "Imposses" who attempt to pass for Heirs. In spite of the warnings issued by WELLFI to stay out of the DE-AX, it acts as a magnet for Heirs like Lazarus, whose final act of suicide vividly highlights the self-defeating structure upon which the U.A. rests. Lazarus, the product of a system that has annihilated a meaningful sense of time, longs for that meaning, and thus embraces time's ultimate expression. In this sense Crone's novel, like *Treme*, calls New Orleans into service as a symbol of death. And yet Malcolm's similarly motivated choice has a different outcome. Having managed to save his Trust, which Lazarus places in the care of Lydia Greenmore, Malcolm, seduced by the thought of a future with the inescapably earthly Camille, decides to remain a Nat. His decision is to live in time. As he refuses Lydia's invitation to escape the oncoming storm via a helicopter ride that will deliver them into a life together as Heirs, he experiences a form of unveiling:

> And, then, all at once, at least for me, Malcolm de Lazarus, for that one man, with his limits, his outline, his tale, this: the air, and the sky, merged—the wood of the pier and the crisp fabric of my jacket, the air going in and out of my mouth, my anger at her, and my adoration of her, and the terror and thrill I felt at the future, and the soft face of my Camille and the journey we had dared to imagine—became all one single thing. My life so far, and in the future, collapsed, closed in—all the boundaries were lines that led to this one instant. There was only the moment, which was a passage, an opening. This was not simple, it was not painless. It was almost too much to know.[88]

The De-Accessioned Gulf Territory thus becomes the scene of embracing not just death but the life that is bound up with that experience. Where Lazarus's is a tragic act of resistance, the outcome of Malcolm's remains deeply uncertain: the novel closes with the oncoming "roar" that might symbolize his future or the storm that annihilates that future. What seems clear is that his gesture is not to inhabit the queer time of Edelman's "no future," but rather to reintroduce the idea of the future into a social world that has banished it. For this "moment" that is not simply fleeting and transitory but which also signifies "a passage, an opening," seems to perform the formal rupture that Fredric Jameson argues is the Utopian gesture. He writes:

The Utopian form itself is the answer to the universal ideological
conviction that no alternative is possible, that there is no alternative to the system. But it asserts this by forcing us to think
the break itself, and not by offering a more traditional picture
of what things would be like after the break.

Jameson glosses this point by insisting that this is not "liberal capitulation
to the necessity of capitalism, however; it is quite the opposite, a rattling of
the bars and an intense spiritual concentration and preparation for another stage which has not yet arrived."[89] In this vein I argue that Malcolm's
gesture is itself profoundly conditioned by his location on the fringes of a
corrupt national project. The DE-AX, and particularly the Islands of New
Orleans, are the staging grounds in this novel not for a particular kind of
politics, but for an alternate temporality that might be the conditions of
possibility for the political as such. Crone achieves this not just by replaying
the disaster of the slow violence wrought by neoliberal capitalism, as in
Sheldon's account of contemporary post-apocalyptic SF, but by gesturing
beyond neoliberalism itself. As Jameson writes:

[T]he most characteristic SF does not seriously attempt to imagine
the "real" future of our social system. Rather, its multiple mock
futures serve the quite different function of transforming our
own present into the determinate past of something that is yet
to come.[90]

Conclusion: Beyond America

In this way *The Not Yet* dramatizes the ways in which liquid capitalism is
always already bound up with liquid precarity, the conditions that might
signify the demise not just of neoliberalism but of capitalism itself. The novel
thus steers us away from the deeply problematic idea that New Orleans'
culture and physical geography have sown the seeds of the city's self-destruction. Rather, the city is "the canary in the coalmine," its peripheral
location—literally and figuratively—paradoxically centralizing its role as a
theatre for the unfolding of capitalism's worst excesses. In this sense the
region is geographically and social predictive, as Crone suggests:

When I was first writing the novel in the nineties, I'd read an
article that said the two places in the country that had the

biggest gap between rich and poor were Louisiana and New York City. The idea that the wealthiest, most advanced part of our nation, New York City, was coming to the same place as a society that emerged from slavery and plantation culture—that was remarkable.[91]

Ironically though, New Orleans emerges in Crone's novel as a vehicle of solidity, of attachments rooted in time and place that transcend the short-term investments of liquid modernity, of the collapsed temporality that I have been calling "Katrina time." In this sense, while this is a way of life under threat, it offers some resistance to the weightless capitalism that arguably drives popular perceptions of New York City (the "most advanced part of our nation"). In a recent piece for the *New Yorker*, reflecting on the tenth anniversary of Hurricane Katrina, Thomas Beller notes the fact that while after 9/11, "We are all New Yorkers now" became a slogan that resonated not just across the United States but around the world, an equivalent slogan professing solidarity with New Orleanians did not take off after Katrina. And yet, Beller suggests that "We are all New Orleanians now" "is much closer to the truth, for America and for the world . . . What happened to New Orleanians on August 29, 2005, is much more likely to happen to most Americans than what happened to New Yorkers on September 11, 2001."[92] As Jarvis DeBerry asks in a piece also reflecting on the ten-year anniversary, alongside the May 2015 floods in Houston, "Let's say a person wanted to escape to a state safe from floods. Tell me, where would that person go?"[93]

The reflections on the tenth anniversary of Hurricane Katrina in the summer of 2015 consistently returned to the apparent contradiction that while post-storm New Orleans is in many respects more prosperous than ever, a significant section of the population has been, once again, left behind. In this vein the *New York Times* reported:

> In a city long marinated in fatalism, optimists are now in ascendance. They promise that an influx of bright newcomers, a burst of entrepreneurial verve and a new spirit of civic engagement have primed the city for an era of greatness, or, at least, reversed a long-running civic-disaster narrative.

And yet, it explains, "as before, there are two cities here . . . old inequities have proved to be resilient."[94] What it fails to fully acknowledge, as did so much of the tenth-anniversary coverage, is that there is something new about these inequities. They are a necessary consequence of a model of wealth creation that relies on the dispossession of society's most vulnerable. This is the truth behind the "giant workshop to test solutions to problems—in housing, education and social mobility"—that the *Times* article admits the post-Katrina city has become. There is no contradiction at work in this "tale of two cities," wherein the success of the one relies on the failure of the other—thus forecasting not the renewal but rather the abandonment of the "American dream."

"We are all New Orleanians now" is estranging precisely because it recenters a city on the fringes of the national imaginary at a moment when that imaginary seems to be losing its center. New Orleans after Katrina offers a unique vantage point from which to consider not simply the environmental and social risks of neoliberal world-making, particularly for the racialized poor. It also proposes new ways of reappraising the notion of progress that fuelled the so-called American Century, with its elision of history and its increasingly privatized understandings of utopia. In contrast, and beyond its tourist spaces, particularly black New Orleans is a place where residents nurture collective memories and public spaces. To borrow a term that has recently soared into public awareness as a result of another confrontation that has put African Americans at the center of a national debate about racism and state violence, that once again highlights the descendants of slaves as whistleblowers vis-à-vis the "American dream," it is a place where "black lives matter," materially and morally. The city's transnational horizons, its imperial and slave legacies, and its environmental precarity open it up geographically and temporally, while depriving it of the taken-for-granted, triumphalist vision of the future that has driven U.S. exceptionalism.

Post-Katrina New Orleans has not been the scene of unified resistance to the neoliberal restructuring that seems to mark the terminus of what I have here been calling "American time." But the interruptive temporality that I have argued New Orleans carries—in which the future is neither colonized by a capitalist rendition of "progress," nor eclipsed by a political economy that has lost its vision of the future—might represent the conditions of possibility for something different, for new ways of thinking not just about survival but political agency. In this sense New Orleans after Katrina seems to promise a window onto that which is yet to come, and therefore becomes a fascinating location from which to "excavate the future"[95] of a post-American world.

Notes

Introduction

1. See Pamela R. Metzger, "Doing Katrina Time," *Tulane Law Review* 81.4 (2007), 1175–1217.

2. See "After the Hurricane: Where Have All the Prisoners Gone?" *Democracy Now*, September 27, 2005, http://www.democracynow.org/2005/9/27/after_the_hurricane_where_have_all (accessed June 25, 2016).

3. See Paul A. Passavant, "Mega-Events, the Superdome and the Return of the Repressed in New Orleans" in *The Neoliberal Deluge: Hurricane Katrina, Late Capitalism, and the Remaking of New Orleans*, ed. Cedric Johnson (Minneapolis: University of Minnesota Press, 2011), 87–129 (108–09).

4. Henry R. Luce, "The American Century," *Life Magazine*, February 17, 1941, 61–65, available at: http://www.informationclearinghouse.info/article6139.htm (accessed June 28, 2016).

5. For more on the origins of this idea see Thomas M. Allen, *A Republic in Time: Temporality and Social Imagination in Nineteenth-Century America* (Chapel Hill: University of North Carolina Press, 2008).

6. See Clyde Woods, "Katrina's World: Blues, Bourbon, and the Return to the Source," *American Quarterly*, 61.3 (2009), 427–53.

7. For analysis of this emerging narrative—that has long been present but which has in recent years gained considerable ground—see George Packer, *The Unwinding: An Inner History of the New America* (London: Faber and Faber, 2013); Chris Hedges and Joe Sacco, *Days of Destruction, Days of Revolt* (New York: Nation Books, 2012); and a July 2013 interview of Barack Obama described by Jackie Calmes and Micheal D. Shear, "Obama Says Income Gap Is Fraying U.S. Social Fabric," *New York Times*, July 27, 2013, http://www.nytimes.com/2013/07/28/us/politics/obama-says-income-gap-is-fraying-us-social-fabric.html?nl=todaysheadlines&emc=edit_th_20130728&_r=0 (accessed June 25, 2016).

8. Articulated on September 2, 2005 by Clarence Page writing for the *Chicago Tribune*, this question has become the title of a musical track by Pat Metheny and Charlie Haden dedicated to the subject of Hurricane Katrina, and it has driven

much academic scholarship that has sought to elucidate Katrina's meaning for the contemporary United States.

9. See especially the discussions in Spike Lee's two epic documentaries on Katrina's aftermath, *When the Levees Broke: A Requiem in Four Acts* (DVD; HBO, 2006) and *If God is Willing and Da Creek Don't Rise* (HBO, 2011).

10. The use of the term "refugee" will be discussed more extensively in chapter 1. See also Anna Hartnell, "Domesticating Katrina: Eliding the International Coordinates of a 'Natural' Disaster," in *Challenging US Foreign Policy: America and the World in the Long Twentieth Century*, eds. Bevan Sewell and Scott Lucas (Basingstoke, UK: Palgrave Macmillan, 2011), 244–59.

11. This will be discussed in detail in chapter 1; also see: Katheryn Russell-Brown, "While Visions of Deviance Danced in Their Heads," in *After the Storm: Black Intellectuals Explore the Meaning of Hurricane Katrina*, ed. David Dante Troutt (New York: The New Press, 2006), 111–23.

12. See Hedges and Sacco, *Days of Destruction, Days of Revolt*.

13. Diane Negra, "Introduction: Old and New Media After Katrina," in Diane Negra, ed., *Old and New Media After Katrina* (New York: Palgrave Macmillan, 2010), 1–21 (16).

14. OED definitions of "crisis": "a time of intense difficulty or danger"; "a time when a difficult or important decision must be made"; "the turning point of a disease when an important change takes place, indicating either recovery or death."

15. See, for example, Barbara Eckstein, *Sustaining New Orleans: Literature, Local Memory, and the Fate of a City* (New York: Routledge, 2006) and Kevin Fox Gotham, *Authentic New Orleans: Tourism, Culture, and Race in the Big Easy* (New York: New York University Press, 2007).

16. Lynnell L. Thomas, *Desire and Disaster in New Orleans: Tourism, Race, and Historical Memory* (Durham, NC: Duke University Press, 2014), 2.

17. Nik Cohn, "Reimagining the City: New Orleans," *BBC Radio 4*, January 5, 2013, 10.30 a.m., http://www.bbc.co.uk/programmes/b01pnfjc (accessed June 25, 2016).

18. Eckstein, 31–63.

19. Tom Piazza, *Why New Orleans Matters* (New York: Harper Perennial, 2008), 3.

20. Piazza, 6.

21. Jacqueline Rose, *States of Fantasy* (Oxford: Clarendon Press, 1998), 3.

22. Donald E. Pease, *The New American Exceptionalism* (Minneapolis: University of Minnesota Press, 2009).

23. Jean Baudrillard, *America* (London: Verso, 2010).

24. Piazza, 31–32.

25. Piazza, 35.

26. Lee Edelman, *No Future: Queer Theory and the Death Drive* (Durham, NC: Duke University Press, 2004), 11.

27. For example, Chris Lloyd, "Exceptional Photographs? Images from America's Dark Side: Lynching to Abu Ghraib" (conference presentation) at American Exceptionalisms, June 15, 2013, Goldsmiths, University of London.

28. Michael P. Bibler, "Always the Tragic Jezebel: New Orleans, Katrina, and the Layered Discourse of a Doomed Southern City," *Southern Cultures*, 14.2 (2008), 6–27 (10).

29. This battle will be explored in chapter 4, but for a full account of this issue see John Arena, *Driven from New Orleans: How Nonprofits Betray Public Housing and Support Privatization* (Minneapolis: University of Minnesota Press, 2012).

30. Cedric Johnson, "Charming Accommodations: Progressive Urbanism meets Privatization in Brad Pitt's Make It Right Foundation," in *The Neoliberal Deluge*, 187–224 (199).

31. Johnson, "Charming Accommodations," 190.

32. Naomi Klein, *The Shock Doctrine: The Rise of Disaster Capitalism* (London: Penguin, 2008), 406–22.

33. Rebecca Solnit, *A Paradise Built in Hell: The Extraordinary Communities that Arise in Disaster* (New York: Penguin, 2010).

34. Klein, *The Shock Doctrine*, 413.

35. Solnit, 305.

36. Solnit, 312.

37. Solnit, 305.

38. See, for example, Rebecca Solnit, "The Ruins of Memory" in *Ruins: Documents of Contemporary Art*, ed. Brian Dillon (London: Whitechapel Gallery; Cambridge, MA: The MIT Press, 2011), 150–52, which is extracted from Solnit's collection, *Storming the Gates of Paradise* (2007).

39. William Faulkner, *Mosquitoes* (New York: Liveright, 2011), 18.

40. Faulkner, 24.

41. Eckstein, 68.

42. Andreas Huyssen, "Authentic Ruins: Products of Modernity," in *Ruins of Modernity* ed. Julia Hell and Andreas Schönle (Durham, NC: Duke University Press, 2010), 17–28 (21).

43. Julia Hell and Andreas Schönle, "Introduction," *Ruins of Modernity*, 1–14 (3–4).

44. Hell and Schönle, 1.

45. George Steinmetz, "Colonial Melancholy and Fordist Nostalgia: Ruinscapes of Namibia and Detroit," in *Ruins of Modernity*, 294–320 (301).

46. Hell and Schönle, "Introduction," 6.

47. Pease, 154.

48. Pease, 161.

49. Pease, 202–203.

50. See, for example, Fritz Breithaupt, "Rituals of Trauma: How the Media Fabricated September 11," *Media Representations of September 11*, ed. Steven Chermak, Frankie Y. Bailey, and Michelle Brown (Westport, CT: Praeger, 2003), 67–81.

51. See, for example, Barack Obama's 2004 Preface to his memoir, *Dreams from My Father: A Story of Race and Inheritance* (Edinburgh: Canongate, 2007), x.

52. George W. Bush, "Second Inaugural Address of George W. Bush," The Avalon Project at Yale Law School, January 20, 2005, http://avalon.law.yale.edu/21st_century/gbush2.asp (accessed June 26, 2016).

53. See Rob Nixon, *Slow Violence and the Environmentalism of the Poor* (Cambridge, MA: Harvard University Press, 2011).

54. Lauren Berlant, *Cruel Optimism* (Durham, NC: Duke University Press, 2011), 1.

55. "In the Wake of Katrina: New Paradigms and Social Visions," ed. Clyde Woods, *American Quarterly* 61.3 (2009).

56. M.B. Hackler, ed., *Cultures after the Hurricanes: Rhetoric and Reinvention on the Gulf Coast* (Jackson: University of Mississippi Press, 2010).

57. Henry A. Giroux, *Stormy Weather: Katrina and the Politics of Disposability* (Boulder, CO: Paradigm Publishers, 2006).

58. Michael Eric Dyson, *Come Hell or High Water: Hurricane Katrina and the Color of Disaster* (New York: Basic Civitas, 2006).

59. In fact one of the most useful literary-cultural studies of representations of New Orleans for this book was written largely prior to Katrina, though it was published just after: Barbara Eckstein's *Sustaining New Orleans* (2006).

60. Bernie Cook, *Flood of Images: Media, Memory, and Hurricane Katrina* (Austin: University of Texas Press, 2015).

61. Russ Castronovo and Susan Gillman, eds., *States of Emergency: The Object of American Studies* (Chapel Hill: University of North Carolina Press, 2009).

62. See Wai Chee Dimock, *Through Other Continents: American Literature Across Deep Time* (Princeton, NJ: Princeton University Press, 2006), 1; and Wai Chee Dimock, "World History According to Katrina," in *States of Emergency*, 143–60.

63. See especially Richard Campanella's *Bienville's Dilemma: A Historical Geography of New Orleans* (Lafayette, LA: Center for Louisiana Studies, 2008).

64. Isabel Allende, *Island Beneath the Sea*, trans. Margaret Sayers Peden (London: Fourth Estate, 2011).

65. *Trouble the Water*, dir. Tia Lessin and Carl Deal (DVD; Louverture films, 2007).

66. *Land of Opportunity*, dir. Luisa Dantas (DVD; JoLu Productions, 2010).

67. Vincanne Adams, *Markets of Sorrow, Labors of Faith: New Orleans in the Wake of Katrina* (Durham, NC: Duke University Press, 2013).

68. Rebecca Solnit and Rebecca Snedeker, eds., *Unfathomable City: A New Orleans Atlas* (Berkeley and Los Angeles: University of California Press, 2013).

69. *Beasts of the Southern Wild*, dir. Benh Zeitlin (DVD; Cinereach Productions, 2012).

70. ArtSpot Productions and Mondo Bizarro, *Cry You One*, first performed in St. Bernard Parish in October 2013, see http://www.cryyouone.com/ (accessed June 26, 2016).

71. David Simon and Eric Overmyer, *Treme* Seasons 1–4 (DVD; HBO 2011–2014).

72. Moira Crone, *The Not Yet* (New Orleans: University of New Orleans Press, 2012).

73. Zygmunt Bauman, *Liquid Modernity* (Cambridge, UK, and Malden, MA: Polity Press, 2000 and 2012); see also Zygmunt Bauman, *Liquid Times: Living in an Age of Uncertainty* (Cambridge, UK, and Malden, MA: Polity Press, 2007).

Chapter 1

1. Dave Eggers, *Zeitoun* (San Francisco: McSweeney's Books, 2009), 229.

2. George Friedman, "The Ghost City," *The New York Review of Books*, October 6, 2005, http://www.nybooks.com/articles/archives/2005/oct/06/the-ghost-city/ (accessed June 26, 2016).

3. Amy Kaplan, "Homeland Insecurities: Some Reflections on Language and Space," *Radical History Review*, 85 (2003), 82–93 (82–83).

4. Kaplan, 83–84.

5. Quoted in Richard Campanella, *Bienville's Dilemma: A Historical Geography of New Orleans* (Lafayette, LA: Center for Louisiana Studies, 2008), 91.

6. Marcus Rediker, "History from Below the Water Line: Sharks and the Atlantic Slave Trade," *New Orleans in the Atlantic World: Between Land and Sea*, ed. William Boelhower (New York: Routledge, 2013), 131–43 (131–32).

7. For a description of these distinctions that have been eroded, see Richard J. Ellis, "'I know for certain . . . that these are bad people': The Intractable Problem of Guantánamo," *Comparative American Studies*, 8.3 (2010), 169–84.

8. Jonathan M. Hansen, *Guantánamo: An American History* (New York: Hill and Wang, 2011), 12–13.

9. Hansen, *Guantánamo*, xi.

10. Niall Ferguson, *Colossus: The Rise and Fall of the American Empire* (London: Penguin, 2005).

11. Michael Hardt and Antonio Negri, *Empire* (Cambridge, MA: Harvard University Press, 2001), xiv.

12. Hardt and Negri, xiv.

13. Hansen, *Guantánamo*, xvii.

14. For example, in December 2009 President Obama told the nation: "unlike the great powers of old, we have not sought world domination. Our union was founded in resistance to oppression. We do not seek to occupy other nations. We will not claim another nation's resources or target other peoples because their faith or ethnicity is different from ours." Barack Obama, "Remarks by the President in Address to the Nation on the Way Forward in Afghanistan and Pakistan," The White House, December 1, 2009, http://www.whitehouse.gov/the-press-office/remarks-president-address-nation-way-forward-afghanistan-and-pakistan (accessed June 26, 2016).

15. Anne McClintock, "Paranoid Empire: Specters from Guantánamo and Abu Ghraib," in *States of Emergency: The Object of American Studies*, ed. Russ Castronovo and Susan Gillman (Chapel Hill: University of North Carolina Press, 2009), 88–115 (104).

16. McClintock, 104.

17. Michelle Alexander, *The New Jim Crow: Mass Incarceration in the Age of Colorblindness* (New York: The New Press, 2012), 180.

18. Alexander, 191.

19. Eggers, 320.

20. As a number of scholars and activists have pointed out, "Slavery has NOT been abolished in the United States. Section 1) of the 13th Amendment to the United States Constitution reads: Neither slavery nor involuntary servitude, except as a punishment for crime whereof the party shall have been duly convicted, shall exist within the United States, or any place subject to their jurisdiction." The House that Herman Built, http://www.hermanshouse.org/pdfs/prisonfacts.pdf (accessed June 26, 2016).

21. Angela Y. Davis, *Are Prisons Obsolete?* (New York: Seven Stories Press, 2003), 31.

22. Angela Davis, "A Lecture by Angela Davis," Tulane University, New Orleans, November 18, 2013. It is important to note here that significant strides have been made in terms of reducing the population of the jail in Orleans Parish itself (which is often misnamed "Orleans Parish Prison"). A June 2015 report by the Data Center explains that "prior to Katrina, and for most of the last 10 years, New Orleans incarcerated residents in the jail at a much higher rate than any other city in the country. In a hopeful sign going forward, the city has reduced the number of people it incarcerates on any given day by more than two-thirds." Judge Calvin Johnson (Ret.), Mathilde Laisne and Jon Wool, "Criminal Justice: Changing Course on Incarceration," The Data Center, June 2015, https://s3.amazonaws.com/gnocdc/reports/The+Data+Center_NOI10_Changing+Course+on+Incarceration.pdf (accessed June 27, 2016). As the *New York Times* reported in August 2015, however, this reduced figure still leaves the city's incarceration rate at more than twice the national average. Campbell Robertson and Richard Fausset, "10 Years After Katrina," *New York Times*, August 26, 2015, http://www.nytimes.com/interactive/2015/08/26/us/ten-years-after-katrina.html?_r=0 (accessed June 27, 2016).

23. James Forman, Jr., "Racial Critiques of Mass Incarceration: Beyond the New Jim Crow," *New York University Law Review*, 87 (2012), 101–46 (104).

24. Forman notes that the victims of this crime wave were largely African-American communities often very vocal about the need for criminal justice solutions.

25. See Ezra Klein and Evan Soltas, "Wonkbook: 11 facts about America's prison population," *Washington Post*, August 13, 2013, http://www.washingtonpost.com/blogs/wonkblog/wp/2013/08/13/wonkbook-11-facts-about-americas-prison-population (accessed June 29, 2016).

26. Alexander, 124.

27. Leonard N. Moore, *Black Rage in New Orleans: Police Brutality and African American Activism from World War II to Hurricane Katrina* (Baton Rouge: Louisiana State University Press, 2010), 2.

28. Cindy Chang, "Louisiana is the World's Prison Capital," *Times-Picayune*, May 13, 2012, http://www.nola.com/crime/index.ssf/2012/05/louisiana_is_the_worlds_prison.html (accessed June 29, 2016).

29. Bill Quigley, "Katrina Pain Index 2013: New Orleans Eight Years Later," *Huffington Post*, August 27, 2013, http://www.huffingtonpost.com/bill-quigley/katrina-pain-index-2013_b_3817165.html (accessed June 29, 2016).

30. Alexander, 205.

31. Forman, 124.

32. Christian Parenti, *Lockdown America: Police and Prisons in the Age of Crisis* (London and New York: Verso, 2008).

33. Parenti, 246.

34. Parenti, 89.

35. Alexander, 193.

36. Alexander, 198.

37. Wajahat Ali, "Dave Eggers Interview: Zeitoun—An American Muslim Hero," August 7, 2009, http://goatmilkblog.com/2009/08/07/dave-eggers-interview-zeitoun-%E2%80%93-an-american-muslim-hero/ (accessed June 29, 2016).

38. See Roopali Mukherjee, "Between Enemies and Traitors: Black Press Coverage of September 11 and the Predicaments of National 'Others,'" in *Media Representations of September 11*, ed. Steven Chermak, Frankie Y. Bailey, and Michelle Brown (Westport, CT: Praeger, 2003), 29–46.

39. Naomi Martin, "Zeitoun found not guilty on charges he tried to kill his ex-wife," *Times-Picayune*, July 30, 2013, http://www.nola.com/crime/index.ssf/2013/07/zeitoun_found_not_guilty_on_bo.html (accessed June 29, 2016).

40. For example, see Victoria Patterson, "Did Dave Eggers get Zeitoun wrong?" *Salon*, December 9, 2012, http://www.salon.com/2012/12/09/did_dave_eggers_get_zeitoun_wrong/ (accessed June 29, 2016).

41. Angela Y. Davis, *The Meaning of Freedom and Other Difficult Dialogues* (San Francisco: City Lights Books, 2012), 75.

42. Davis, *The Meaning of Freedom*, 50.

43. See Hansen, *Guantánamo*, 266–89.

44. Kaplan, 89.

45. Jonathan M. Hansen, "Guantánamo to the Rescue," *New York Times*, January 16, 2010, http://www.nytimes.com/2010/01/17/opinion/17hansen.html?_r=0 (accessed June 29, 2016).

46. Eggers, 205–06.

47. Rebecca Solnit, *A Paradise Built in Hell: The Extraordinary Communities that Arise in Disaster* (New York: Penguin, 2010), 234.

48. Linda Robertson, "How Shall We Remember New Orleans? Comparing News Coverage of Post-Katrina New Orleans and the 2008 Midwest Floods," in *Neoliberal Deluge: Hurricane Katrina, Late Capitalism, and the Remaking of New Orleans*, ed. Cedric Johnson (Minneapolis: University of Minnesota Press, 2011), 269–99 (274).

49. Quoted in Solnit, 237.

50. Rush Limbaugh referred to a "welfare state mentality" and claimed that "the nonblack population was just as devastated, but apparently they were able to get out." Quoted in Michael Eric Dyson, *Come Hell or High Water: Hurricane Katrina and the Color of Disaster* (New York: Basic Civitas, 2006), 181.

51. Dyson, 180.

52. See, for example, Al Sharpton's appearance in Act III of *When the Levees Broke: A Requiem in Four Acts*, dir. Spike Lee (DVD; HBO, 2006).

53. See "The Guiding Principles on Internal Displacement," United Nations, 2004, http://www.unhcr.org/43ce1cff2.html (accessed June 29, 2016).

54. Henry A. Giroux, *Stormy Weather: Katrina and the Politics of Disposability* (Boulder, CO: Paradigm Publishers, 2006), 10.

55. Giroux, 15.

56. Alexander, 218.

57. Alexander, 218.

58. Pamela R. Metzger, "Doing Katrina Time," *Tulane Law Review* 81.4 (2007), 1175–1217 (1176). It is worth noting here that "Orleans Parish Prison" is actually a commonly used misnomer for the city jail which, unlike a prison, is not set up for long-term inmates.

59. Metzger, 1177.

60. Giroux, 22.

61. Alexander 142.

62. See Orlando Patterson, *Slavery and Social Death* (Cambridge, MA: Harvard University Press, 1982).

63. Giroux, 23.

64. Alexander, 219.

65. A term that has also been applied to the Deepwater Horizon oil spill of 2010, Hurricane Sandy in 2012, and the roll-out of Obama's health care reforms in 2013.

66. Mark Thompson, "The U.S. Military in Haiti: A Compassionate Invasion," *Time*, January 16, 2010, http://content.time.com/time/specials/packages/article/0,28804,1953379_1953494_1954326,00.html (accessed June 29, 2016).

67. See Dan Kennedy, "Obama's Haiti is not Bush's Katrina," *Guardian*, January 14, 2010, http://www.theguardian.com/commentisfree/cifamerica/2010/jan/14/haiti-earthquake-robertson-obama-katrina (accessed June 29, 2016).

68. Beverly Bell, "7.0 On the Horror Scale: Notes on the Haitian Earthquake," in *Haiti Rising: Haitian History, Culture, and the Earthquake of 2010*, ed. Martin Munro (Liverpool: Liverpool University Press, 2010), 155–65 (163).

69. In the 1990s NGOs worldwide increased tenfold, from an estimated six thousand in 1990 to an estimated sixty thousand in 1998.

70. Paul Farmer, "Foreword," in Mark Schuller, *Killing with Kindness: Haiti, International Aid, and NGOs* (New Brunswick, NJ: Rutgers University Press, 2012), xi–xii.

71. See Schuller, *Killing with Kindness*.

72. The United Nations forces in post-earthquake Haiti have taken the lead in demonstrating the ways in which "aid" engenders new disasters: it is now widely believed that they are responsible for the cholera epidemic that has killed thousands of Haitians over the last few years, hospitalizing many more, and which has now spread to the neighboring countries of the Dominican Republic and Cuba.

73. Jonathan M. Katz, *The Big Truck That Went By: How the World Came to Save Haiti and Left Behind a Disaster* (New York: Palgrave Macmillan, 2013), 281.

74. Deborah Sontag, "Earthquake Relief Where Haiti Wasn't Broken," *New York Times*, July 5, 2012, http://www.nytimes.com/2012/07/06/world/americas/earthquake-relief-where-haiti-wasnt-broken.html?pagewanted=all (accessed June 29, 2016).

75. See Douglas Brinkley's contribution to Act IV of *When the Levees Broke*.

76. This involves neglect of the levees as well as a failure to enact policies that would counteract Louisiana's land loss; for a detailed discussion of these issues see chapter 5.

77. Anna Brickhouse, " 'L'Ouragan de Flammes' ('The Hurricane of Flames'): New Orleans and Transamerican Catastrophe, 1866/2005," *American Quarterly*, 59.4 (2007), 1097–1127 (1099).

78. Brickhouse, 1098.

79. Rachel Hope Cleves, "Transatlantic Revolution, National Identity, and American Exceptionalism in the Early Republic," *Reviews in American History*, 39.4 (2011), 607–16 (612).

80. See Lawrence N. Powell, *The Accidental City: Improvising New Orleans* (Cambridge, MA: Harvard University Press, 2012), 318.

81. For a recent account of this historically neglected migration, see Nathalie Dessens, *From Saint-Domingue to New Orleans: Migration and Influences* (Gainesville: University Press of Florida, 2007).

82. It was a sign of the U.S. commitment to slavery in the early nineteenth century that in this case it made an exception to the 1808 law that banned the entry of foreign slaves into the United States, in the aftermath of the abolition of the transatlantic slave trade in the British Parliament in 1807 (which itself occurred in the wake of the Haitian Revolution).

83. Brickhouse, 1106.

84. Mary A. Renda, *Taking Haiti: Military Occupation and the Culture of U.S. Imperialism 1915–1940* (Chapel Hill and London: The University of North Carolina Press, 2001).

85. J. Michael Dash, *Haiti and the United States: National Stereotypes and the Literary Imagination*, 2nd ed. (Basingstoke, UK: Macmillan Press Ltd, 1997), 1–2.

86. C. L. R. James, *The Black Jacobins: Toussaint L'Ouverture and the San Domingo Revolution* (London: Penguin, 2001).

87. See Michael P. Bibler and Jessica Adams, "Introduction: Race, Romance and Revolution," in Arna Bontemps, *Drums at Dusk* (Baton Rouge: Louisiana State University, 2009), vii–lii.

88. Michael Le Bris, "Finding the Words," in *Haiti Rising*, 29–34 (32).

89. Isabel Allende, *Island Beneath the Sea*, trans. Margaret Sayers Peden (London: Fourth Estate, 2011).

90. Allende, 6–7.

91. Ned Sublette: *The World that Made New Orleans: From Spanish Silver to Congo Square* (Chicago: Lawrence Hill Books, 2009), 143.

92. Allende, 50.

93. Allende, 228.

94. Allende, 248.

95. Allende, 221.

96. Allende, 223.

97. Rediker, 131–43.

98. Allende, 296.

99. John D. Garrigus, "The Legacies of Pre-revolutionary Saint-Domingue," in *Haiti Rising*, 115–25 (119).

100. See Deborah McDermott, "A Closer Look at Haiti," Seacoast Online, April 18, 2010, http://www.seacoastonline.com/articles/20100418-ENTERTAIN-100419801 (accessed June 27, 2016).

101. Sublette, 135.

102. See, for example, Gaiutra Bahadur, "All Souls Rising," *New York Times*, April 29, 2010, http://www.nytimes.com/2010/05/02/books/review/Bahadur-t.html?_r=0 (accessed June 27, 2016).

103. Homi Bhabha quoted in Stephen M. Hart and Wen-chin Ouyang, "Introduction: Globalization of Magical Realism: New Politics of Aesthetics," in *A Companion to Magical Realism*, ed. Stephen M. Hart and Wen-chin Ouyang (Woodbridge, UK: Tamesis, 2005), 1–22 (1).

104. Alejo Carpentier, *The Kingdom of This World*, trans. Harriet de Onís (New York: Farrar, Straus and Giroux, 2006), 45–46.

105. James Wilson, "Alejo Carpentier's Re-invention of América Latina as Real and Marvellous," in *A Companion to Magical Realism*, 67–78 (70).

106. Allende, 58.

107. Allende, 62.

108. Allende, 106.

100. Allende, 256.

110. Allende, 203.

111. Allende, 192–93.

112. Allende, 450.

113. Allende, 268.

114. Allende, 329.

115. Allende, 457.

116. Sublette, 156.

117. Sublette, 200.

118. Sublette, 109.

110. Sublette, 74.

120. Sublette, 73.

121. The theme of New Orleans exceptionalism will be returned to in chapter 6.

122. See, for example, Michael Eric Dyson, *Come Hell or High Water: Hurricane Katrina and the Color of Disaster* (New York: Basic Civitas, 2006), 179–81.

123. Scholars of the U.S. South are increasingly interested in the ways in which this seemingly all-American geography relates to the region just below it. As

the collection *Just Below South* shows, New Orleans, and in particular its links with Haiti, loom large in this reconceptualized geography. *Just Below South: Intercultural Performance in the Caribbean and the U.S. South*, ed. Jessica Adams, Michael P. Bibler and Cécile Accilien (Charlottesville and London: University of Virginia Press, 2007).

124. Emily Clark, *The Strange History of the American Quadroon: Free Women of Color in the Revolutionary Atlantic World* (Chapel Hill: The University of North Carolina Press, 2013), 9.

125. Clark, *The Strange History of the American Quadroon*, 194; 9.

126. "The Arrivals Series, Part 1: Colonial New Orleans and the Louisiana Purchase," Louisiana Endowment for the Humanities, New Orleans, October 16, 2013.

127. See, for example, Emily Clark, "How American Is New Orleans? What the Founding Era Has to Tell Us," in Samuel C. Ramer and Blair A. Ruble, *Place, Identity, and Urban Culture: Odesa and New Orleans*, Kennen Institute Occasional Paper #31 (Washington, DC, Woodrow Wilson International Center for Scholars, 2008).

128. Eggers, 335.

129. See Alexander, 40–58.

130. Clyde Woods, "Katrina's World: Blues, Bourbon, and the Return to the Source," *American Quarterly*, 61.3 (2009), 427–53.

Chapter 2

1. Jesmyn Ward, *Men We Reaped* (New York: Bloomsbury, 2013).

2. Anna Hartnell, "When Cars Become Churches: Jesmyn Ward's Disenchanted America. An Interview," *Journal of American Studies*, 50.1 (2016), 205–18.

3. See, for example, Michael Eric Dyson, *Come Hell or High Water: Hurricane Katrina and the Color of Disaster* (New York: Basic Civitas, 2006).

4. Thomas M. Allen, *A Republic in Time: Temporality and Social Imagination in Nineteenth-Century America* (Chapel Hill: University of North Carolina Press, 2008).

5. See Richard Campanella, *Bourbon Street: A History* (Baton Rouge: Louisiana State University Press, 2014), 95.

6. Barbara Eckstein, *Sustaining New Orleans: Literature, Local Memory, and the Fate of a City* (New York: Routledge, 2006), 212.

7. For details of some of the post-Katrina population changes, see Richard Campanella, "Gentrification and its Discontents: Notes from New Orleans," *New Geography*, March 1, 2013, http://www.newgeography.com/content/003526-gentrification-and-its-discontents-notes-new-orleans (accessed June 28, 2016).

8. Nativity being defined here as anybody born in Louisiana.

9. The Arrivals Series, "Part 1: Colonial New Orleans and the Louisiana Purchase," October 16, 2013, "Part 2: New Orleans in the Nineteenth Century," October 30, 2013, and "Part 3: Late Twentieth Century through Post-Katrina," November 11, 2013, Louisiana Endowment for the Humanities, New Orleans.

10. Ned Sublette: *The World that Made New Orleans: From Spanish Silver to Congo Square* (Chicago: Lawrence Hill Books, 2009), 276.

11. For an account of this particular construct, see J. Mark Souther, "Making the 'Birthplace of Jazz,'" *New Orleans on Parade: Tourism and the Transformation of the Crescent City* (Baton Rouge: Louisiana State University Press, 2006), 102–31.

12. Sublette, 275.

13. Sublette, 280.

14. Joseph G. Tregle, Jr., "Creoles and Americans," in *Creole New Orleans: Race and Americanization*, ed. Arnold R. Hirsch and Joseph Logsdon (Baton Rouge: Louisiana State University Press, 1992), 131–85.

15. John Hope Franklin interviewed in *Fauborg Tremé: The Untold Story of Black New Orleans*, dir. Dawn Logsdon and Lolis Eric Elie (DVD; Serendipity Films, 2008).

16. Sublette, 262.

17. Sublette, 262; see also Gwendolyn Midlo Hall, "The Formation of Afro-Creole Culture," in *Creole New Orleans*, 58–87 (59).

18. Sublette, 220–39.

19. Central protagonist in and author-narrator of the 1853 slave narrative, *Twelve Years a Slave* (London: Collins, 2014).

20. For an account of *Plessy vs. Ferguson*, its contexts and consequences for New Orleans, see Joseph Logsdon and Caryn Cossé Bell, "The Americanization of Black New Orleans, 1850–1900," 201–61 and Arnold R. Hirsch, "Simply a Matter of Black and White: The Transformation of Race and Politics in Twentieth-Century New Orleans," in *Creole New Orleans*, 262–319.

21. Arnold R. Hirsch and Joseph Logsdon, Introduction to "Part II: The American Challenge," *Creole New Orleans*, 91–100 (96).

22. Referring to the nation's "God-given" right to expand spatially, westwards.

23. Allen, 17–58.

24. See Allen, 54–57.

25. For a discussion of the vexed analogy between the United States and the Roman Republic, see Margaret Malamud, *Ancient Rome and Modern America* (Chichester, UK: Wiley-Blackwell, 2009).

26. Allen, 49.

27. Richard Campanella, *Bienville's Dilemma: A Historical Geography of New Orleans* (Lafayette, LA: Center for Louisiana Studies, 2008), 41.

28. Anthony J. Stanonis, *Creating the Big Easy: New Orleans and the Emergence of Modern Tourism, 1918–1945* (Athens and London: University of Georgia Press, 2006).

29. Campanella, *Bourbon Street*, 60.

30. Stanonis, 41.

31. Stanonis, 41–43.

32. Stanonis, 40.

33. Stanonis, 28.

34. Kevin Fox Gotham, *Authentic New Orleans: Tourism, Culture, and Race in the Big Easy* (New York and London: New York University Press, 2007), 96.

35. Stanonis, 65.

36. Stanonis, 30.

37. Stanonis, 56.

38. Eckstein, 31–63.

39. See Michael P. Bibler, "Always the Tragic Jezebel: New Orleans, Katrina, and the Layered Discourse of a Doomed Southern City," *Southern Cultures*, 14.2 (2008), 6–27.

40. Sublette, 135.

41. Michael E. Crutcher, Jr., *Tremé: Race and Place in a New Orleans Neighborhood* (Athens, GA: University of Georgia Press, 2010), 7.

42. This argument is initiated in Lynnell L. Thomas, "'Roots Run Deep Here': The Construction of Black New Orleans in Post-Katrina Tourism Narratives," *American Quarterly*, 61.3 (2009), 749–68, and more fully elaborated in her book-length study, *Desire and Disaster in New Orleans: Tourism, Race, and Historical Memory* (Durham, NC: Duke University Press, 2014).

43. Thomas, "'Roots Run Deep Here,'" 750–51.

44. See Logsdon and Bell, "The Americanization of Black New Orleans," *Creole New Orleans*, 230.

45. Crutcher, 37.

46. For a full account of this movement, see Alecia P. Long, *The Great Southern Babylon: Sex, Race, and Respectability in New Orleans, 1865–1920* (Baton Rouge: Louisiana State University Press, 2004).

47. Crutcher, 44.

48. Quoted in Crutcher, 60.

49. Crutcher, 50–51.

50. See Souther, *New Orleans on Parade*, 111.

51. For an account of the emergence of Mardi Gras in New Orleans, see Gotham, 22–44.

52. See Andrei Codrescu, *Hail Babylon! In Search of the American City at the End of the Millennium* (New York: St. Martin's Press, 1998).

53. Author visits to Oak Alley Plantation, Louisiana, March 2011 and November 2013.

54. Quoted in Jessica Adams, *Wounds of Returning: Race, Memory, and Property on the Postslavery Plantation* (Chapel Hill: University of North Carolina Press, 2007), 67.

55. Author visits to Oak Alley Plantation, Louisiana, March 2011 and November 2013.

56. For a full account, see Thomas, *Desire and Disaster in New Orleans*, 27–52.

57. Jessica Adams, 62.

58. *Reconstructing Creole*, dir. Jennifer John Block (DVD; Fresh Media Productions, 2007).

59. Laura functions in not dissimilar ways in the Laura Plantation's sister tour in New Orleans run by Le Monde Tours, discussed extensively in Thomas's *Desire and Disaster in New Orleans*, 53–91.

60. "Afro-Louisiana History and Genealogy 1719–1820," based on the research of Gwendolyn Midlo Hall, http://www.ibiblio.org/laslave/ (accessed June 29, 2016).

61. Jessica Adams, 55.

62. See Eric Porter, "Jazz and Revival," *American Quarterly*, 61.3 (2009), 593–613 (595–6).

63. *Faubourg Tremé: The Untold Story of Black New Orleans*, dir. Dawn Logsdon (DVD; Serendipity Films, 2008).

64. For an account of gentrification in Tremé, see Crutcher, 96–113.

65. Jessica Adams, 5.

66. Attica Locke, *The Cutting Season* (London: Serpent's Tail, 2013).

67. Christian Parenti, *Lockdown America: Police and Prisons in the Age of Crisis* (London and New York: Verso, 2008), 96.

68. For an account of the tourist industry's role in gentrification and the demolition of public housing in post-Katrina New Orleans, see John Arena, *Driven From New Orleans: How Nonprofits Betray Public Housing and Promote Privatization* (Minneapolis: University of Minnesota Press, 2012).

60. Rachel Carrico, "On Thieves, Spiritless Bodies, and Creole Soul: Dancing Through the Streets of New Orleans," *TDR: The Drama Review*, 57.1 (2013), 70–87 (78).

70. Carrico, 82.

71. Thomas, *Desire and Disaster in New Orleans*, 3.

72. Thomas, *Desire and Disaster in New Orleans*, 127–57.

73. J. Mark Souther, "The Disneyfication of New Orleans: The French Quarter as Facade in a Divided City," *Journal of American History*, 94.3 (2007), 804–11 (811).

74. Campanella, "Gentrification and its Discontents."

75. For a sense of this threat, see Mike Davis, "Foreword: Sittin' on the Porch with a Shotgun," in *New Orleans Under Reconstruction: The Crisis of Planning*, ed. Carol McMichael Reese, Michael Sorkin and Anthony Fontenot (London and New York: Verso, 2014), ix–xv.

76. Carrico, 82.

77. Gotham, 196.

78. See Nick Slie's contribution to "Session 1: Art after Katrina," Transnational Perspectives on the Futures of the Gulf South, Tulane University, November 15, 2013; Audio available online: http://media.bloomsburymediacloud.org/media/roundable-1-art-after-katrina (accessed May 29, 2014).

79. Campanella, "Gentrification and its Discontents."

80. Carol Bebelle, Interview with the author, December 4, 2013.

81. See Campanella, "Nativity as Ethnicity in America: Dynamics Between Natives and Transplants Within the United States," *Bienville's Dilemma*, 274–78.

82. This idea was most famously articulated by Barbara Bush who, on witnessing Katrina evacuees at a Houston relocation site, commented that these people were "underprivileged anyway . . . so this is working very well for them." See "Barbara Bush Calls Evacuees Better Off," *New York Times*, September 7, 2005, http://www.nytimes.com/2005/09/07/national/nationalspecial/07barbara.html?_r=0 (accessed June 29, 2016).

83. Marshall Berman, *All that is Solid Melts into Air: The Experience of Modernity* (New York: Penguin, 1988), 291.

84. Berman, 326.

85. Berman, 327.

86. Quoted in Jessica Adams, above.

87. Northup, 3.

88. *12 Years a Slave*, dir. Steve McQueen (DVD; Entertainment One, 2014).

89. David Brooks, "Katrina's Silver Lining," *New York Times*, September 8, 2005, http://www.nytimes.com/2005/09/08/opinion/08brooks.html (accessed June 29, 2016).

90. David Brooks, "The Underlying Tragedy," *New York Times*, January 14, 2010, http://www.nytimes.com/2010/01/15/opinion/15brooks.html (accessed June 29, 2016).

91. John Kennedy Toole, *A Confederacy of Dunces* (New York: Grove Press, 1980), 6; 2–3.

92. Codrescu, xxi.

93. Jane Jacobs, *The Death and Life of Great American Cities* (New York: Vintage Books, 1992).

Chapter 3

1. *Wendy and Lucy*, dir. Kelly Reichardt (DVD; Oscilloscope Laboratories, 2008).

2. Alison Willmore, "Interview: Kelly Reichardt on 'Wendy and Lucy,'" *IFC*, December 10, 2008, http://www.ifc.com/fix/2008/12/interview-kelly-reichardt-on-w (accessed June 28, 2016).

3. Gus Van Sant, "Kelly Reichardt," *BOMB* 105, Fall 2008, http://bomb-magazine.org/article/3182/kelly-reichardt (accessed June 28, 2016).

4. Lauren Berlant, *Cruel Optimism* (Durham, NC: Duke University Press, 2011).

5. Gus Van Sant.

6. Berlant, 11.

7. Berlant, 200.

8. *Trouble the Water*, dir. Tia Lessin and Carl Deal (DVD; Louverture films, 2007.

9. *Land of Opportunity*, dir. Luisa Dantas (DVD; JoLu Productions, 2010); Vincanne Adams, *Markets of Sorrow, Labors of Faith: New Orleans in the Wake of Katrina* (Durham, NC: Duke University Press, 2013).

10. *When the Levees Broke: A Requiem in Four Acts*, dir. Spike Lee (DVD; HBO, 2006) and *If God is Willing and Da Creek Don't Rise* (HBO, 2011).

11. Though here it should be noted that these images were rapidly censored in the United States, particularly with respect to the bodies falling from the towers; see Tom Junod, "The Falling Man," *Esquire*, September 2003, http://classic.esquire.com/the-falling-man/ (accessed June 29, 2016).

12. Fritz Breithaupt, "Rituals of Trauma: How the Media Fabricated September 11," in *Media Representations of September 11*, ed. Steven Chermak, Frankie Y. Bailey, and Michelle Brown (Westport, CT: Praeger, 2003), 67–81.

13. Ian McEwan, "Only Love and Then Oblivion," *Guardian*, September 15, 2001, http://www.theguardian.com/world/2001/sep/15/september11.politicsphilosophyandsociety2 (accessed June 29, 2016).

14. I am referring to John Updike, *Terrorist* (New York: Alfred A. Knopf, 2006), and Don DeLillo, *Falling Man* (New York: Scribner, 2007).

15. See especially Richard Gray, *After the Fall: American Literature Since 9/11* (Malden, MA: Wiley-Blackwell, 2011) and Michael Rothberg, "A Failure of the Imagination: Diagnosing the Post-9/11 Novel: A Response to Richard Gray," *American Literary History*, 21.1 (2009), 152–58.

16. Kamila Shamsie, "The Storytellers of Empire," *Guernica*, February 1, 2012, http://www.guernicamag.com/features/shamsie_02_01_2012/ (accessed June 29, 2016).

17. Most notably Jesmyn Ward's *Salvage the Bones* (New York: Bloomsbury, 2011), which is set not in New Orleans but on the Mississippi Gulf Coast; Tom Piazza's *City of Refuge* (New York: Harper Perennial, 2008) is set in New Orleans and was one of the first to appear.

18. See Diane Negra, "Introduction: Old and New Media After Katrina," in Diane Negra, ed., *Old and New Media After Katrina* (New York: Palgrave Macmillan, 2010), 1–21; and Bernie Cook, *Flood of Images: Media, Memory, and Hurricane Katrina* (Austin: University of Texas Press, 2015).

19. David Brooks, "Katrina's Silver Lining," *New York Times*, September 8, 2005, http://www.nytimes.com/2005/09/08/opinion/08brooks.html (June 29, 2016).

20. Dave Eggers, *Zeitoun* (San Francisco: McSweeney's Books, 2009); Lola Vollen and Chris Ying, eds., *Voices from the Storm: The People of New Orleans on Hurricane Katrina and its Aftermath* (San Francisco: McSweeney's Books, 2008).

21. Chris Rose, *1 Dead in Attic: After Katrina* (New York: Simon & Schuster, 2007).

22. Dan Baum, *Nine Lives: Death and Life in New Orleans* (New York: Spiegel & Grau, 2009).

23. Josh Neufeld, *A.D. New Orleans After the Deluge* (New York: Pantheon Books, 2009).

24. This point is also made by Bernie Cook in *Flood of Images*, which notes the different temporal framework that shapes the documentary feature, with its investments in historical material, in contrast to news footage which "prioritizes the moment and the future over the past," 126.

25. Robert Polidori, *After the Flood* (Gottingen: Steidl, 2006).

26. See, for example, Derrick Price, "Surveyors and Surveyed: Photography Out and About," in Liz Wells, ed., *Photography: A Critical Introduction*, 4th ed. (New York: Routledge, 2009), 65–115.

27. See "Documenting 'The Other Half': The Social Reform Photography of Jacob Riis and Lewis Hine," University of Virginia, http://xroads.virginia.edu/~ma01/davis/photography/riis/lanternslides.html (accessed June 29, 2016).

28. John Grierson quoted by Jonathan Kahana, *Intelligence Work: The Politics of American Documentary* (New York: Columbia University Press, 2008), 1.

29. Bill Nichols, *Introduction to Documentary*, 2nd ed. (Bloomington and Indianapolis: Indiana University Press, 2010), 212–13.

30. Brian Winston, "The Tradition of the Victim in Griersonian Documentary," in *New Challenges for Documentary*, ed. Alan Rosenthal (Berkeley: University of California Press, 1988), 269–87 (269).

31. David Shields, *Reality Hunger* (London: Penguin, 2010), 81.

32. Kimberly Rivers Roberts's voiceover to her own Katrina footage in *Trouble the Water*.

33. Jane Elliott, "Life Preservers: The Neoliberal Enterprise of Hurricane Katrina Survival in *Trouble the Water*, *House M.D.*, and *When the Levees Broke*," in *Old and New Media After Katrina*, ed. Diane Negra (New York: Palgrave MacMillan, 2010), 89–111 (92).

34. Elliott, 92.

35. Peter Grier, "The Great Katrina Migration," *Christian Science Monitor*, September 12, 2005, http://www.csmonitor.com/2005/0912/p01s01-ussc.html (accessed June 29, 2016).

36. Rebecca Solnit, *A Paradise Built in Hell: The Extraordinary Communities that Arise in Disaster* (New York: Penguin, 2010), 231–304.

37. Elliott, 96.

38. Referenced above.

39. Berlant, 240.

40. Elliott, 99.

41. Jay Ruby, "The Ethics of Image Making; or, 'They're Going to Put Me in the Movies. They're Going to Make a Big Star Out of Me . . .'" in *New Challenges for Documentary*, 2nd ed., ed. Alan Rosenthal and John Corner (Manchester, UK: Manchester University Press, 2005), 209–19.

42. Trouble the Water, http://www.troublethewaterfilm.com/ (accessed June 29, 2016).

43. Land of Opportunity, http://www.landofopportunitymovie.com/ (accessed June 29, 2016).

44. Land of Opportunity interactive, http://landofopportunityinteractive.com/ (accessed June 29, 2016).

45. Vincanne Adams, 173.

46. Vincanne Adams, 149.

47. See, for example, Karyn Trader-Leigh, "Understanding the Role of African American Churches and Clergy in Community Crisis Response," Joint Center for

Political and Economic Studies, Health Policy Institute, Washington, DC, 2008, http://jointcenter.org/sites/default/files/UnderstandingRoleofChurches.pdf (accessed June 29, 2016).

48. Luisa Dantas, Interview with the author, December 5, 2013.

40. Vincanne Adams, 52.

50. Vincanne Adams, 38–39.

51. Vincanne Adams, 123.

52. Vincanne Adams, 171–72.

53. Kahana, 9–11.

54. Kahana, 358.

55. Kahana, 323.

56. Solnit, 231–304.

57. Kahana, 8.

58. I am borrowing this term from Cedric Johnson, editor of *The Neoliberal Deluge: Hurricane Katrina, Late Capitalism, and the Remaking of New Orleans* (Minneapolis: University of Minnesota Press, 2011).

Chapter 4

1. William P. Quigley, *Storms Still Raging: Katrina, New Orleans and Social Justice* (BookSurge Publishing, 2008), 183.

2. Deborah Cotton, "NOPD Bait, then Arrests, the Homeless," *Times-Picayune*, July 14, 2008, http://blog.nola.com/notesonneworleans/2008/07/nopd_baits_then_arrests_the_ho.html (accessed June 29, 2016).

3. For illustrative statistics, see Bill Quigley's "New Orleans Katrina Pain Index at Ten: Who Was Left Behind," July 20, 2015, https://billquigley.word-press.com/2015/07/20/new-orleans-katrina-pain-index-at-ten-who-was-left-behind/ (accessed June 29, 2016).

4. See Henri Lefebvre, *Writings on Cities*, trans. and ed. Eleonore Kofman and Elizabeth Lebas (Malden, MA: Blackwell Publishing, 2006).

5. See, for example, Naomi Klein, "Let the People Rebuild New Orleans," *The Nation*, September 8, 2005, http://www.thenation.com/article/let-people-rebuild-new-orleans (accessed June 29, 2016).

6. Cedric Johnson, "Watching the Train Wreck or Looking for the Brake?" *Souls: A Critical Journal of Black Politics, Culture, and Society*, 14:3–4 (2013), 207–26 (209).

7. David Theo Goldberg, *The Threat of Race: Reflections on Racial Neoliberalism* (Malden, MA: Wiley-Blackwell, 2009), 70–75.

8. Goldberg, 91.

9. Quigley, *Storms Still Raging*, 254.

10. Quigley, *Storms Still Raging*, 139–41.

11. Loïc Wacquant, *Punishing the Poor: The Neoliberal Government of Social Insecurity* (Durham, NC: Duke University Press, 2009).

12. For example, the then Secretary for Housing and Urban Development, Alphonso Jackson, claimed in September 2005 that "New Orleans is not going to be as black as it was for a long time, if ever again," quoted by Lori Rodriguez and Zeke Minaya, "HUD Chief Doubts New Orleans will be as Black," *Houston Chronicle*, September 29, 2005, http://www.chron.com/news/hurricanes/article/HUD-chief-doubts-New-Orleans-will-be-as-black-1919882.php (accessed June 29, 2016).

13. John Arena, *Driven From New Orleans: How Non-Profits Betray Public Housing and Promote Privatization* (Minneapolis: University of Minnesota Press, 2012), xxv.

14. Clyde Woods, "Les Misérable of New Orleans: Trap Economics and the Asset Stripping Blues, Part 1," *American Quarterly*, 61.3 (2009), 769–96.

15. Naomi Klein, *The Shock Doctrine: The Rise of Disaster Capitalism* (London: Penguin, 2008), 415.

16. Cedric Johnson, "Introduction: The Neoliberal Deluge," in *The Neoliberal Deluge: Hurricane Katrina, Late Capitalism, and the Remaking of New Orleans*, ed. Cedric Johnson (Minneapolis: University of Minnesota Press, 2011), xvii–I (xxxii).

17. I borrow this term from Rob Nixon's book, *Slow Violence and the Environmentalism of the Poor* (Cambridge, MA: Harvard University Press, 2011).

18. Sheila Crowley quoted by M. Christine Boyer, "New Orleans Under Reconstruction: A Crisis in Planning and Human Security," in *New Orleans Under Reconstruction: The Crisis of Planning*, ed. Carol McMichael Reese, Michael Sorkin, and Anthony Fontenot (London and New York: Verso, 2014), 121–53 (145–46).

19. Lauren Berlant, *Cruel Optimism* (Durham, NC: Duke University Press, 2011); also see the discussion of this term in chapter 3.

20. Rowland Atkinson and Gary Bridge, "Introduction," *Gentrification in a Global Context: The New Urban Colonialism*, ed. Rowland Atkinson and Gary Bridge (London and New York: Routledge, 2005), 1–17.

21. Erin K. Wyly and Daniel J. Hammel, "Mapping Neo-liberal American Urbanism," in *Gentrification in a Global Context*, 18–38.

22. Neil Smith, *The New Urban Frontier: Gentrification and the Revanchist City* (London and New York: Routledge, 1996), xiii.

23. Smith, xiv.

24. Smith, 23.

25. Arena, xxii.

26. See, for example, Nicolai Ouroussoff, "High Noon in New Orleans: The Bulldozers Are Ready," *New York Times*, December 19, 2007, http://www.nytimes.com/2007/12/19/arts/design/19hous.html?_r=0 (accessed June 29, 2016).

27. Arena, xxxi.

28. Arena, xxii.

29. Al Gore quoted by Arena, xxii.

30. Arena, 87.

31. Friedrich Engels quoted by David Harvey, *Rebel Cities: From the Right to the City to the Urban Revolution* (London and New York: Verso, 2013), 16.

32. Harvey, *Rebel Cities*, 17.

33. Arena, xxxii.

34. Arena, xxxiii.

35. Arena, 55–116.

36. William P. Quigley, "Thirteen Ways of Looking at Katrina: Human and Civil Rights Left Behind Again," *Tulane Law Review*, 81.4 (2007), 955–1017 (1007).

37. Arena, 211.

38. Bill Quigley, Interview with the author, November 11, 2013.

39. Quigley, Interview.

40. Oliver Thomas quoted by Jordan Flaherty, *Floodlines: Community and Resistance from Katrina to the Jena Six* (Chicago: Haymarket Books, 2010), 186.

41. Alphonso Jackson quoted in Part 1 of *If God is Willing and Da Creek Don't Rise*, dir. Spike Lee (DVD; HBO, 2011).

42. Quigley, Interview.

43. Adrienne Dixson, "Whose Choice? A Critical Race Perspective on Charter Schools," in *The Neoliberal Deluge*, 130–51 (135).

44. Diane Ravitch, *The Death and Life of the Great American School System: How Testing and Choice are Undermining Education* (New York: Basic Books, 2010), 9.

45. Donald E. Devore and Joseph Logsdon, *Crescent City Schools: Public Education in New Orleans 1841–1991* (New Orleans: Center for Louisiana Studies, 1991), 1.

46. Scott Cowen, *The Inevitable City: The Resurgence of New Orleans and the Future of Urban America* (New York: Palgrave Macmillan, 2014), 12.

47. Cowen, 11.

48. Cowen, 19.

49. Sarah Carr, *Hope Against Hope: Three Schools, One City, and the Struggle to Educate America's Children* (New York: Bloomsbury Press, 2013).

50. Cowen, 83.

51. Carr, 104.

52. Carr, 103.

53. Carr, 246.

54. Carr, 254.

55. After Katrina, as well as supporting an overhaul of the public school system as chair of the education committee of the Bring New Orleans Back Commission, Cowen established a program that made it compulsory for all Tulane undergraduates to take a service-learning class through the Center for Public Service. While this program had the admirable aim of encouraging Tulane students to be more involved with communities in New Orleans, Cowen's account of his own misgivings about sending "his kids" onto the "frontline" are revealing. He recounts a day in August 2010 on the site of the former Iberville Housing project. "His kids" have set up a "pink Slip 'n Slide, and they're jumping and sliding right beside the kids who have all come out to play": "I approach a man leaning against a chain-link fence, swaying back and forth. I wonder if he's on drugs, or a dealer, or maybe he's just passing the time. I introduce myself and he nods . . . I clear

my throat; I may as well ask him. 'Are my kids safe here?' I send students into the city all the time, sometimes to high-crime districts. I'm responsible." Cowen, 61.

56. See Catherine Michna, "Why I Stopped Writing Recommendation Letters for Teach for America," *Slate*, October 9, 2013, http://www.slate.com/articles/life/education/2013/10/teach_for_america_recommendations_i_stopped_writing_them_and_my_colleague.html (accessed June 29, 2016).

57. Ashana Bigard, Interview with the author, October 15, 2014.

58. Bigard, Interview.

59. Bigard, Interview.

60. Kenneth J. Saltman and David A. Gabbard, eds., *Education as Enforcement: The Militarization and Corporatization of Schools* (New York: RoutledgeFalmer, 2003).

61. Devore and Logsdon, 1.

62. Catherine Michna, "Stories at the Center: Story Circles, Educational Organizing, and Fate of Neighborhood Public Schools in New Orleans," *American Quarterly*, 61.3 (2009), 529–55 (547).

63. See Kristen L. Buras, *Charter Schools, Race, and Urban Space: Where the Market Meets Grassroots Resistance* (New York: Routledge, 2014).

64. Klein, "Let the People Rebuild New Orleans."

65. Harvey, *Rebel Cities*, 4.

66. "Letter from the People of New Orleans to Our Friends and Allies," The Louisiana Justice Institute, December 15, 2006, http://louisianajusticeinstitute.blogspot.co.uk/2012/12/post-katrina-funders-and-foundations.html (accessed June 29, 2016).

67. Flaherty, *Floodlines*, 124.

68. Cedric Johnson, "The City that Care Forgot: The 'People's Reconstruction' and the Limits of Anarcho-Liberalism," conference paper delivered at "New Orleans as Subject: Against Authenticity and Exceptionalism," Tulane University, September 18–20, 2014.

69. Rebecca Solnit, *A Paradise Built in Hell: The Extraordinary Communities that Arise in Disaster* (New York: Penguin, 2010), 231–304.

70. Johnson, "The City that Care Forgot."

71. Bigard, Interview.

72. Johnson, "The City that Care Forgot."

73. Joel Dinerstein, "Second Lining Post-Katrina: Learning Community from the Prince of Wales Social Aid and Pleasure Club," *American Quarterly*, 61.3 (2009), 615–37.

74. Helen A. Regis, "Second Lines, Minstrelsy, and the Contested Landscapes of New Orleans' Afro-Creole Festivals," *Cultural Anthropology*, 14.4 (1999), 472–504.

75. Brice Miller, Interview with the author, October 17, 2014.

76. Thomas Jessen Adams and Matt Sakakeeny, organizers of "New Orleans as Subject," a conference that took place at Tulane University in September 2014.

77. Quigley, Interview.

78. Brice Miller, contributions to a roundtable on "Post-Katrina Futures" at "After Katrina: Transnational Perspectives on the Futures of the Gulf South," Tulane University, November 25, 2013.

79. Miller, "Post-Katrina Futures."

80. Abram Himelstein, Interview with the author, October 1, 2014.

81. See Rachel Breunlin, Abram Himelstein, and Ashley Nelson, "'Our Stories Told by US:' The Neighborhood Story Project in New Orleans," in *Telling Stories to Change the World: Global Voices on the Power of Narrative to Build Community and Make Social Justice Claims*, ed. Rickie Solinger, Madeline Fox, and Kayhan Irani (New York: Routledge, 2008), 75–89.

82. Paulo Freire quoted by Kristen L. Buras, "'We Have to Tell Our Story': Neo-Griots, Schooling, and the Legacy of Racial Resistance in the Other South," in Kristen L. Buras with Jim Randels, Kalamu ya Salaam, and Students at the Center, *Pedagogy, Policy, and the Privatized City: Stories of Dispossession and Defiance from New Orleans* (New York: Teachers College Press, 2010), 17–45 (17).

83. Michna, "Stories at the Center," 537–40.

84. Harvey, *Rebel Cities*, 25.

85. Jim Randels and Kalamu ya Salaam, "Scorching the Earth Isn't the Way: New Orleans Before and After," in *Pedagogy, Policy, and the Privatized City*, 15–16 (15).

86. S. Sayid and Barnor Hesse, "A War Against Politics?" Open Democracy, November 29, 2001, https://www.opendemocracy.net/democracy-war_on_terror/article_179.jsp (accessed June 29, 2016).

87. Lauren Berlant, *Cruel Optimism* (Durham, NC: Duke University Press, 2011), 259.

88. Henry A. Giroux, "Democracy, Schooling, and the Culture of Fear after September 11," in *Education as Enforcement*, ix–xxiv (xviii).

89. Kenneth Saltman, "Introduction," in *Education as Enforcement*, 1–23 (5).

90. Giroux, "Democracy, Schooling, and the Culture of Fear after September 11," xii.

91. Janice Taylor quoted in *Coming Out the Door for the Ninth Ward*, by Nine Times Social Aid and Pleasure Club (New Orleans: Neighborhood Story Project, 2006), 183.

92. Rachel Breunlin and Helen Regis, "Putting the Ninth Ward on the Map: Race, Place, and Transformation in Desire, New Orleans," *American Anthropologist*, 108.4 (2006), 744–64 (745).

93. Himelstein, Interview.

94. Regis and Breunlin, 760.

95. *Coming Out the Door for the Ninth Ward*, 9.

96. Berlant, 262.

Chapter 5

1. *When the Levees Broke: A Requiem in Four Acts*, dir. Spike Lee (DVD; HBO, 2006), Act I.

2. In this case, those deliberately flooded out of their homes were largely poor whites, although black suffering across the Mississippi valley was severe, disproportionate, and in many cases deliberately inflicted.

3. Although wealthy, powerful people do of course reside here.

4. John. M. Barry, *Rising Tide: The Great Mississippi Flood of 1927 and How it Changed America* (New York: Simon & Schuster, 1997), 374.

5. Bill Clinton, State of the Union Address, January 23, 1996, available at: http://www.washingtonpost.com/wp-srv/politics/special/states/docs/sou96.htm (accessed June 29, 2016).

6. http://levees.org/mission-and-goals-of-levees-org/ (accessed June 29, 2016).

7. http://www.leveesnotwar.org/ (accessed June 29, 2016).

8. Craig E. Colten, "Meaning of Water in the American South: Transatlantic Encounters," in *New Orleans in the Atlantic World: Between Land and Sea*, ed. William Boelhower (New York: Routledge, 2013), 51–70 (63).

9. Stephanie Houston Grey, "(Re)Imagining Ethnicity in the City of New Orleans: Katrina's Geographical Allegory," in *Seeking Higher Ground: The Hurricane Katrina Crisis, Race, and Public Policy Reader*, ed. Manning Marable and Kristen Clarke (New York: Palgrave Macmillan, 2008), 129–40 (133).

10. See Monique Verdin, "Southward into the Vanishing Lands," in *Unfathomable City: A New Orleans Atlas*, ed. Rebecca Solnit and Rebecca Snedeker (Berkeley and Los Angeles: University of California Press, 2013), 19–24.

11. Wai Chee Dimock, *Through Other Continents: American Literature Across Deep Time* (Princeton, NJ: Princeton University Press, 2006), 1.

12. Richard Campanella, *Bienville's Dilemma: A Historical Geography of New Orleans* (Lafayette, LA: Center for Louisiana Studies, 2008), 147–54.

13. *Beasts of the Southern Wild*, dir. Benh Zeitlin (DVD; Cinereach Productions, 2012).

14. Craig E. Colten, *An Unnatural Metropolis: Wresting New Orleans from Nature* (Baton Rouge: Louisiana State University Press, 2005), 2.

15. Lawrence N. Powell, *The Accidental City: Improvising New Orleans* (Cambridge, MA: Harvard University Press, 2012), 7.

16. Barry, 16.

17. Quoted by Campanella, *Bienville's Dilemma,* 15.

18. Powell, 31–32.

19. Campanella, *Bienville's Dilemma*, 112–13.

20. Campanella, *Bienville's Dilemma*, 114.

21. Powell, 3.

22. Barry, 21.

23. See Lydia Pelot-Hobbs, "Lockdown Louisiana," in *Unfathomable City*, 55–61 (59).

24. See Barry, 312–17.

25. Campanella, *Bienville's Dilemma*, 229–33.

26. Campanella, *Bienville's Dilemma*, 207.

27. Campanella, *Bienville's Dilemma*, 213.

28. Richard Campanella, "Disaster as Educator: Responses and Lessons in New Orleans, 1722–2012," keynote address delivered to "After Katrina: Transnational Perspectives on the Futures of the Gulf South," Tulane University, November 15, 2013.

29. Lauren Berlant, *Cruel Optimism* (Durham, NC: Duke University Press, 2011), 9–10.

30. Wai Chee Dimock, "World History According to Katrina," in *States of Emergency: The Object of American Studies*, ed. Russ Castronovo and Susan Gillman (Chapel Hill: University of North Carolina Press, 2009), 143–60 (147).

31. David Waggonner quoted in Rebecca Snedeker, "The Cement Lily Pad," in *Unfathomable City*, 154–58 (157).

32. David Waggonner, Interview with the author, October 13, 2014.

33. Snedeker, 158.

34. Nathaniel Rich, "Bodies," in *Unfathomable City*, 34–36 (35).

35. Carol Bebelle, Interview with the author, December 4, 2013.

36. Billy Sothern, "On a Strange Island," *Unfathomable City*, 37–47 (37).

37. Rebecca Snedeker and Rebecca Solnit, "Sinking In and Reaching Out," *Unfathomable City*, 1–12 (2; 12).

38. "The Floating Cushion: George Porter Jr. on the City's Low End," *Unfathomable City*, 116–20 (120).

39. Nathaniel Rich, "Jungleland: The Lower Ninth Ward in New Orleans Gives New Meaning to 'Urban Growth,'" *New York Times Magazine*, March 21, 2012, http://www.nytimes.com/2012/03/25/magazine/the-lower-ninth-ward-new-orleans.html?pagewanted=all&_r=0 (accessed June 28, 2016).

40. Juliette Landphair, "'The Forgotten People of New Orleans': Community, Vulnerability, and the Lower Ninth Ward," *Journal of American History*, 94.3 (2007), 837–45.

41. See, for example, Jenga Mwendo, "'Jungleland,' Really? A Lower 9th Ward Response," A Blog of the Lower 9th Ward Center for Sustainable Engagement and Development, May 2, 2012, http://blog.sustainthenine.org/2012/05/jungleland-really-a-lower-9th-ward-response.html (accessed June 28, 2016).

42. See Charles Babington, "Hastert Tries Damage Control After Remarks Hit a Nerve," *Washington Post*, September 3, 2005, http://www.washingtonpost.com/wp-dyn/content/article/2005/09/02/AR2005090202156.html (accessed June 28, 2016).

43. For a discussion of these various stages in post-Katrina planning see Carol McMichael Reese, Michael Sorkin, and Anthony Fontenot, eds., *New Orleans Under Reconstruction: The Crisis of Planning* (London and New York: Verso, 2014); for a discussion of the contexts of the "Bring New Orleans Back" Commission, see Campanella, *Bienville's Dilemma*, 344–53.

44. Dan Baum, "The Lost Year: Behind the Failure to Rebuild," *New Yorker*, August 21, 2006, http://www.newyorker.com/magazine/2006/08/21/the-lost-year

(accessed June 27, 2016).

45. Tom Wooten, *We Shall Not Be Moved: Rebuilding Home in the Wake of Katrina* (Boston: Beacon Press, 2012), 44.

46. Wooten, 112–24.

47. Campanella, *Bienville's Dilemma*, 149.

48. See Landphair, 839.

49. Campanella, *Bienville's Dilemma*, 152.

50. See Campanella, *Bienville's Dilemma*, 147–54.

51. Quoted in Baum, "The Lost Year."

52. Wooten, 119.

53. Roberta Brandes Gratz, "It Takes a Neighborhood," *New York Times*, September 28, 2010, http://opinionator.blogs.nytimes.com/2010/09/28/it-takes-a-neighborhood/ (accessed June 29, 2016).

54. See, for example, the literature produced by the nonprofit lowernine.org.

55. This abstraction stands in contrast to the sense that renters had no rights, in spite of the fact that, as with the case of public housing, the structures had often remained firmly in place.

56. Quoted in Baum, "The Lost Year."

57. See Vincanne Adams, *Markets of Sorrow, Labors of Faith: New Orleans in the Wake of Katrina* (Durham, NC: Duke University Press, 2013).

58. Quoted in Wooten, 193.

59. Richard Campanella, Interview with the author, October 10, 2014.

60. Baum, "The Lost Year."

61. Campanella, Interview.

62. Michael Blum, Interview with the author, September 30, 2014.

63. Blum, Interview.

64. Detail informed by Darryl Malek-Wiley, Interview with the author, December 3, 2013. See also Stéphane Tonnelat, "Making Sustainability Public: The Bayou Observation Deck in the Lower 9th Ward of New Orleans," trans. Eric Rosencrantz, Metropolitics, June 20, 2011, http://www.metropolitiques.eu/Making-sustainability-public-the.html (accessed June 27, 2016).

65. Ben Kenigsberg, "Beasts of the Southern Wild: A Republican Fantasy?" *Time Out Chicago*, July 6, 2012, http://www.timeout.com/chicago/film/beasts-of-the-southern-wild-a-republican-fantasy (accessed June 27, 2016).

66. Narrator in the "Making Of" film that is included in the "Extras" section of the DVD.

67. Richard Campanella, "Beneficial Use: Toward Balancing America's (Sediment) Budget," The Design Observer Group, January 2013, http://richcampanella.com/assets/pdf/article_Campanella_Beneficial%20Use%20of%20Sediment_Places%20Journal.pdf (accessed June 28, 2016).

68. A. O. Scott, "She's the Man of this Swamp: 'Beasts of the Southern Wild,'" Directed by Beinh Zeitlin," *New York Times*, June 26, 2012, http://www.nytimes.com/2012/06/27/movies/beasts-of-the-southern-wild-directed-by-benh-zeitlin.html

(accessed June 29, 2016).

69. See Kenigsberg.

70. Cedric Johnson, "Watching the Train Wreck or Looking for the Brake?" *Souls: A Critical Journal of Black Politics, Culture, and Society*, 14:3–4 (2013), 207–26.

71. And it should be noted that, as mentioned in the previous chapter, there is a fine line, but nonetheless a difference, between "self-reliance" and "self-determination." The first is a hallmark of American mythology and its neoliberal accentuation; the latter is an often left-identified aspiration that has notably been central to black nationalist ideology, but which has also more recently been cannibalized by right-identified rhetoric and the forces of neoliberalism.

72. Johnson, "Watching the Train Wreck," 212.

73. Johnson, "Watching the Train Wreck," 212.

74. Patricia Yaeger, "*Beasts of the Southern Wild* and Dirty Ecology," *Southern Spaces*, February 13, 2013, http://southernspaces.org/2013/beasts-southern-wild-and-dirty-ecology (accessed June 28, 2016).

75. Johnson, "Watching the Train Wreck," 210.

76. bell hooks, "No Love in the Wild," NewBlackMan (in Exile), September 6, 2012, http://newblackman.blogspot.co.uk/2012/09/bell-hooks-no-love-in-wild.html (accessed June 28, 2016).

77. *Louisiana Story*, dir. Robert J. Flaherty (DVD; Home Vision Entertainment, 2003).

78. *Oil and Water*, dir. Alan Robert Davis (Rob Davis Photography, 2014).

79. See Alan Robert Davis, "About: *Oil and Water*," May, 20, 2014, http://www.watchoilandwater.com/about/ (June 28, 2016).

80. Catherine Michna, "Performance and Cross-Racial Storytelling in Post-Katrina New Orleans: Interviews with John O'Neal, Carol Bebelle, and Nicholas Slie," *TDR: The Drama Review*, 57.1 (2013), 48–69. (67).

81. *Cry You One*, produced by ArtSpot Productions and Mondo Bizarro, see http://www.cryyouone.com/ (accessed June 26, 2016).

82. This account is adapted from a longer version written by the author: Anna Hartnell, "*Cry You One*: A Front-Row View of Louisiana's Slow Death," *Times Higher Education*, November 7, 2013, http://www.timeshighereducation.co.uk/features/culture/a-front-row-view-of-louisianas-slow-death/2008687.article (accessed June 29, 2016).

83. Rob Nixon, *Slow Violence and the Environmentalism of the Poor* (Cambridge, MA: Harvard University Press, 2011), 6.

84. Naomi Klein, *This Changes Everything: Capitalism vs. the Climate* (London: Allen Lane, 2014), 19.

85. See, for example, Robert D. Bullard and Beverly Wright, eds., *Race, Place, and Environmental Justice After Hurricane Katrina* (Boulder, CO: Westview Press, 2008).

86. Campanella, Interview.

Chapter 6

1. Moira Crone, *The Not Yet* (New Orleans: University of New Orleans Press, 2012); Zygmunt Bauman, *Liquid Modernity* (Cambridge, UK, and Malden, MA: Polity Press, 2000 and 2012); see also Zygmunt Bauman, *Liquid Times: Living in an Age of Uncertainty* (Cambridge, UK, and Malden, MA: Polity Press, 2007).

2. Bauman, *Liquid Modernity*, 115.

3. Bauman, *Liquid Modernity*, 120.

4. Bauman, *Liquid Modernity*, 135–36.

5. I borrow this term from Cedric Johnson, ed., *The Neoliberal Deluge: Hurricane Katrina, Late Capitalism, and the Remaking of New Orleans* (Minneapolis: University of Minnesota Press, 2011).

6. Lee Edelman, *No Future: Queer Theory and the Death Drive* (Durham, NC.: Duke University Press, 2004).

7. Nina Power, "Non-Reproductive Futurism: Rancière's Rational Equality against Edelman's Body Apolitic," *Borderlands*, 8.2 (2009), http://www.borderlands.net.au/vol8no2_2009/power_futurism.pdf (accessed June 29, 2016).

8. Chris Hedges and Joe Sacco, *Days of Destruction, Days of Revolt* (New York: Nation Books, 2012).

9. *Treme* Seasons 1–4, directed and produced by David Simon and Eric Overmyer (DVD; HBO 2011–2014).

10. Hedges and Sacco, 96.

11. Robert McClendon, "New Orleans is 2nd Worst for Income Inequality in the U.S., Roughly on Par with Zambia, Report Says," *Times-Picayune*, August 19, 2014, http://www.nola.com/politics/index.ssf/2014/08/new_orleans_is_2nd_worst_for_i.html (accessed June 29, 2016).

12. For illustrative statistics, see Bill Quigley's "New Orleans Katrina Pain Index at Ten: Who Was Left Behind," July 20, 2015, https://billquigley.wordpress.com/2015/07/20/new-orleans-katrina-pain-index-at-ten-who-was-left-behind/ (accessed June 26, 2016).

13. Hedges and Sacco, 65; 72.

14. Mike Davis, *Dead Cities and Other Tales* (New York: The New Press, 2002), 386.

15. Davis, *Dead Cities*, 389.

16. Davis, *Dead Cities*, 387.

17. Kevin Rozario, "Making Progress: Disaster Narratives and the Art of Optimism in Modern America," in *The Resilient City: How Modern Cities Recover from Disaster*, ed. Lawrence J. Vale and Thomas J. Campanella (Oxford: Oxford University Press, 2005), 27–54 (29; 28). Diane Negra also analyses Rozario's essay in relation to post-Katrina New Orleans in her introduction to her edited volume, *Old and New Media After Katrina* (New York: Palgrave Macmillan, 2010).

18. Rozario, 34.

19. Rozario, 31.

20. I borrow this term from Vincanne Adams, *Markets of Sorrow, Labors of Faith: New Orleans in the Wake of Katrina* (Durham, NC: Duke University Press, 2013).

21. According to Rozario the rebuilding of Chicago after the 1871 fire took more lives than the fire itself; see Rozario, 41.

22. Rozario, 33.

23. Hedges and Sacco, 68.

24. Joseph E. Stiglitz, *The Price of Inequality* (London: Penguin, 2013), 5.

25. Stiglitz, 7–9.

26. Stiglitz, 17.

27. Stiglitz, 11.

28. Stiglitz, 16.

29. Patrick Sharkey, *Stuck in Place: Urban Neighborhoods and the End of Progress toward Racial Equality* (Chicago: University of Chicago Press, 2013).

30. Sharkey, 21.

31. Sharkey, 33.

32. Sharkey, 169.

33. Friedrich Engels quoted by David Harvey, *Rebel Cities: From the Right to the City to the Urban Revolution* (London and New York: Verso, 2013), 17.

34. Hedges and Sacco, 77; 78.

35. Hedges and Sacco, 108.

36. Hedges and Sacco, 226–27.

37. Hedges and Sacco, 232.

38. David Simon quoted by Julia Leyda, " 'This Complicated, Colossal Failure': The Abjection of Creighton Bernette in HBO's *Treme*," *Television & New Media*, 13.3 (2012), 243–60 (247).

39. For a discussion of this idea, see Kevin Fox Gotham, *Authentic New Orleans: Tourism, Culture, and Race in the Big Easy* (New York and London: New York University Press, 2007).

40. *The Wire*, dir. David Simon (DVD; HBO, 2002–2008).

41. See Kecia Driver Thompson, " 'Deserve Got Nothing to Do With It': Black Urban Experience and the Naturalist Tradition in *The Wire*," *Studies in American Naturalism*, 7.1 (2012), 80–120.

42. Fredric Jameson, "Realism and Utopia in *The Wire*," *Criticism*, 52. 3–4 (2010), 359–72 (369).

43. Ronald Geerts, "Naturalism and Reality in *Treme*," *Excavatio*, 23 (2014), https://www.ualberta.ca/~aizen/excavatio/articles/v24/Geertsfinal.pdf (accessed May 31, 2015).

44. "HBO's 'Treme' creator David Simon explains it all for you," *Times-Picayune*, April 11, 2010, http://www.nola.com/treme-hbo/index.ssf/2010/04/hbos_treme_creator_david_simon.html (accessed June 26, 2016).

45. See, for example, Joy V. Fuqua, " 'In New Orleans, We Might Say It Like This . . .': Authenticity, Place, and HBO's *Treme*," *Television & New Media*,

13.3 (2012), 235–42 and Courtney George, "Keeping it 'Reals': Narratives of New Orleans Jazz History as represented in HBO's *Treme*," *Television & New Media*, 13.3 (2012), 235–42.

46. It is interesting that it is largely the series' male characters who assume these roles as cultural guardians, and I am conscious that my discussion almost entirely overlooks *Treme*'s female characters, who tend to bear more complicated—and indeed less patriarchal—relationships to New Orleans culture. I am thinking mainly of Davis McAlary, Creighton Bernette, and Albert Lambreaux, all of whom are explored briefly here.

47. Marc Augé, *Non-Places: An Introduction to Supermodernity*, trans. John Howe (London and New York: Verso, 2008), 35.

48. Augé, 39.

49. Creighton Bernette in *Treme*, Season 1, Episode 7, "Smoke My Peace Pipe."

50. Leyda, 245.

51. Leyda, 248.

52. Creighton Bernette in *Treme*, Season 1, Episode 8, "All on a Mardi Gras Day."

53. *Treme*, Season 1, Episode 9, "Wish Someone Would Care."

54. Leyda, 253.

55. Nik Cohn, "Reimagining the City: New Orleans," *BBC Radio 4*, January 5, 2013, 10.30am, http://www.bbc.co.uk/programmes/b01pnfjc (accessed June 28, 2016).

56. David Simon, "Preface," in Lolis Eric Elie, *Treme: Stories and Recipes from the Heart of New Orleans* (San Francisco: Chronicle Books, 2013), 8–9.

57. Simon, "Preface."

58. Lynnell L. Thomas, "'People Want to See What Happened': *Treme*, Tele-visual Tourism, and the Racial Remapping of Post-Katrina New Orleans," *Television & New Media*, 13.3 (2012), 213–24.

59. Thompson, 81.

60. Jameson, "Realism and Utopia in *The Wire*," 371; 372.

61. *Treme*, Season 4, Episode 4, "Sunset on Louisianne."

62. *Treme*, Season 4, Episode 5, "To Miss New Orleans."

63. Augé, 59.

64. Walter Benn Michaels, *The Trouble With Diversity: How We Learned to Love Identity and Ignore Inequality* (New York: Metropolitan Books/Henry Holt and Company, 2006), 201.

65. Thomas Jessen Adams, "New Orleans Brings it All Together," *American Quarterly*, 66.1 (2014), 245–56 (247).

66. *The Not Yet*, 224; 237.

67. *The Not Yet*, 113; 215.

68. *The Not Yet*, 207.

69. Thomas Jessen Adams, "The Political Economy of Invisibility in Twenty-First Century New Orleans: Security, Hospitality, and the Post-Disaster City," in

Hurricane Katrina in Transatlantic Perspective, ed. Romain Huret and Randy J. Sparks (Baton Rouge: Louisiana State University Press, 2014), 121–36 (129).

70. See Vicki Mayer, "Yeah You Rite: The *Treme* Issue," *Television & New Media*, 13.3 (2012), 191–192.

71. Thomas Jessen Adams, "The Political Economy of Invisibility in Twenty-First Century New Orleans," 130–31.

72. Tom Andes, "An Interview with Moira Crone," *Bookslut*, May 2014, http://www.bookslut.com/features/2014_05_020635.php (accessed June 29, 2016).

73. *The Not Yet*, 63.

74. *The Not Yet*, 156.

75. *The Not Yet*, 263,

76. Bauman, *Liquid Modernity*, 128.

77. *The Not Yet*, 271–72.

78. *The Not Yet*, 264.

79. Gerry Canavan and Eric Carl Link, "Introduction," in *The Cambridge Companion to American Science Fiction*, ed. Eric Carl Link and Gerry Canavan (New York: Cambridge University Press, 2015), 1–13 (4).

80. Aldous Huxley quoted in "Introduction by David Bradshaw," in Aldous Huxley, *Brave New World* (London: Vintage, 2007), xvii–xxvii (xix).

81. Huxley quoted in "Introduction by David Bradshaw," xix.

82. Fredric Jameson quoted by Rebekah C. Sheldon, "After America," in *The Cambridge Companion to American Science Fiction*, 206–18 (207).

83. Sheldon, 207.

84. Wendy Brown, *Walled States, Waning Sovereignty* (New York: Zone Books, 2014), 22.

85. Brown, 24.

86. Brown, 25.

87. *The Not Yet*, 203.

88. *The Not Yet*, 274.

89. Fredric Jameson, *Archaeologies of the Future: The Desire Called Utopia and Other Science Fictions* (London and New York: Verso, 2007), 232–33.

90. Jameson, *Archaeologies of the Future*, 288.

91. Tom Andes, "An Interview with Moira Crone."

92. Thomas Beller, "Don't Call it Katrina," *New Yorker*, May 29, 2015, http://www.newyorker.com/culture/cultural-comment/dont-call-it-katrina (accessed June 29, 2016).

93. Jarvis DeBerry, "Texas, Louisiana, Colorado, You Name It; It Floods All Over America," *Times-Picayune*, May 28, 2015, http://www.nola.com/opinions/index.ssf/2015/05/flood_houston_new_orleans.html (accessed June 29, 2016).

94. Campbell Robertson and Richard Fausset, "10 Years After Katrina," *New York Times*, August 26, 2015, http://www.nytimes.com/interactive/2015/08/26/us/ten-years-after-katrina.html?_r=0 (accessed February 25, 2016).

95. I borrow this term from Mike Davis' book, *City of Quartz: Excavating the Future in Los Angeles* (New York: Verso, 1990).

Select Bibliography

Adams, Jessica. *Wounds of Returning: Race, Memory, and Property on the Postslavery Plantation* (Chapel Hill: University of North Carolina Press, 2007).

Adams, Jessica, Michael P. Bibler, and Cécile Accilien, eds. *Just Below South: Intercultural Performance in the Caribbean and the U.S. South* (Charlottesville and London: University of Virginia Press, 2007).

Adams, Thomas Jessen. "New Orleans Brings it All Together," *American Quarterly*, 66.1 (2014), 245–56.

Adams, Vincanne. *Markets of Sorrow, Labors of Faith: New Orleans in the Wake of Katrina* (Durham, NC: Duke University Press, 2013).

Alexander, Michelle. *The New Jim Crow: Mass Incarceration in the Age of Colorblindness* (New York: The New Press, 2012).

Allen, Thomas M. *A Republic in Time: Temporality and Social Imagination in Nineteenth-Century America* (Chapel Hill: University of North Carolina Press, 2008).

Allende, Isabel. *Island Beneath the Sea*, trans. Margaret Sayers Peden (2009; London: Fourth Estate, 2011).

Arena, John. *Driven from New Orleans: How Nonprofits Betray Public Housing and Support Privatization* (Minneapolis: University of Minnesota Press, 2012).

ArtSpot Productions and Mondo Bizarro. *Cry You One*, first performed in St. Bernard Parish in October 2013, see http://www.cryyouone.com/ (accessed June 26, 2016).

Atkinson, Rowland, and Gary Bridge, eds. *Gentrification in a Global Context: The New Urban Colonialism* (London and New York: Routledge, 2005).

Augé, Marc. *Non-Places: An Introduction to Supermodernity*, trans. John Howe (1992; London and New York: Verso, 2008).

Barry, John. M. *Rising Tide: The Great Mississippi Flood of 1927 and How it Changed America* (New York: Simon & Schuster, 1997).

Baudrillard, Jean. *America*, trans. Chris Turner (1986; London: Verso, 2010).

Baum, Dan. *Nine Lives: Death and Life in New Orleans* (New York: Spiegel & Grau, 2009).

———. "The Lost Year: Behind the Failure to Rebuild," *New Yorker*, August 21, 2006, http://www.newyorker.com/magazine/2006/08/21/the-lost-year (accessed June 27, 2016).

Bauman, Zygmunt. *Liquid Times: Living in an Age of Uncertainty* (Cambridge, UK, and Malden, MA: Polity Press, 2007).

———. *Liquid Modernity* (Cambridge, UK and Malden, MA: Polity Press, 2000 and 2012).

Berlant, Lauren. *Cruel Optimism* (Durham, NC: Duke University Press, 2011).

Berman, Marshall. *All that is Solid Melts into Air: The Experience of Modernity* (1982; New York: Penguin, 1988).

Bibler, Michael P. "Always the Tragic Jezebel: New Orleans, Katrina, and the Layered Discourse of a Doomed Southern City," *Southern Cultures*, 14.2 (2008), 6–27.

Block, Jennifer John, dir. *Reconstructing Creole* (DVD; Fresh Media Productions, 2007).

Boelhower, William, ed. *New Orleans in the Atlantic World: Between Land and Sea*, (2010; New York: Routledge, 2013).

Breunlin, Rachel, Abram Himelstein, and Ashley Nelson. " 'Our Stories Told By US:' The Neighborhood Story Project in New Orleans," in *Telling Stories to Change the World: Global Voices on the Power of Narrative to Build Community and Make Social Justice Claims*, ed. Rickie Solinger, Madeline Fox, and Kayhan Irani (New York: Routledge, 2008), 75–89.

Breunlin, Rachel, and Helen A. Regis. "Putting the Ninth Ward on the Map: Race, Place, and Transformation in Desire, New Orleans," *American Anthropologist*, 108.4 (2006), 744–64.

Brickhouse, Anna. " 'L'Ouragan de Flammes' ('The Hurricane of Flames'): New Orleans and Transamerican Catastrophe, 1866/2005," *American Quarterly*, 59.4 (2007), 1097–1127.

Brown, Wendy. *Walled States, Waning Sovereignty* (2010; New York: Zone Books, 2014).

Bullard, Robert D. and Beverly Wright, eds. *Race, Place, and Environmental Justice After Hurricane Katrina* (Boulder, CO: Westview Press, 2008).

Buras, Kristen L. *Charter Schools, Race, and Urban Space: Where the Market Meets Grassroots Resistance* (New York: Routledge, 2014).

Buras, Kristen L. with Jim Randels, Kalamu ya Salaam, and Students at the Center. *Pedagogy, Policy, and the Privatized City: Stories of Dispossession and Defiance from New Orleans* (New York: Teachers College Press, 2010).

Campanella, Richard. "Beneficial Use: Toward Balancing America's (Sediment) Budget," The Design Observer Group, January 2013, http://richcampanella. com/assets/pdf/article_Campanella_Beneficial%20Use%20of%20Sediment_ Places%20Journal.pdf (accessed June 28, 2016).

———. *Bourbon Street: A History* (Baton Rouge: Louisiana State University Press, 2014).

———. "Gentrification and its Discontents: Notes from New Orleans," *New Geography*, March 1, 2013, http://www.newgeography.com/content/003526-gentrification-and-its-discontents-notes-new-orleans (accessed June 28, 2016).

———. *Bienville's Dilemma: A Historical Geography of New Orleans* (Lafayette, LA: Center for Louisiana Studies, 2008).

Carpentier, Alejo. *The Kingdom of This World*, trans. Harriet de Onís (1949; New York: Farrar, Straus and Giroux, 2006).

Carr, Sarah. *Hope Against Hope: Three Schools, One City, and the Struggle to Educate America's Children* (New York: Bloomsbury Press, 2013).

Carrico, Rachel. "On Thieves, Spiritless Bodies, and Creole Soul: Dancing Through the Streets of New Orleans," *TDR: The Drama Review*, 57.1 (2013), 70–87.

Castronovo, Russ and Susan Gillman, eds. *States of Emergency: The Object of American Studies* (Chapel Hill: University of North Carolina Press, 2009).

Chermak, Steven, Frankie Y. Bailey, and Michelle Brown, eds. *Media Representations of September 11* (Westport, CT: Praeger, 2003).

Clark, Emily. *The Strange History of the American Quadroon: Free Women of Color in the Revolutionary Atlantic World* (Chapel Hill: University of North Carolina Press, 2013).

———. "How American Is New Orleans? What the Founding Era Has to Tell Us," in Samuel C. Ramer and Blair A. Ruble, *Place, Identity, and Urban Culture: Odesa and New Orleans*, Kennen Institute Occasional Paper #31 (Washington, DC, Woodrow Wilson International Center for Scholars, 2008).

Cleves, Rachel Hope. "Transatlantic Revolution, National Identity, and American Exceptionalism in the Early Republic," *Reviews in American History*, 39.4 (2011), 607–16.

Codrescu, Andrei. *Hail Babylon! In Search of the American City at the End of the Millennium* (New York: St. Martin's Press, 1998).

Cohn, Nik. "Reimagining the City: New Orleans," *BBC Radio 4*, January 5, 2013, 10.30am, http://www.bbc.co.uk/programmes/b01pnfjc (accessed June 28, 2016).

Colten, Craig E. *An Unnatural Metropolis: Wresting New Orleans from Nature* (Baton Rouge: Louisiana State University Press, 2005).

Cook, Bernie. *Flood of Images: Media, Memory, and Hurricane Katrina* (Austin: University of Texas Press, 2015).

Cowen, Scott. *The Inevitable City: The Resurgence of New Orleans and the Future of Urban America* (New York: Palgrave Macmillan, 2014).

Crone, Moira. *The Not Yet* (New Orleans: University of New Orleans Press, 2012).

Crutcher, Michael E. Jr. *Tremé: Race and Place in a New Orleans Neighborhood* (Athens, GA: University of Georgia Press, 2010).

Dantas, Luisa, dir. *Land of Opportunity* (DVD; JoLu Productions, 2010).

Dash, J. Michael. *Haiti and the United States: National Stereotypes and the Literary Imagination*, 2nd ed. (Basingstoke, UK: Macmillan Press Ltd, 1997).

Davis, Angela Y. *The Meaning of Freedom and Other Difficult Dialogues* (San Francisco: City Lights Books, 2012).

———. *Are Prisons Obsolete?* (New York: Seven Stories Press, 2003).

Davis, Mike. *Dead Cities and Other Tales* (New York: The New Press, 2002).

———. *City of Quartz: Excavating the Future in Los Angeles* (New York: Verso, 1990).

Davis, Alan Robert, dir. *Oil and Water* (Rob Davis Photography, 2014).

Dessens, Nathalie. *From Saint-Domingue to New Orleans: Migration and Influences* (Gainesville: University Press of Florida, 2007).

Devore, Donald E., and Joseph Logsdon. *Crescent City Schools: Public Education in New Orleans 1841–1991* (New Orleans: Center for Louisiana Studies, 1991).

Dimock, Wai Chee. *Through Other Continents: American Literature Across Deep Time* (Princeton, NJ: Princeton University Press, 2006).

Dinerstein, Joel. "Second Lining Post-Katrina: Learning Community from the Prince of Wales Social Aid and Pleasure Club," *American Quarterly*, 61.3 (2009), 615–37.

Dyson, Michael Eric. *Come Hell or High Water: Hurricane Katrina and the Color of Disaster* (New York: Basic Civitas, 2006).

Eckstein, Barbara. *Sustaining New Orleans: Literature, Local Memory, and the Fate of a City* (New York: Routledge, 2006).

Edelman, Lee. *No Future: Queer Theory and the Death Drive* (Durham, NC: Duke University Press, 2004).

Eggers, Dave. *Zeitoun* (San Francisco: McSweeney's Books, 2009).

Elie, Lolis Eric. *Treme: Stories and Recipes from the Heart of New Orleans* (San Francisco: Chronicle Books, 2013).

Faulkner, William. *Mosquitoes* (New York: Liveright, 2011).

Ferguson, Niall. *Colossus: The Rise and Fall of the American Empire* (2004; London: Penguin, 2005).

Flaherty, Jordan. *Floodlines: Community and Resistance from Katrina to the Jena Six* (Chicago: Haymarket Books, 2010).

Flaherty, Robert J., dir. *Louisiana Story* (1948; DVD; Home Vision Entertainment, 2003).

Forman, James, Jr. "Racial Critiques of Mass Incarceration: Beyond the New Jim Crow," *New York University Law Review*, 87 (2012), 101–46.

Friedman, George, "The Ghost City," *New York Review of Books*, October 6, 2005, http://www.nybooks.com/articles/archives/2005/oct/06/the-ghost-city/ (accessed June 26, 2016).

Geerts, Ronald. "Naturalism and Reality in *Treme*," *Excavatio*, 23 (2014), https://www.ualberta.ca/~aizen/excavatio/articles/v24/Geertsfinal.pdf (accessed June 28, 2016).

Giroux, Henry A. *Stormy Weather: Katrina and the Politics of Disposability* (Boulder, CO: Paradigm Publishers, 2006).

Goldberg, David Theo. *The Threat of Race: Reflections on Racial Neoliberalism* (Malden, MA: Wiley-Blackwell, 2009).

Gotham, Kevin Fox. *Authentic New Orleans: Tourism, Culture, and Race in the Big Easy* (New York and London: New York University Press, 2007).

Gotham, Kevin Fox, and Miriam Greenberg. *Crisis Cities: Disaster and Redevelopment in New York and New Orleans* (New York: Oxford University Press, 2014).

Gratz, Roberta Brandes. *The Battle for Gotham: New York in the Shadow of Robert Moses and Jane Jacobs* (New York: Nation Books, 2010).

Gray, Richard. *After the Fall: American Literature Since 9/11* (Malden, MA: Wiley-Blackwell, 2011).

Hackler, M.B., ed. *Cultures after the Hurricanes: Rhetoric and Reinvention on the Gulf Coast* (Jackson: University of Mississippi Press, 2010).

Hansen, Jonathan M. *Guantánamo: An American History* (New York: Hill and Wang, 2011).

Hardt, Michael, and Antonio Negri. *Empire* (2000; Cambridge, MA: Harvard University Press, 2001).

Hart, Stephen M., and Wen-chin Ouyang, eds. *A Companion to Magical Realism* (Woodbridge, UK: Tamesis, 2005).

Harvey, David. *Rebel Cities: From the Right to the City to the Urban Revolution* (2012; London and New York: Verso, 2013).

Hedges, Chris, and Joe Sacco. *Days of Destruction, Days of Revolt* (New York: Nation Books, 2012).

Hell, Julia and Andreas Schönle, eds. *Ruins of Modernity* (Durham, NC: Duke University Press, 2010).

Hirsch, Arnold R., and Joseph Logsdon, eds. *Creole New Orleans: Race and Americanization* (Baton Rouge: Louisiana State University Press, 1992).

hooks, bell. "No Love in the Wild," NewBlackMan (in Exile), September 6, 2012, http://newblackman.blogspot.co.uk/2012/09/bell-hooks-no-love-in-wild.html (accessed June 28, 2016).

Huret, Romain, and Randy J. Sparks, eds. *Hurricane Katrina in Transatlantic Perspective* (Baton Rouge: Louisiana State University Press, 2014).

Huxley, Aldous. *Brave New World* (1932; London: Vintage, 2007).

Jacobs, Jane. *The Death and Life of Great American Cities* (1961; New York: Vintage Books, 1992).

James, C. L. R. *The Black Jacobins: Toussaint L'Ouverture and the San Domingo Revolution* (1938; London: Penguin, 2001).

Jameson, Fredric. "Realism and Utopia in *The Wire*," *Criticism*, 52. 3–4 (2010), 359–72.

———. *Archaeologies of the Future: The Desire Called Utopia and Other Science Fictions* (2005; London and New York: Verso, 2007).

Johnson, Cedric. "Watching the Train Wreck or Looking for the Brake?" *Souls: A Critical Journal of Black Politics, Culture, and Society*, 14:3–4 (2013), 207–26.

———, ed. *The Neoliberal Deluge: Hurricane Katrina, Late Capitalism, and the Remaking of New Orleans* (Minneapolis: University of Minnesota Press, 2011).

Kahana, Jonathan. *Intelligence Work: The Politics of American Documentary* (New York: Columbia University Press, 2008).

Kaplan, Amy. "Homeland Insecurities: Some Reflections on Language and Space," *Radical History Review*, 85 (2003), 82–93.

Katz, Jonathan M. *The Big Truck That Went By: How the World Came to Save Haiti and Left Behind a Disaster* (New York: Palgrave Macmillan, 2013).

Klein, Naomi. *This Changes Everything: Capitalism vs. the Climate* (London: Allen Lane, 2014).

———. *The Shock Doctrine: The Rise of Disaster Capitalism* (2007; London: Penguin, 2008).

Landphair, Juliette. "'The Forgotten People of New Orleans': Community, Vulnerability, and the Lower Ninth Ward," *Journal of American History*, 94.3 (2007), 837–45, http://www.journalofamericanhistory.org/projects/katrina/ Landphair.html (accessed January 24, 2015).

Lee, Spike, dir. *If God is Willing and Da Creek Don't Rise* (2010; DVD; HBO, 2011).

———, dir. *When the Levees Broke: A Requiem in Four Acts* (DVD; HBO, 2006).

Lefebvre, Henri. *Writings on Cities*, trans. and ed. Eleonore Kofman and Elizabeth Lebas (Malden, MA: Blackwell Publishing, 2006).

Lessin, Tia, and Carl Deal, dirs. *Trouble the Water* (DVD; Louverture films, 2007).

Leyda, Julia. "'This Complicated, Colossal Failure': The Abjection of Creighton Bernette in HBO's Treme," *Television & New Media*, 13.3 (2012), 243–60.

Link, Eric Carl. and Gerry Canavan, eds. *The Cambridge Companion to American Science Fiction* (New York: Cambridge University Press, 2015).

Locke, Attica. *The Cutting Season* (2012; London: Serpent's Tail, 2013).

Logsdon, Dawn, dir. *Fauborg Tremé: The Untold Story of Black New Orleans* (DVD; Serendipity Films, 2008).

Long, Alecia P. *The Great Southern Babylon: Sex, Race, and Respectability in New Orleans, 1865–1920* (Baton Rouge: Louisiana State University Press, 2004).

Luce, Henry R. "The American Century," *Life Magazine*, February 17, 1941, 61–65, available at: http://www.informationclearinghouse.info/article6139. htm (accessed June 28, 2016).

Marable, Manning, and Kristen Clarke, eds. *Seeking Higher Ground: The Hurricane Katrina Crisis, Race, and Public Policy Reader* (New York: Palgrave Macmillan, 2008).

McMichael Reese, Carol, Michael Sorkin, and Anthony Fontenot, eds. *New Orleans Under Reconstruction: The Crisis of Planning* (London and New York: Verso, 2014).

McQueen, Steve, dir. *12 Years a Slave* (2013; DVD; Entertainment One, 2014).

Metzger, Pamela R. "Doing Katrina Time," *Tulane Law Review*, 81.4 (2007), 1175–1217.

Michaels, Walter Benn. *The Trouble With Diversity: How We Learned to Love Identity and Ignore Inequality* (New York: Metropolitan Books/Henry Holt and Company, 2006).

Michna, Catherine. "Performance and Cross-Racial Storytelling in Post-Katrina New Orleans: Interviews with John O'Neal, Carol Bebelle, and Nicholas Slie," *TDR: The Drama Review*, 57:1 (2013), 48–69.

———. "Stories at the Center: Story Circles, Educational Organizing, and Fate of Neighborhood Public Schools in New Orleans," *American Quarterly*, 61.3 (2009), 529–55.

Moore, Leonard N. *Black Rage in New Orleans: Police Brutality and African American Activism from World War II to Hurricane Katrina* (Baton Rouge: Louisiana State University Press, 2010).

Munro, Martin, ed. *Haiti Rising: Haitian History, Culture, and the Earthquake of 2010* (Liverpool: Liverpool University Press, 2010).

Negra, Diane, ed. *Old and New Media After Katrina* (New York: Palgrave Macmillan, 2010).

Neufeld, Josh. *A.D. New Orleans After the Deluge* (New York: Pantheon Books, 2009).

Nichols, Bill. *Introduction to Documentary*, 2nd ed. (2001; Bloomington and Indianapolis: Indiana University Press, 2010).

Nine Times Social Aid and Pleasure Club. *Coming Out the Door for the Ninth Ward* (New Orleans: Neighborhood Story Project, 2006).

Nixon, Rob. *Slow Violence and the Environmentalism of the Poor* (Cambridge, MA: Harvard University Press, 2011).

Packer, George. *The Unwinding: An Inner History of the New America* (London: Faber and Faber, 2013).

Parenti, Christian. *Lockdown America: Police and Prisons in the Age of Crisis* (London and New York: Verso, 2008).

Pease, Donald E. *The New American Exceptionalism* (Minneapolis: University of Minnesota Press, 2009).

Piazza, Tom. *City of Refuge* (New York: Harper Perennial, 2008).

———. *Why New Orleans Matters* (2005; New York: Harper Perennial, 2008).

Polidori, Robert. *After the Flood* (Gottingen: Steidl, 2006).

Porter, Eric. "Jazz and Revival," *American Quarterly*, 61.3 (2009), 593–613.

Powell, Lawrence N. *The Accidental City: Improvising New Orleans* (Cambridge, MA: Harvard University Press, 2012).

Power, Nina. "Non-Reproductive Futurism: Rancière's Rational Equality against Edelman's Body Apolitic," *Borderlands*, 8.2 (2009), http://www.borderlands.net.au/vol8no2_2009/power_futurism.pdf (accessed June 28, 2016).

Quigley, William P. *Storms Still Raging: Katrina, New Orleans and Social Justice* (BookSurge Publishing, 2008).

———. "Thirteen Ways of Looking at Katrina: Human and Civil Rights Left Behind Again," *Tulane Law Review*, 81.4 (2007), 955–1017.

Ravitch, Diane. *The Death and Life of the Great American School System: How Testing and Choice are Undermining Education* (New York: Basic Books, 2010).

Regis, Helen A. "Second Lines, Minstrelsy, and the Contested Landscapes of New Orleans' Afro-Creole Festivals," *Cultural Anthropology*, 14.4 (1999), 472–504.

Reichardt, Kelly, dir. *Wendy and Lucy* (DVD; Oscilloscope Laboratories, 2008).

Renda, Mary A. *Taking Haiti: Military Occupation and the Culture of U.S. Imperialism 1915–1940* (Chapel Hill and London: University of North Carolina Press, 2001).

Rich, Nathaniel. "Jungleland: The Lower Ninth Ward in New Orleans Gives New Meaning to 'Urban Growth,'" *New York Times Magazine*, March 21, 2012, http://www.nytimes.com/2012/03/25/magazine/the-lower-ninth-ward-new-orleans.html?pagewanted=all&_r=0 (accessed June 28, 2016).

Rose, Chris. *1 Dead in Attic: After Katrina* (New York: Simon & Schuster, 2007).

Rose, Jacqueline. *States of Fantasy* (1996; Oxford: Clarendon Press, 1998).

Rosenthal, Alan, ed. *New Challenges for Documentary* (Berkeley: University of California Press, 1988).

Rosenthal, Alan and John Corner, eds. *New Challenges for Documentary*, 2nd ed. (Manchester: Manchester University Press, 2005).

Saltman, Kenneth J., and David A. Gabbard, eds. *Education as Enforcement: The Militarization and Corporatization of Schools* (New York: RoutledgeFalmer, 2003).

Schuller, Mark. *Killing with Kindness: Haiti, International Aid, and NGOs* (New Brunswick, NJ: Rutgers University Press, 2012).

Sharkey, Patrick. *Stuck in Place: Urban Neighborhoods and the End of Progress toward Racial Equality* (Chicago: University of Chicago Press, 2013).

Shields, David. *Reality Hunger* (London: Penguin, 2010).

Simon, David, and Eric Overmyer. *Treme* Seasons 1–4 (2010–2013; DVD; HBO 2011–2014).

Simon, David, dir. *The Wire* (DVD; HBO, 2002–2008).

Smith, Neil. *The New Urban Frontier: Gentrification and the Revanchist City* (London and New York: Routledge, 1996).

Solnit, Rebecca. *A Paradise Built in Hell: The Extraordinary Communities that Arise in Disaster* (2009; New York: Penguin, 2010).

Solnit, Rebecca, and Rebecca Snedeker, eds. *Unfathomable City: A New Orleans Atlas* (Berkeley and Los Angeles: University of California Press, 2013).

Souther, J. Mark. "The Disneyfication of New Orleans: The French Quarter as Facade in a Divided City," *Journal of American History*, 94. 3 (2007), 804–11.

———. *New Orleans on Parade: Tourism and the Transformation of the Crescent City* (Baton Rouge: Louisiana State University Press, 2006).

Stanonis, Anthony J. *Creating the Big Easy: New Orleans and the Emergence of Modern Tourism, 1918–1945* (Athens, GA: University of Georgia Press, 2006).

Stiglitz, Joseph E. *The Price of Inequality* (2012; London: Penguin, 2013).

Sublette, Ned. *The World that Made New Orleans: From Spanish Silver to Congo Square* (Chicago: Lawrence Hill Books, 2009).

Thomas, Lynnell L. *Desire and Disaster in New Orleans: Tourism, Race, and Historical Memory* (Durham, NC: Duke University Press, 2014).

———. "'People Want to See What Happened': *Treme*, Televisual Tourism, and the Racial Remapping of Post-Katrina New Orleans," *Television & New Media*, 13.3 (2012), 213–24.

———. "'Roots Run Deep Here': The Construction of Black New Orleans in Post-Katrina Tourism Narratives," *American Quarterly*, 61.3 (2009), 749–68.

Thompson, Kecia Driver. "'Deserve Got Nothing to Do With It': Black Urban Experience and the Naturalist Tradition in *The Wire*," *Studies in American Naturalism*, 7.1 (2012), 80–120.

Toole, John Kennedy. *A Confederacy of Dunces* (New York: Grove Press, 1980).

Troutt, David Dante, ed. *After the Storm: Black Intellectuals Explore the Meaning of Hurricane Katrina* (New York: The New Press, 2006).

Vale, Lawrence J., and Thomas J. Campanella, eds. *The Resilient City: How Modern Cities Recover from Disaster* (Oxford: Oxford University Press, 2005).

Wacquant, Loïc. *Punishing the Poor: The Neoliberal Government of Social Insecurity* (2004; Durham, NC: Duke University Press, 2009).

Ward, Jesmyn. *Men We Reaped* (New York: Bloomsbury, 2013).

———. *Salvage the Bones* (New York: Bloomsbury, 2011).

Wells, Liz, ed. *Photography: A Critical Introduction*, 4th ed. (New York: Routledge, 2009).

Woods, Clyde. "Katrina's World: Blues, Bourbon, and the Return to the Source," *American Quarterly*, 61.3 (2009), 427–53.

———. "Les Misérables of New Orleans: Trap Economics and the Asset Stripping Blues, Part 1," *American Quarterly*, 61. 3 (2009), 769–96.

Wooten, Tom. *We Shall Not Be Moved: Rebuilding Home in the Wake of Katrina* (Boston: Beacon Press, 2012).

Yaeger, Patricia. "*Beasts of the Southern Wild* and Dirty Ecology," *Southern Spaces*, February 13, 2013, http://southernspaces.org/2013/beasts-southern-wild-and-dirty-ecology (accessed June 28, 2016).

Zeitlin, Benh, dir. *Beasts of the Southern Wild* (DVD; Cinereach Productions, 2012).

Index

Names enclosed in quotation marks indicate fictitious characters. They are followed by the titles of works in which they appear.

Printed in Great Britain
by Amazon